ENGLISH LANGUA

Adverbs and Modality in English

ENGLISH LANGUAGE SERIES
General Editor: Randolph Quirk

Adverbs and Modality in English

LEO HOYE

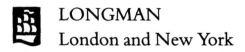

LONGMAN
London and New York

Addison Wesley Longman Limited
Edinburgh Gate
Harlow, Essex CM20 2JE
England
and Associated Companies throughout the world

*Published in the United States of America
by Addison Wesley Longman Inc., New York*

First published 1997

ISBN 0 582 21535-8 Paper

British Library Cataloguing-in-Publication Data
A catalogue record for this book is
available from the British Library

Library of Congress Cataloguing-in-Publication Data
Hoye, Leo, 1954–
        Adverbs and modality in English / Leo Hoye.
            p.   cm. — (English language series)
        Includes bibliographical references (p.   ) and index.
        ISBN 0-582-21535-8
        1. English language—Adverb.   2. English language—Modality.
    I. Title.   II. Series: English language series
    PE1325.H69   1997
    425—dc20   96-33240
                                                                      CIP

Set by 33

Transferred to digital print on demand, 2005

Printed and bound by Antony Rowe Ltd, Eastbourne

Contents

For my Romanian, English, Danish and Dutch families

Doamne ajută

Preface

There is a wealth of publications dealing with modality in English, and in particular with the small set of auxiliary verbs, known as the 'modals'. The focus here is not only on the modals but on the nature of their association with different categories of adverb which are also concerned with the expression of modality. The aim is to offer an accessible introduction to the subject, a comprehensive account of modal–adverb co-occurrence, and a reappraisal of the English modal system. This book is therefore designed to meet the demands of the specialist with research interests in the field of modality, yet, at the same time, to function as a general introduction to this notoriously complex and challenging area of language study.

The book would never have come into being without the support and encouragement of my Romanian friends, colleagues and students alike, at the Universities of Cluj-Napoca and Bucharest, in the latter part of the 1980s. First and foremost, this work is a tribute to their generosity and friendship, given freely in hard and sometimes desperate times. Thank you then to: Dumitru Chiţoran, Sever Trifu and Mihai Zdrenghea. I must also thank Carl James for his timely intervention and assistance at an earlier stage of the work, and to the staff of the British Embassy and the British Council in Bucharest for their forbearance and co-operation. I would also like to record my debt to Roy Bird whose encouragement and advice in the very first stages of the project were invaluable.

I am very grateful to the late Sidney Greenbaum, Director of the Survey of English Usage at University College, London for granting me access to the Survey facilities when I undertook my original research.

Thank you to my former students at the University of Concepción, Chile, and to staff and students of the Chilean–British Institute in Santiago for acting as informants in connection with the later stages of this study.

I am grateful to Odense University for providing me with the necessary facilities and time to see the project through to its completion, and to Carl Bache and Nils Davidsen-Nielsen for reading the manuscript in its draft form and making helpful comments which have led to a number of useful revisions. Special thanks to Christina Herslev Jeppesen for her expert and generous help with the compilation of the indices.

The editor of the series, Randolph Quirk, deserves particular mention for his advice and encouragement in the preparation of this book, as do the editorial team at Longman for their guidance and patience.

Finally, I should like to thank those family, friends and colleagues, in Romania, England, Denmark, Holland and further afield, too numerous to mention by name, whose support and encouragement helped me survive the ordeal with a smile.

LEO HOYE

Odense, Denmark
1996

One

The scope of the study and some earlier proposals

Her terrible tale you can't assail
With Truth it quite agrees;
Her taste exact for faultless fact
Amounts to a disease.
(W. S. Gilbert, 'The Mikado')

1.1 GENERAL INTRODUCTION

The study of modality in English remains one of the most pervasive and intriguing areas of philosophical and linguistic inquiry. The wealth of literature on the subject, much of it recent, attests the continuing need for new insights into the definition, description and analysis of this elusive and fundamental category of human language and thought. The notion of modality is tantalizingly problematic in that its scope and treatment depend on whether the inquiry is essentially philosophical or language based. The question 'What is modality?' produces different answers according to the orientation of the approach adopted. The philosophical treatment of modality and the modal concepts of possibility, probability, and necessity takes place at a relatively high level of abstraction and the problems raised are not typically susceptible to solution by observation and experiment. Linguistic investigation, however, is founded in empirical and scientific method and examines these same concepts in terms of the human attitudes and behaviour from which they are extrapolated. There is considerable interpenetration between the philosophical and linguistic approaches, but they have fundamentally different research aims and proceed at different levels of abstraction. The present book is primarily a linguistic study of modality in natural language, namely, modern spoken and written English.

Linguists normally take as the basic modal notions those expressed by the central modal auxiliary verbs MAY, MIGHT; CAN, COULD; WILL, WOULD; SHALL, SHOULD; MUST. In general, the modal auxiliaries are used not to express statements of fact but events or actions which exist only as conceptions of the mind and which may or may not eventuate in the future. The modals express a wide range of meanings which grammars usually describe in terms of the modal concepts of possibility, probability, necessity and the related notions of permission, obligation, volition. For example, related to MAY are the ideas of possibility and permission:

(1)   I think that actually may be his name. (CG/107)[1]

(2)   mi "lord# "may I 'very re'spectfully at this stàge# ex"plain 'what this màn dìd# (S.12.3.798/9)[2]

Related to MUST are the ideas of necessity and obligation:

(3)   He couldn't believe his box had been taken away altogether; they must simply have been moved around. (PH/231)

(4)   But now we really must get down to business. (CG/167)

Linguistic discussions of modality in English have traditionally focused on an examination of the behaviour of the modal auxiliaries, also referred to in the literature as 'modal verbs', or 'modals' for short, and the ways in which they affect the meaning of the sentence or clause in which they appear. In comparison with other modal expressions, the modals readily lend themselves to formal definition and analysis and are the most grammaticalized exponents of the system of modality in English. Indeed, the category of modal auxiliary is more readily established in English than in other European languages, be they Germanic or Romance in origin. As Palmer (1986: 33) points out: 'There is no doubt that English has a set of modal verbs that can be formally defined' and Perkins (1983: 25) observes that 'the modals are syntactically distinct from other modal expressions . . .'. The study of the modals is often regarded as synonymous with the study of modality itself 'for the meanings expressed by the modal verbs in English represent, to a large degree, those that are to be included in a typological account of modality' (Palmer 1990: 2). However, this is not to imply that linguists fail to recognize the existence of other carriers of modality: English has a variety of means by which it can signal modal contrasts. These would include, for instance, the use of: modal idioms such as HAD BETTER, WOULD RATHER, WOULD SOONER; adjectives such as POSSIBLE, LIKELY, SURE; nouns such as POSSIBILITY, LIKELIHOOD, CERTAINTY; adverbs such as PERHAPS, PROBABLY, DEFINITELY; and modal lexical verbs such as DOUBT, RECKON, BELIEVE. In speech, the prosodic features of intonation and stress interact with the lexical carriers of modality and can be associated with a range of modal meanings; the speaker's doubt or uncertainty, for instance, is regularly conveyed by a fall–rise intonation pattern.

There are many ways in which modality can manifest itself and there is rich potential for the association of diverse modal elements within the sentence. Palmer (1986: 45) suggests that 'Modality is not, then, necessarily marked in the verbal element, nor is there any obvious reason why it should be, apart from the fact that the verb is the most central part of the sentence'. It is of course this very centrality which has caused linguists to rehearse modal concepts almost exclusively in terms of the modal auxiliaries and at the expense of other modal expressions. Given that the underlying concern of linguistics is with linguistic form and that the modals are a syntactically coherent and distinct class of items, the predilection is understandable. But the picture of modality which emerges as a result of this bias is skewed and wanting in descriptive scope. Despite widespread recognition that modal contrasts are not signalled by the modals alone, other modal expressions available in English tend to be used heuristically to elucidate the meanings of the modals, rarely attracting much attention in their own right. On occasions, a group of expressions such as MAY, PERHAPS, IT IS POSSIBLE THAT, THERE'S A POSSIBILITY THAT are seen as synonymous, merely representing characteristic variations in style. The semantic category of modality cannot be adequately accounted for by focusing on the modals alone, nor by discussing them in isolation from other modal elements which may be functioning synergetically within the same environment; analysis of language corpora supports the view that modal elements frequently combine and interact dynamically, there seldom being one carrier of modality operating in isolation within the clause: 'modality ... does not relate semantically to the verb alone or primarily, but to the whole sentence' (Palmer 1986: 2). Different realizations of modality do combine, having a cumulative effect on the modality expressed.

The present work is meant to examine in detail a specific type of modal realization as expressed through the combination of modals with their adverb satellites. Its motivation is due to a complex of reasons. Modal–adverb collocations remain a largely neglected area, even though the study of co-occurrence restrictions and regularities has always been an essential aspect of grammatical description.[3] In recent years, important advances have been made in the field of lexicology based upon the study of co-occurrence and collocation. The now widespread use of language corpora, which involves the study of naturally occurring written text and transcribed recorded speech, has revolutionized the way linguists approach the analysis and description of linguistic phenomena. The present study is very much the product of a corpus approach to the subject of modality. It endorses the view that 'the majority of text is made of the occurrence of common words in common patterns, or in slight variants of those common patterns. Most everyday words do not have an independent meaning, or meanings, but are components of a rich repertoire of multi-word patterns that make up text. This is totally obscured by the procedures of conventional grammar' (Sinclair 1991: 108). Modal–adverb collocations conform to lexicographical principles of patterning and tendency; there is little that is random or that cannot be predicted with assurance. Indeed, we would argue that profiles of the modals' behaviour with their various adverb satellites is yet a further defining characteristic of the modals themselves. Modal–adverb collocations therefore play a relatively central role in the expression of modality in English.

The incidence and nature of modal–adverb combinations vary considerably according to which modal auxiliary is involved (some are more common than others) and the basic meaning it conveys: possibility, permission, obligation and so forth. The grammar and semantics of co-occurrence are dealt with in detail later, but the following prototypical examples illustrate the broad characteristics of modal–adverb synergism which are the central focus of this study. This sample is purely illustrative and at this juncture is not meant as an exhaustive typology of the modal–adverb combinations to be found in English.

(5)   He might – just might – succeed in reaching the woods.
        (CG/243)

(6)   it "may wèll bé# that "there were faùlts#
        (S. 12.4 1120/1)

(7)   That she could quite possibly identify him was something
        he didn't stop to consider . . . (AA/337-8)

(8)   We'll send a car . . . as soon as we possibly can. (CG/268)

(9)   By the time you come back from honeymoon, probate
        will probably be granted. (W. 7.10.25)

(10)   Perhaps you would bring to the notice of those who
        instructed you to write to me the custom of sending
        stamped envelopes in making requests of this sort.
        (W. 17.2.36)

(11)   As prices go on rising and the value of money declines (as,
        it seems to me, must inevitably happen) . . . (W. 11.2.147)

In each instance the modality expressed undergoes some form of
modification, complementation or even transformation. In (5) the
adverb JUST has a lowering or diminishing effect on the force of the
modal meaning of possibility expressed by the auxiliary, and this
contrasts with the situation in (7) and (8) where the effect of the
adverb is to strengthen or heighten the force of the verb. In (6),
WELL, operating within the restricted environment of MAY, actually
transforms the modal's inherent meaning of possibility into one of
probability. In association with other modals, such as CAN, for
instance, WELL behaves quite differently and modifies not the modal
but the main verb; in 'I can well understand', the lexical verb is
intensified and the phrase could be glossed: 'I have no difficulty
whatsoever in understanding.'[4] In (9), PROBABLY approximates in
meaning to the modal notion of probability expressed by the
auxiliary and thus complements rather than alters the modality
expressed. In (10), PERHAPS, which shares no obvious semantic
feature with WOULD, is used tentatively to introduce what could be
best described as a sardonic recommendation. PERHAPS regularly
co-occurs with the modals in the making of suggestions, whatever
the overtones. Finally, in (11), INEVITABLY reinforces the notion of

inference or plausible assumption conveyed by MUST, complement-
ing that modal's widespread use in expressing the strength of the
speaker's attitude or opinion to what he or she is saying.
Furthermore, example (6) also demonstrates how in speech
prosodic contrasts may interact with and highlight the modal
elements already present, thereby signalling their importance to the
message of the utterance.

Adverbial mobility and position within the sentence have
implications for their formal classification and the manner in which
they function in harness with their modal verb heads. Because of
its close association with the modal which it clearly modifies, WELL
in (6) is relatively integrated in the structure of the sentence; moved
to, say, initial position: 'Well, it may be that there were faults', that
association is entirely disrupted. The adverb loses all vestiges of
modal meaning and becomes a speech initiator (Quirk *et al.* 1985:
444 and 852)[5] on a par with other formulae used in stereotyped
communication, such as reaction signals 'Yeah!', 'Right' or expletives 'Blast', 'Fiddlesticks'! By contrast, in (9), even though there is
an obvious semantic link between the adverb PROBABLY and the
modal WILL, the adverb retains its modal status regardless of
whether it occurs in initial position or, for that matter, is tagged on
at the end, almost as an afterthought: 'By the time you come back
from honeymoon probate will be granted, probably.' Given its
potential for mobility within the sentence, PROBABLY seems
relatively peripheral in terms of sentence structure; it is a typical
sentence adverb. The range and nature of the adverbials involved in
co-occurrence with the modals, their transmobility within the
structure of the sentence and the importance of this to their
classification in terms of formal and notional criteria, are explored
in detail in Chaper 4.

In his study *Verb–Intensifier Collocations in English*, Greenbaum
(1970: 9) opens with the comment that 'A complete linguistic
description needs to take account of the restrictions on the
collocability of one lexical item with another in certain syntactic
relationships.' He continues, 'In addition to establishing the
restrictions on collocability, we may also wish to take account of the
tendency for certain collocations rather than others to be likely in
the language.' This study seeks to demonstrate that modal–adverb
co-occurrences follow identifiable trends; patterns emerge, and
collocational restrictions and tendencies come into force. Investiga-

tion into the cohesiveness between the two word classes means we are dealing with probabilities rather than absolutes; the syntactic and semantic association between the modals and their adverb satellites is therefore a matter of degree. The modal–verb combination we saw in (6) above, MAY WELL, is fixed in form and sequence; its holophrastic nature suggests we are dealing with a type of modal idiom on a par with what grammars commonly recognize as modal idioms such as WOULD RATHER or HAD BETTER. The semantic cohesion between modal and adverb is weaker in (9), where adverbs such as MAYBE or PERHAPS, which express possibility rather than probability, also have the potential to combine, or are collocable, with the modal. Collocations are important in the grammatical and lexical structure of the language because they are repeated with regularity; a large part of our mental lexicon is made up of combinations of words which customarily co-occur and where the occurrence of one enables prediction of the other in the more idiomatic combinations, as with MAY WELL, or where the occurrence of one word suggests the company of another derived from a finite set of choices, as in the association of WILL with either MAYBE or PERHAPS.

The descriptive need to examine modal–adverb combinations must by now be apparent. By primarily focusing on the modals alone, linguistic inquiry into the workings of modality in English is incomplete. Rarely is there just one exponent of modality at work in the clause or sentence but often two or more elements operating interdependently and dynamically. The range of adverbs which keeps company with the modals is a finite set of items but there are a number of different grammatical and semantic processes involved. The linguistic description of modality at its higher levels of abstraction must take into account the collocational bonds and tendencies revealed through an explicit examination of modal–adverb co-occurrence.

1.2 THE NATURE AND ORGANIZATION OF THE STUDY

In general terms, this study is a corpus-based, descriptive account of native speaker performance across the modal–adverb domain as attested by authenticated instances of language data.[6] The focus is on surface structure and potential as well as actual use. This study does not embrace the theory of any one specific school nor does it adopt a particular syntactic theory such as transformational grammar or systemic grammar. Our approach is typically eclectic. Given the complexity of the subject and the vast array of analyses currently available, we draw on the reasearch of others whose works and findings are considered central.

The language data used for exemplificatory purposes is mostly drawn from the Survey of English Usage (SEU) corpus which contains representative samples of modern, standard, British English: historical precedence, dialectal and national varieties are specifically excluded, as to examine co-occurrence in terms of these would have taken us well beyond our present brief.[7] Moreover, rarely is reference made to differences obtaining between British and American English, although it is recognized that there are corresponding variations in patterns of usage.

We examine both the modals and their adverb satellites in accordance with their formal identification and definition, and then consider the grammatical and semantic processes at work when the two word classes combine. At a syntactic level, we investigate the distributional properties of the relevant categories of adverb within or in relation to clause structure and explore the positional and semantic implications transmobility has for co-occurrence. We thus distinguish between sentence adverb, where the adverb is peripheral to clause structure and its scope is mainly sentential, and verb phrase adverb, where the adverb is integrated in clause structure and its scope is primarily the modal verb head. At a semantic level, we provide an analysis of the collocational patterns and restrictions which emerge and on this basis seek to identify the extent to which trends in co-occurrence are predictable. Our concern, therefore, is not only to describe the phenomenon of modal–adverb co-occurrence but also to offer an explanation of the underlying system. At a pragmatic level, co-occurrence is examined in terms of speaker meaning and context of utterance. The nuances introduced by particular modal–adverb associations and the influences that motivate their selection offer further insights into how modal–adverb collocations may be accounted for and eventually formulated. In the absence of a coherent theory of pragmatics, we do not attempt to relate co-occurrence to a comprehensive overview of current pragmatic theories and the often conflicting approaches to communication they embrace; this would amount to several studies in itself! Mey (1993: 43) comments on the difficulty of defining pragmatics when it 'apparently is in a steady evolutionary flux'. We try to steer a middle course by focusing primarily on the linguistic aspects of the context and by making reference to the extra-linguistic, social dimension only where this offers particular insights into the nature of modality itself. For instance, we devote an entire section to a discussion of the relationship between modality and power at a societal level (2.6), and elsewhere we examine the role of modal expressions in politeness strategies (3.5). Our approach is chiefly language-based and 'pragmalinguistic' in scope, but also recognizes the association between the conditions of language use and the wider social context, normally the province of 'sociopragmatics' or 'societal pragmatics'.

Through relying on corpus-derived material, we avoid the pitfalls of an exclusively introspective approach citing examples of attested modal–adverb combinations.[8] We distinguish between spoken and written discourse, taking into consideration the effect of medium on performance. This also enables us to investigate intonational aspects of co-occurrence.

The book is divided into six chapters: the first two serve as an introduction to central theoretical issues where relevant previous research is critically examined and related to the present study. The next two chapters establish formal, semantic and pragmatic frameworks for the descriptive treatment of co-occurrence between modal verb heads and their adverb satellites. Chapter 4 includes a discussion of prosodic features attributable to co-occurrence; for this reason, examples deriving from speech are almost always accompanied by appropriate diacritical markings. The first four chapters lay the essential theoretical foundation for the final part of the book. Chapter 5 examines the patterns in co-occurrence described in Chapters 3 and 4, and these are then used as a framework for describing collocational restrictions and associations. Native and non-native (Spanish) speaker sensitivity in this area is subsequently investigated by elicitation experiments; differences in their performance permit a number of Spanish–English contrastive observations, which form the basis of an outline exercise typology for developing and improving awareness and use of this aspect of the modal system. The work thus proceeds from theoretical to more practical issues for teaching modal–adverb expressions. The final chapter presents the overall conclusions and implications of the study. Each chapter is accompanied by notes which provide further details and references for readers wishing to pursue the issues in greater depth. An abundance of illustrative material is used throughout the work and examples are numbered consecutively within each chapter. A list of written texts that were used to supplement the material obtained from the SEU corpus is provided at the end of the book, before the main bibliography.

1.3 THE LANGUAGE DATA AND THE SURVEY OF ENGLISH USAGE

Recourse to the use of authentic spoken and and written texts in linguistic enquiry is not new but there has been a vast increase in corpus-based studies since Randolph Quirk originally launched the seminal Survey of English Usage (SEU) in 1959 at the University of Durham, England.[9] The aim of that pioneering corpus, presently housed on computer at University College, London, was the systematic collection of a large body of spoken and written English texts, covering a wide variety of styles. Two main points can be made about the use of a corpus which are relevant to this study. Firstly, because the data record instances of language in actual use, the illustrations they provide are more realistic and reliable than much material used in the past, which was all too often the product of armchair introspection. Secondly, the data promote examination of the quantitative and probabilistic features of the language which were all but impossible to research previously.[10]

Most of the illustrative material used in the preparation of this study has been obtained from the SEU corpus.[11] This consists of a million words, comprising 200 samples or 'texts', each of 5000 words, distributed equally between spoken and written English, and covering a wide range of subject matter, situations, and degrees of formality. Each text has been analysed and tagged for a large number of grammatical features, and the spoken material includes detailed prosodic and paralinguistic information.[12]

The corpus is an obvious source for making judgements about how often particular modals and adverbs combine, but it can also be used in a more interesting and revealing way to identify tendencies in the association of the two forms and to help explain why certain combinations occur and others do not. Commenting on the role of corpora generally, de Beaugrande (1996: §27; 514) observes that: 'Among all the possible combinations of English words and phrases that might be intuitively judged "grammatical", we can finally see which ones are more likely to be realised and at least some of the reasons why.' The language data are always contextualized and so it is often possible to identify the particular syntactic, semantic and pragmatic factors which make certain modal–adverb collocations more or less likely to occur than others. The real data offered by a corpus demonstrate how these components of language description actually interact and converge, allowing for a description which covers both form and function in a more meaningful way than a non-corpus approach would allow.[13]

To some extent the data do support quantitative observations about co-occurrence, particularly as regards the frequency and predictability of the more common or idiomatic modal–adverb collocations, such as WOULD PROBABLY and CAN'T POSSIBLY. Where modal–adverb combinations are infrequent, as, for instance, when READILY and EASILY operate as emphasizers within the restricted environments of CAN or COULD:

(12)   A similar disaster can/could easily happen again, unless precautions are taken.

it is difficult to ascertain whether or not the sample is either sufficiently large or representative for a statement about their frequency to have any validity or particular significance. While it can thus be argued that the absence of such items as DEFINITELY in the environment of MUST reflects more the limitations of the corpus than a peculiarity of modal–adverb co-occurrence in the language, it could also be argued that this suggests that MUST favours other types of adverb satellite, such as REALLY (a relatively common emphasizer which operates in harness with the modals generally), where there is no modal synergy at work. The question of frequency and its potential significance is dealt with more fully in the body of our description. We make appeal to statistical evidence only where it is felt that reference to the relative frequency of particular modal–adverb combinations or types of combination augments the descriptive adequacy of the study. The corpus material is thus treated with circumspection.

To supplement the SEU corpus-derived data, relevant examples are taken from other sources, and chiefly randomly selected published works (a list of these texts appears before the main bibliography).[14] Sometimes, modified versions of authenticated examples are used, either to accord with the outline presentation of a particular section, as in the data profile of modal–adverb co-occurrence given in Chapter 5, or to clarify basic principles where the use of the original material would have proved unwieldy. The occasional invented example is used where neither the SEU corpus nor the other sources of data provided an attested alternative. Modified or invented examples are signalled by the absence of any source reference.

Not even the largest corpus can provide for all the potentialities of a particular set or string of linguistic features, and modal–adverb combinations attested in the SEU is no exception. For instance, there are 78 instances of MUST in co-occurrence with such adverbs as CERTAINLY, INDEED, SURELY. Yet there are no instances documented of collocations with DEFINITELY or UNDOUBTEDLY; intuition tells us that combinations with these adverbs are possible, even though they may well be relatively infrequent. Both adverbs belong syntactically and semantically to the same set of attested collocates. Do we omit reference to unattested collocations or do we include them on the grounds of analogy, for the sake of descriptive accuracy and completeness? This study aims to be comprehensive in its coverage and is 'corpus-based' rather than 'corpus-restricted' in the use it makes of the available linguistic data. The SEU is more than just a source of examples: it has a heuristic function in that it provides a framework or paradigmatic context for describing potential modal–adverb collocations not actually represented in the data. Potential as well as actual instances of co-occurrence need to be accounted for. Consequently, the SEU data, while forming the core of the study, do not stand alone; illustrative material is drawn from elsewhere and intuitions on the idiomaticity and predictability of certain modal–adverb combinations are tested through recourse to native speaker informants. The ensuing description is broader in scope than a purely corpus-based approach would allow, or at least one relying solely on the SEU (or any other corpus for that matter), and is more reliable than an account founded uniquely in introspection.

Introspection cannot be done away with altogether, however, even though its role in a corpus-motivated description is greatly reduced. As de Beaugrande (1996: §63; 527) observes: 'The data have already passed the introspection of the text producers . . . . Our task now is to explore how our own introspecting can help us understand *why* these data did pass . . . .' At this stage, intuitions arising from examination of the data can be tested through recourse to native speaker informants, similar to those who generated the original data constituting the corpus. The need to recruit such informants has long been recognized. With reference to the SEU corpus, Quirk (1995: 120) states that it 'has never been solely a corpus-based project. . . . A corpus representative of the repertoire of the mature, educated native speaker would be subjected to analysis in terms of total accountability. And there would be techniques for eliciting the required features. . . .' Elsewhere (1995: 129) he reiterates the place of elicitation in the work of the Survey and, quoting from an earlier essay (Quirk and Svartvik 1979: 207), remarks that: 'It was never envisaged that any corpus, *necessarily finite* [my italics], would of itself be adequate for a comprehensive description of English grammar.'[15] Rather, elicitation tests conducted among educated native speaker informants have always been considered as 'an essential tool for enlarging upon corpus-derived information and for investigating features not perhaps found in the corpus at all'.

In this study, elicitation and translation experiments are used as a basis for comparing native and non-native speaker performance in the modal–adverb domain. Where the corpus records instances of actual usage, elicitation experiments produce supplementary data about native speaker attitudes towards potential use.[16] The results indicate native speaker awareness of the linguistic choices that are available and, together with the corpus data, point to the structure and use of the underlying modal–adverb system. The results of the experiments also indicate the extent to which non-native speaker performance deviates from that of their native speaker counterparts and they suggest ways for increasing the former group's awareness of this area of modality. Both corpus and elicitation data clearly have implications for the teaching of modal–adverb expressions: learning a modal verb might well entail learning the adverbial baggage which accompanies it in actual usage – that is, its more usual and characteristic collocations. Pedagogical proposals are reserved for Chapter 5 after thorough discussion of all the relevant language data.[17]

The book is not primarily a textual study of the SEU; only very occasionally is modal–adverb co-occurrence characteristic of a particular style. But reference is made, where appropriate, in the course of our description. For instance, combinations of SHALL with adverbs like HENCEFORTH, THEREAFTER, WHEREUPON reflect peculiarities in that modal's patterns of co-occurrence which are to be found uniquely in certain formal varieties of English, such as legal contexts.[18, 19]

Illustrations drawn from the Survey of English Usage are followed by a reference such as 'S.7.3.588' or 'W.5.1.36'. The initial letter, 'S' or a 'W', indicates that the corpus material derives from either spoken (SEUS) or written (SEUW) samples respectively. The first number indicates the number of the text; the second the tone unit (SEUS) or script code (SEUW); and the third the computerized reference. Specific examples can be retrieved by keying in the appropriate reference.

In a few examples we have edited out material which is not directly relevant to an appreciation of the context and where its inclusion would make the whole unwieldy and obfuscate the commentary. Dots (. . .) are used to signal omission and to indicate that only a part of the sentence or utterance is being quoted. In all other respects, the quotations are cited unabridged and unmodified as they appear recorded in the SEU. The language material is thus attested and 'real'; the authenticity of the illustrations gives them a poignancy the inventions of grammarians can rarely match, and by being selective it has been possible to avoid inclusion of examples with topical reference, as these date quickly.[20]

1.3.1 The prosodic notation

Examples drawn from the SEUS are accompanied by diacritical markings, indicating the intonational contours and stress patterns for the tone units in question. The prosodic information available on the computerized corpus has been simplified and coded reference to paralinguistic features omitted: to have done otherwise would have encumbered the text and involved the inclusion of otiose detail. But the prosodic information provided is, we believe, adequate for the purposes of demonstrating the interaction between intonation and modality. Prosodic notation is included wherever an illustration derives from the SEUS: a key to the symbols used and an outline of the semantic associations of the various nuclear tones is given below.

While the material is necessarily presented in the form of the printed word, it must always be remembered that language is primarily spoken and heard. The prosodic transcription used is intended to convey for spoken English what the system of punctuation and the spaces between words express in a less sophisticated fashion for written English. The transcription system relates to three interrelated prosodic features: stress, rhythm and intonation.

Stress refers to the relative degree of force used in producing a syllable within a word, or a word within a phrase. A distinction is usually made between stressed and unstressed syllables, the former being perceived as more prominent and uttered with greater emphasis or strength. In the transcription, the stressed segment is marked either with a single vertical stroke, ', where normal stress is involved, or with a double vertical stroke, ", where onset stress is involved and used to mark the first prominent syllable in a tone unit (see below).

The regularity with which stressed syllables are interspersed with unstressed ones in connected speech is referred to as rhythm. Although English may be described as a stress-timed language, there is no absolute regularity of rhythm as this would sound intolerably mechanical. However, in animated speech, successive items may be stressed if a speaker is being unusually insistent or assertive.

Intonation, like stress, is a means of signalling relative prominence but now the variable is pitch or melody, the aspect of auditory sensation perceived in terms of 'low' or 'high'. Spoken English is realized by short stretches or sequences of stressed and unstressed syllables, known as tone units or tone groups, and these are usually co-extensive with a simple or complex grammatical unit, such as an initially placed sentence adverb, a clause, or a sentence. In each tone unit there is at least one syllable which is maximally marked for pitch prominence and referred to as the nucleus. The first prominent syllable in a tone unit is called the onset, and it is often preceded by one or more unstressed syllables. The end of the tone unit, the tone unit boundary, is indicated by #.

Pitch prominence is the central prosodic feature of intonation and is usually associated with changes in pitch. The most prominent pitch movement in a tone unit is referred to as the nuclear tone and, according to variations in the direction of pitch movement, the following categories of nuclear tone can be discriminated: the falling or fall (`) and the rising or rise (´), known as simple tones; the fall–rise (ˇ) and the rise–fall (ˆ), called complex tones; and, finally, the multi-nuclear patterns, fall-plus-rise (`+´), and rise–plus–fall (´+`), which are also referred to as compound tones.

Intonation performs several functions in English. Its most important is to signal grammatical structure, such as the marking of a clause or a sentence, and the contrast between a statement and a question. A second role is to communicate personal attitude, such as the speaker's relative doubt or certainty about what he is saying. Intonation also co-occurs with lexical meanings which have a reinforcing or limiting effect and this is particularly important in the case of adverbs. Ascribing meaning to different nuclear tones is a complex issue, since the meanings associated with any one particular tone often vary, sometimes considerably, according to context. We outline only their basic meanings in relation to declarative utterances here and postpone more detailed discussion of the semantic and pragmatic aspects of intonation until Chapter 4, section 4.6.

The commonest pitch change or tone is a fall (`) and is the least attitudinally marked; it generally conveys an impression of completeness, matter-of-factness, or assertiveness and is most usual on sentence final tone units:

(13)   oh "maps 'must have exǐsted# "cèrtainly# (S.2.3.72/73)

The CGEL (1599) suggests that it operates as a default mode: 'It might be said that . . . a tone unit has a falling nuclear tone unless there is some specific reason why it should not.'

The rising tone (´) is the next most frequently used after the fall and communicates an element of uncertainty or inconclusiveness. It is sometimes used with overtones of politeness:

(14)   I "thought they'd 'prŏbably al'low me to infringe on their
hospi'tality júst 'once 'more# (S.2.12.566)

The other nuclear tones are nowhere near as frequent as either
the fall or the rise but are nevertheless important. The fall–rise (ˇ)
conveys a variety of meanings, in particular, a sense of reservation,
doubt or uncertainty. It can be regularly associated with certain
types of modal–adverb combination and is especially common with
sentence-initial adverbs:

(15)   "prŏbably#   I   "would   im'agine   she   ĭs   in   'fact#
(S.2.14.719)

The rise–fall (ˆ) is a somewhat emotive variant of the fall, which
may involve a sense of finality or completeness, but may also
indicate that the speaker is genuinely impressed, feigning surprise,
or just being sarcastic:

(16)   of course it may "wêll be absurd# it depends on what he
"mèans by absurd# (S.5.2.63/64)

In contrast to other nuclear tones, the multi-nuclear patterns,
fall–plus–rise ('+') and the less common rise–plus–fall ('+'), have
two nuclei and therefore two peaks of prominence and potential
information interest. They tend to combine and set in contrast the
basic meanings conveyed by the individual tones when these
constitute the sole nucleus in a tone unit:

(17)   it "may wèll bé# that "there were fàults# (S.12.4.1120/1)

(18)   you "múst and you 'will go#

The fall occurs on the item which receives the marked focus when
special emphasis is required.
    The prosodic notation used throughout can now be summarized
as follows:

Onset stress	"
Normal stress	'
Tone unit boundary	#
Nuclear stress	
Fall	`
Rise	´
Fall–rise	ˇ

Rise–fall	^
Fall + Rise	ˋ+ˊ
Rise + Fall	ˊ+ˋ

1.4 REVIEW OF THE LITERATURE

A vast number of linguistic and philosophical accounts of modality have been written, but these have primarily focused on the syntactic and semantic behaviour of the modal auxiliaries, or treated the concept and phenomenon of modality in terms of modal logic. Linguistic research still tends to dwell on the semantic rather than the syntactic aspects of the modals, as it is primarily in the domain of meaning that firm and often conflicting theoretical positions have been taken. The present study has an obvious debt to previous research in the field and although, as we have said, this book is primarily a linguistic work, it must be acknowledged that it is impossible to write on modality without making allusion to the underlying philosophical system, which is also the source of much of the terminology linguists currently use. While detailed analysis of modal–adverb co-occurrence has never before been undertaken, recent years have seen the publication of a few works which have set out to analyse and describe modal expressions in general. These are of particular interest. We consider here research where explicit reference is made to modal–adverb co-occurrence or whose treatment of either word class has had a significant influence on the present study. We offer a potted survey: the literature is too vast to review in depth in an introductory treatment such as this. Quite detailed synopses of previous work can be found in Hermerén (1978), Perkins (1983) and Palmer (1986, 1990) in connection with the modals, and Buysschaert (1982) and Virtanen (1992) with regard to adverbials.

Halliday (1970: 322f) recognizes the significance of the potential interplay between the verbal and non-verbal elements or 'forms' of modality, where verbal forms are the modal auxiliaries and non-verbal forms are lexical items such as the adverbs POSSIBLY or CERTAINLY. He argues that the two forms do not correspond one to one, even though there may be a measure of semantic overlap:

> Nor do the different non-verbal forms of the same lexical item necessarily correspond with each other: *obviously* is not the same

as *it is obvious that, surely* as *I am sure that*. But there are discernible groupings, and a clear distinction can be drawn between pairs which are felt to be equivalent, and thus reinforce each other ('as concord') when both are present, as in *perhaps he might have built it*, and those which are not equivalent and are thus cumulative in meaning, as in *certainly he might have built it* ('I insist that it is possible' or 'I grant that it is possible').'

(Halliday 1970: 331)

In Halliday's view, the various exponents of modality, be they verbal or non-verbal, do not exist paradigmatically, as a finite set of mutually exclusive choices. A modality may be expressed by either verbal or non-verbal means or by a combination or combinations of both. For this reason, he concludes: 'There is thus no single place in the clause where modality is located' (1970: 331). A set of expressions like CERTAINLY, IT IS CERTAIN THAT, I AM CERTAIN THAT, HE IS CERTAIN TO, THERE IS A CERTAINTY THAT represent different 'patterns' of modality and are not simply matters of stylistic variation. The accumulation of modal forms within the same utterance or clause is a matter for modal concord or cumulative modality and cannot be explained away as mere pleonastic reiteration of the same modal theme. The premise on which Halliday based his article was that to explain language structure – and therefore the choices we make between this or that structure, this or that modal combination – we have to consider its use: 'language is as it is because of the functions it is required to serve' (1970: 324).[21]

Lyons (1977: ch. 17) offers a major treatment of modality at a semantic and philosophical level, but his aim is not to provide a systematic notional or theoretical account of how modality is expressed in any given language, although he uses English for his illustrations. His main concern is the logical characterization of necessity and possibility, and the discussion of such theoretical topics as the potential distinction between subjective and objective epistemic modality, which we examine in the next chapter. Referring to Halliday (1970), he acknowledges that '... both a modal verb and a modal adverb may be combined' provided that 'they both express the same degree of modality ...' (1977: 807). In this context he talks of 'modally harmonic' and 'modally non-harmonic' combinations, where the modal verb head and its adverb satellite have to complement or reinforce each other. Hence combinations, such as the following, are incompatible on the grounds of modal harmony, or rather disharmony:

(19)   *He must possibly go.
(20)   *She might definitely come.

The factors governing the acceptability or otherwise of modal–adverb combinations is a matter of collocational restriction, which we explore in 5.2.

The Romanian linguist Bîră (1979) offers a systematic and theoretically motivated account of not just the English modals but modal expressions in general, and focuses on a wide variety of linguistic forms: the use of nouns, adjectives, adverbs, main verbs. Although she does not dwell for long on modal–adverb combinations, she echoes Halliday's observations: 'quite often they [modal adverbs] co-occur with modal verbs, thus reinforcing each other or cumulating in meaning' (1979: 211). An interesting feature of Bîră's work is her treatment of the meanings and uses of the modal auxiliaries against the backdrop of speech act theory and pragmatics. This is an area we explore in Chapter 2 in our discussion of mood and modality.

In a similar integrative approach, Perkins (1983) notes that 'most linguistic studies of modal expressions begin and end with an analysis of the modals'; he argues that 'a much broader analysis of a wide range of expressions and other linguistic devices . . . are also available for the expression of modality in English' (1983: 25). The chief merit of this work is the way the author establishes a wide-ranging typology of modal expressions, and yet the nature and extent of the interdependency between the diverse modal elements he describes is left largely unexplored. While an entire chapter is devoted to modal adverbs (1983: ch. 6) – the prime but by no means the sole candidates for co-occurrence with the modals – it is mostly only those items considered to have 'distinguishing features' that attract commentary. In a rather simplistic, formal treatment, modal adverbs are classified as being exclusively sentential. This viewpoint is challenged in our account of modal adverb behaviour in Chapter 4.

In a later synopsis of modal expressions (1983: ch. 8), Perkins does refer briefly to modal–adverb combinations. These he classifies according to how the adverb satellite operates on the modality expressed by the modal, but the three semantic processes he describes – 'thematization', 'interpolation' and 'adjunction' – apply only to those instances where the adverb functions sententially. As examples of each, he offers the following: 'Possibly he will go' (thematization); 'He will possibly go' (interpolation); 'He will go, possibly' (adjunction) (1983: 102). Collocational patterns and trends, and co-occurrence at verb phrase level, are left undiscussed. Yet Perkins was among the first to recognize that a descriptive account of non-verbal as well as verbal modal expressions was necessary, and that the former are more than just periphrastic options:

> It was only when such a wide range of expressions and other linguistic devices was submitted to a close scrutiny at the same time that it became clear that there were semantic grounds for isolating the modal auxiliaries from other modal expressions, and that no two modal expressions could be said to have exactly the same meaning.
>
> (Perkins 1983: 2)

Palmer (1979, 1990) still provides one of the fullest accounts in the literature, but his primary focus is the systematic classification of modal meaning almost exclusively in relation to the modal auxiliaries.[22] As with the present study, he too relies on the SEU corpus but uses the data selectively, preferring to rely on invented examples when discussing more theoretical issues. Illustrations drawn from the spoken texts have their prosodic and paralinguistic information excluded because 'it is almost completely irrelevant to a study of the modals' (1979: 19; 1990: 26). Our own findings indicate the contrary (see 4.6) and, as example (6) above demonstrates, intonation can interact with modal elements already present in the sentence. Palmer pays scant attention to co-occurrence, claiming that few adverbs co-occur with the modals and that those that do are primarily concerned with expressing judgements or the speaker's confidence and are thus pleonastic. He concludes '. . . in general, epistemic modals cannot be modified by adverbs, or at least the true modals cannot' (1979: 57). Admittedly, he later revises his position, omitting reference to 'the true modals' (1990: 68) but he remains dismissive of the subject.

Palmer's later work (1986) is broader in focus and, on the basis of language data drawn from many different languages and not just

English, he discusses the various ways in which modality is grammaticalized in language, the range of its functions, and its relation to other grammatical categories such as tense, aspect, gender or number. His discussion of the scope of modality encompasses definitions in terms of speech act theory; the attitude or opinion of the speaker; subjectivity; factivity and assertion; and the traditional concepts of modal logic, possibility and necessity. Again, this typological survey dwells on the modal–verb system and only fleeting reference is made to adverbs. In contrast to his observations elsewhere, Palmer (1986: 64) notes the interaction of MUST with adverbs like CERTAINLY and DEFINITELY: '...there is a clear difference between MUST and adverbs such as CERTAINLY, the modal expressing inference and the adverb confidence'. However, Palmer only pursues this argument in his discussion of the inference/confidence distinction (see 3.3) and how this might be marked grammatically. He does not investigate modal–adverb synergy on its own account.

Coates (1983) again focuses on the semantic system of the modals, although reference is made to co-occurrence in terms of 'harmonic combinations', and adverbs are treated as 'hedges' (1983: passim). Her approach differs markedly from previous research in its reliance on corpus-derived, spoken and written data to inform the framework for analysis. The study contains an abundance of language material drawn from the then Lancaster corpus as well as the Survey of English Usage. Along with a number of other scholars, Coates' strategy is to identify and then isolate for each modal a basic or 'core' meaning which is independent of its context of use. In his treatment of the modals, Perkins (1983) also adopts what is known as a 'monosemantic' or 'monosemic' approach. The underlying principle is that the basic meaning is the one which applies at all times, accompanied by subsidiary meanings or modifications or, as Ehrman (1966: 10) calls them, 'overtones'. Coates, like Perkins, argues against modal polysemy or at least the range and multiplicity of meanings promulgated by some linguists. Whether in fact it is possible to argue in favour of relatively precise core meanings is very much in dispute. Palmer argues that 'there is no clear evidence of such precise core or basic meanings, nor is there any theoretical or descriptive requirement for them' (1990: 17). His accounts veer towards 'polysemy' and the view that each modal has a range of different, but not necessarily unrelated, meanings. However, the strength of Coates' work lies in its reliance on attested spoken and written language data rather than on the whims of intuition, and on its account of the association between prosodic features and modality. This allows her to draw fresh insights into the relative frequencies of the modal verbs, and the core and associated meanings they convey. Throughout the work, Coates makes explicit reference to the indeterminacy of modal meanings, which is unavoidable once their semantic complexity is recognized.

The practice adopted by the CGEL, and the one which we follow in this book, is to assign each modal a set of major meanings (as opposed to a single core meaning) with the rider that the distinctions between them are gradual rather than absolute. WILL and WOULD, for example, are described in terms of prediction, under which heading three related uses are identified, and volition where, again, three subsenses are distinguished (1985: 228f). The virtue of such an approach is that the semantic complexity of the modals is thereby recognized but within a structured framework which allows for the principle of what the CGEL refers to as 'gradience': the various senses described are not necessarily discrete and meanings may overlap.

Matthews' (1991) examination of modality in English, which includes reference to German, largely centres on the modals, referred to as 'modal expressions'. In the main, his study adopts Lyons' (1977) linguistic and philosophical proposals as an analytical framework and the approach he adopts is based in speech act theory and the specification of different utterance types. The modals remain the focus of the study, although other types of modal expression are examined: lexical verbs, such as BELIEVE, THINK, SUPPOSE; adjectival patterns, such as IT IS POSSIBLE THAT; and, significantly, modal–adverb combinations. The latter are treated as 'synthetic' modal expressions and their grammatical and semantic roles discussed in relation to epistemic modality. Variations in adverbial position and the nature of the semantic association between modal and adverb are explored in some detail. Matthews summarizes his findings by establishing a paradigm of modal–adverb combinations, such as WILL CERTAINLY, MIGHT POSSIBLY, and WON'T NECESSARILY, which are then described as 'genuine cases of reinforcing or submodifying adverbs with modal expressions' (1990: 59). Matthews clearly does not endorse Palmer's view that

such combinations are pleonastic and his observation that co-
-occurrence 'may be taken to represent, at least in part, the
"natural" conceptualization of modality in English' (1990: 62)
attests its significance within the English system of modality.

The formal and semantic description of adverbs and adverbials
in English has been a no less fertile ground for research, and as
challenging as the investigation of modal expressions and modality.
In general, most works on the adverbial in English have focused on
questions of placement or position, syntactic status, semantic and
formal classification. Latterly, studies have adopted a contextual
bias, examining adverbial behaviour in terms of speech act theory
and discourse functions. Nearly all the major studies considered
below, recent and not so recent, have relied heavily on the use of
corpora.

In his pioneering work on English adverbial usage, Greenbaum
notes the confusion and disagreement surrounding the definition
of adverb as 'sentence modifier' or 'sentence adverb', stating that
these terms 'have been used imprecisely and in various ways' (1969:
2). Using syntactic criteria, Greenbaum distinguishes three categories of adverb, 'conjuncts', 'disjuncts', and 'adjuncts', a classification which was to be subsequently refined and used as the
framework for adverbial description in the CGEL. Adverbs may
function intersententially (where they have a linking function and
conjoin clauses), sententially (where they are relatively peripheral
to clause structure) or intrasententially (where they are relatively
integrated within clause structure): 'there is a gradient of integration of adverbs in the clause and not a sharp break between the
integrated and the unintegrated' (Greenbaum 1969: 15). This study
put the lie to the then still widely held, yet mistaken, view that
adverbs are peripheral items and sentential in scope (see Chapter 4,
sections 4.1.2 and 4.5.1). A further merit of the work is its reliance
on data drawn from the SEU (see 1.3), supplemented by material
obtained from a series of elicitation experiments.[23]

The largest empirical investigation of English adverbials, and in
particular their placement, is the series of studies carried out by
Jacobson (1964, 1975, 1978). His works merit more detailed
attention in this section because of their centrality to adverbial
studies as a whole. Like Greenbaum, Jacobson (1964) focuses on
adverbial positions and the implications transmobility has for
adverbial classification. Again a central distinction is drawn

between adverbs of sentential and intrasentential orientation. Both Jacobson and Greenbaum are primarily concerned with the syntactic behaviour of adverbs and the formal criteria by which the different categories can be established. However, Jacobson explicitly draws attention to adverbs of mood by acknowledging that certain attitudes of the mind of the speaker or writer towards the contents of the sentence 'can also be expressed by some adverbs and adverbial phrases, and these can then be said to have a modal character' (1964: 24). He goes on to describe three main categories of 'mood' (thus using that term semantically): distinguishing between 'certainty' (as expressed by CERTAINLY, NO DOUBT, etc.); 'supposition' (PROBABLY, PERHAPS, etc.); and 'opinion' (UNFORTUNATELY, BEST OF ALL, etc.) (1964: 25). At the same time, he implies that there is an overlap in function between such adverbs and grammatical exponents of modality, namely the modals. But his concern is adverbial placement rather than verb–adverb collocations.

The second part of the study is given over to a dictionary of adverb placement which contains a number of entries for modal adverbs. The purpose of each entry is to give the relative frequency of the various adverbial positions in relation to clause structure, including verb heads and occasionally the modal auxiliaries where these are attested in the data: Jacobson's material derives from a corpus of present-day written British English, all texts dating from 1935 on. The same adverb is often treated under more than one heading when it has different meanings or functions, especially where such differences are significant to the placement of the adverb. Jacobson thus distinguishes different types of adverbial modification and the scope of that modification. According to Jacobson's analysis, INEVITABLY favours mid-position, accounting for 67 per cent of all occurrences. Two of his examples include co-occurrence with MUST:

(21)   Faith in Christ is the only thing to save you from despair at that point: and out of Faith in Him good actions must inevitably come. (J 1964: 282)

(22)   Without it he may be just but he must inevitably be cold. (J 1964: 282)

Elsewhere, entries referring to 'adverbs of mood' often include in illustration a modal–adverb combination. However, the declared aim of the dictionary is to demonstrate only how 'adverbs are actually placed in some works of written English prose' (1964: 205); the entries thus deal exclusively with positional norms and no attempt is made to examine the nature of the association between adverb satellites and particular types of verb head. A brief section in the body of Jacobson's description also covers the placement of 'phrases of mood' (1964: 92f) where adverbials, as opposed to adverbs, are considered. Common phrases examined include: OF COURSE, NO DOUBT, IN FACT and TO BE FRANK. The most significant aspect of Jacobson's research for our own study is the recognition that adverbs of mood occur mostly in mid-position or a variant of mid-position, in close proximity to the verb head: it seems natural that a modifier should come as close as possible to the head it modifies. The second part of the study is also a valuable independent source of data which is frequently used in this study in order to supplement the Survey material.

In a later work, Jacobson (1975) investigates the influence of contextual factors on adverbial placement in relation to auxiliaries, and the use, meaning and syntax of what he refers to as 'preverbal adverbs'. Whilst adverbs remain the focus of both studies, the syntactic relationship between adverb and verb head is extensively researched. The 1975 study is again corpus-based, except that now the data derive solely from samples of spoken and written American English. The aim of the study is fourfold: syntactic, taxonomic, language-specific and linguistic. The syntactic aim is to give a comprehensive description of preverb (essentially adverbs in preverbal position) placement in surface structure and to elaborate on the factors determining this placement; arising out of this, the taxonomic aim is to establish a classificational procedure which, in aiming to be discrete, does not ignore borderline cases less susceptible to ready categorization; the language-specific aim is to account for the positioning of preverbs in modern American English (British English was the focus of his 1964 study); and, finally, the general linguistic aim is to marry empirical and rationalist approaches to language study on the grounds that they are not necessarily incompatible. The book relates positional variations to language medium (spoken or written), different text categories ('newspapers', 'fiction', 'non-fiction', 'magazines', etc.), and to a variety of 'stylistic provinces' ('sports', 'news', 'business letters', 'narrative prose', 'religion' and so forth). An assessment of the relative frequencies of certain types of 'preverb exponents' in combination with auxiliary verbs such as PROBABLY with WILL in contrast with PROBABLY with DO is used as the basis for establishing and predicting positional norms and tendencies. Two central modal adverbs, PROBABLY and CERTAINLY, figure tantalizingly amongst the twelve most common 'preverb exponents' listed. However, as before, the point at issue is not the nature of the relation between the modifier and the modified but the central factors conditioning preverbal placement.

In a companion study (1978), Jacobson continues his treatment of preverbal adverbs. Whereas before he was concerned with a quantitative analysis of preverb placement in relation to auxiliaries, he now offers a classification of preverbs based on their pragmatic, semantic and syntactic functions. The syntactic function is concerned with the way preverbs operate on or within the sentence; these operations involve three main processes: 'modification', 'focalization' and 'connection'. On this basis, Jacobson distinguishes three main categories of preverb: sentence-modifiers which characterize the utterance as a whole; focalizers which characterize and focus on a particular constituent; and conjuncts which connect sentences or constituents. The semantic function is measured in terms of the abstract notional components of 'quality', 'relationship', 'degree' and 'time'. Modal concepts are covered under 'quality' but the basis of this categorization is extraordinarily vague. For instance, the preverbs TRULY, VERITABLY, GENUINELY, FALSELY, which relate to 'trueness' or 'falseness', are viewed as a 'physical quality' which 'can be ascribed to all kinds of phenomena, including animate beings' (1978: 73). An interesting feature of the work is its treatment of pragmatic functions, described in terms of 'marking a conclusion', 'marking confirmation or correction', 'marking sincerity' and so on. The pragmatics of making a conclusion involves treatment of such modal–adverb combinations as WILL PROBABLY, where the speaker signals that the evidence available to him is insufficient to make a categorical assertion. Hence, instead of 'The car will be ready tomorrow', he can utter 'The car will probably be ready tomorrow', where the strength of his conviction is modified by an element of doubt. We examine common uses of modal–adverb combinations in Chapter 3, section 3.5, and Chapter 4, section 4.5.4.

Probably the most consistently useful aspect of Jacobson's series of studies is its collection of attested data rather than any account it offers of the underlying principles which determine adverbial classification.[24] A more theoretically rigorous treatment of adverbials is provided in the CGEL, to which we refer below and discuss in more detail in Chapter 4.

Buysschaert (1982) eschews traditional approaches to the classification of adverbials and bases his proposals within a generative-transformational framework, in which he acknowledges the importance of semantics. He establishes three main sets of dictinctions. Firstly, a distinction is made between adverbials which function as 'essential complements' and are obligatory as in: 'He treats his servants *well*' and adverbs which function as 'free modifiers' and are optional as in: 'They may *well* leave for Bangkok tomorrow.' 'Ultimately,' it is argued, 'the decisive criterion is of a semantic nature' (1982: 7); when obligatory the adverbial is inherently required by the meaning of the verb, when omissible it is not. The second set of distinctions focuses on sentence adverbials ('sentence modifiers') and non-sentence adverbials ('verb modifiers', 'noun phrase modifiers' and 'adverb modifiers'). Again Buysschaert argues that semantics is crucial: whereas sentence adverbials qualify 'the event, act, circumstance, claim or fact described in an entire sentence; V-modifiers [verb modifiers] only qualify the action or process described in the verb' (1982: 8). Finally, the third set of distinctions, which are the most innovative aspect of Buysschaert's account, relates adverbial behaviour and intonation to the information structure of utterances: 'Adverbials behave differently according to whether they are the comment or the topic of the utterance (or have no function in information structure), and to whether they have the focus or not' (1982: 8). By 'topic' is meant that part of the utterance which is introduced as being the subject-matter; the 'comment' is what is actually said about the subject-matter; and 'focus' is that part of the utterance realized as the location of the tonic or nuclear stress (see 4.6). Obligatory and optional adverbials, sentential and non-sentential modifiers can all function as the topic (focused or non-focused) as well as the comment of an utterance. The analysis of adverbial behaviour in terms of information structure allows for a categorization of adverbials which cuts across distinctions drawn according to the more traditional semantic and grammatical criteria of scope and optionality. Buysschaert's treatment has obvious implications for our own study, even though he is nowhere concerned with the specific issue of modality: the natural association between modal adverbs and their modal verb heads indicates an 'inherent' relationship or collocational bonding (see Chapter 5); modal adverbs which express the speaker's comment towards his utterance and may, for instance, serve as 'theme-setters' have an important discourse function (see 4.4).

Virtanen (1992) adopts a not dissimilar framework for her work on adverbial placement in English and, like Buysschaert, notes that adverbial positions cannot be adequately accounted for by reference to sentence structure alone: 'Several of the factors that may influence the placement of adverbials in their clause or sentence are textual or discoursal in character' (1992: 1). The focus of the study is on clause-initial adverbials of time and place but observations on the relationship between discourse function and initial position are of particular relevance to our treatment of sentential modal adverbs.

The CGEL offers a detailed account of the adverbial in English and incorporates the findings of much previous research. The grammar does account for some modal–adverb combinations, particularly those which occur in restricted environments. Whilst the authors do not at any point give an explicit, descriptive account of modal–adverb co-occurrence, their allusions to this area again support the view that the need for a fuller description exists. The influence of this work and its centrality to English grammatical description is recognized frequently throughout this study. Since the framework we use for our treatment of modal adverbs is based on the system of classification elaborated there, a more detailed examination of the CGEL approach is postponed until Chapter 4.

Finally, in addition to these major works on modals and adverbials, there are other, shorter studies of significance to which we refer in the course of our description. The scope of this review of background literature does not allow a detailed treatment of all relevant research: we have referred to only the most salient accounts.

NOTES

1   A number of illustrations which are not drawn from the Survey of English corpus derive from a range of written material whose source is indicated by a code, consisting of two letters and a page reference, e.g. MD/157. A list of texts with their corresponding codes is provided immediately before the main bibliography.

2   Details of the prosodic notation used in the corpus examples and an explanation of the accompanying codes which appear in brackets are provided in section 1.3.1 of the main text.

3   See, for example, Zellig Harris (1957).

4   See Chapter 3, note 15.

5   Henceforth, Quirk *et al.* (1985) is referred to as the CGEL, with the relevant page reference(s) given in brackets, e.g. CGEL (475).

6   See Sinclair (1991) for a succinct introduction to the role of corpus linguistics in language description.

7   Some of the written data used in this book derive from Jacobson (1975), which is based exclusively on samples of American English. See Coates and Leech (1980) for a brief account of the modals in American and British English.

8   Introspection involves ideas about language rather than facts of actual usage; it is best suited to the evaluation rather than the generation of linguistic evidence. See Greenbaum and Quirk (1970: ch. 1) and Sinclair (1991: 39).

9   There now exist, worldwide, nearly twenty computerized English language corpora, varying in size from around 52,000 to 30 million words. Others, such as 'The International Corpus of English', in preparation by thirteen national groups, are under development and yet others, such as the 'Bank of English' (see note 11 below), fluctuate in the size of the sample which forms the active corpus. The proliferation of corpora and the ease with which they can be accessed has given rise to a wave of research projects that it would have been impossible to imagine a few years ago. The collection of articles on corpus linguistics, compiled and edited by Karin Aijmer and Bengt Altenberg (1991), attests the virility of the field and embodies the orthodoxy of a new generation of specialists in the field of corpus linguistics.

See also the collection of papers edited by Jenny Thomas and Mick Short (1996) on the use of corpora for language research. Of particular interest are the series of corpus-based case studies in syntax, semantics and stylistics it contains, and four articles which discuss the application of corpus-based approaches to more applied areas of language research, such as language teaching and language testing.

For a direct application of corpus techniques to the description of modality, see Stubbs (1996: ch. 8).

10 A third advantage of using corpora is that, by exemplifying different registers, they facilitate comparison between different varieties of English. Sociolinguistic aspects of co-occurrence are not explored in this study. See McDonald (1981) for an account of research into regional language variation and its impact on the use of modal verbs.

11 The Survey material was consulted in the academic year 1987/1988, when the computerization of the data was not complete. This may account for slight discrepancies in statistical figures for the frequency of individual modals and modal–adverb co-occurrences now attested in the data. However, the present work is not a textual analysis of the Survey, and it is also most unlikely that the probabilistic tendencies observed then have in any way been significantly affected.

Other corpora are much larger than the SEU and, because of the size of the sample involved, might validly claim to be more representative. For instance, the 'Bank of English' (the 'Cobuild' corpus of spoken and written English), developed at the University of Birmingham under the guidance of John Sinclair (see the bibliography) and which, at the time of writing, comprises some 200 million words of running text, gives, in principle, greater coverage and represents an even closer approximation to the real language in its entirety. How extensive a language corpus has to be in order to provide enough data for a valid linguistic description must vary according to the feature(s) being described: certainly, the sample size of the SEU has been sufficient to reveal the range and type of modal–adverb collocations that are functionally significant and it has been mostly adequate in revealing the more detailed regularities of association the two forms exhibit. Furthermore, a particular strength of the SEU is that a sizeable proportion of its spoken sample consists of surreptitiously recorded speech as opposed to the scripted commentaries of television and radio broadcasts or the premeditated delivery of lectures, public speeches and sermons: it is therefore especially valuable for the instances of spontaneous, unscripted interaction it attests. For further general discussion of the value of 'large corpus linguistics', see de Beaugrande (1996: 622f), and also note 15 below.

12 The fields of discourse covered by the Survey are very broad. The written texts of the Survey include material intended for spoken delivery, such as drama, news broadcasts, lectures; handwritten and typed materials, such as examination essays, social and business correspondence; and printed publications, such as journalistic

writing, prose fiction, administrative and legal reports. The spoken texts include surreptitiously recorded telephone conversations, face-to-face exchanges, interviews, broadcast commentaries on sport and on ceremonial occasions, lectures, speeches and sermons. Both spoken and written types of discourse therefore represent authenticated instances of real English.

When the Survey was consulted for this investigation (1987), the entire corpus had been analysed in terms of 65 grammatical categories and the occurrence of over 400 specified words and phrases, such as the modals, adverbs, determiners and prepositions that belong to closed class grammatical categories. For spoken texts, the Survey additionally included about 100 prosodic and paralinguistic features.

Originally, the data were available only in hard copy, on catalogued slips, making it slow to search. However, the data are now fully computerized and access to them is much quicker and more reliable than ever before. It was in this format that the Survey was consulted for this study: a concordance browser, which makes it possible to retrieve all occurrences of particular lexical and grammatical strings, proved especially useful in the identification of modal–adverb combinations present in the corpus.

13   See Stubbs (1996: 172f) on the application of quantitative methods in corpus analysis, especially in connection with techniques aimed at the analysis of the meaning and use of cultural keywords in the domain of British culture.

14   Jacobson (1964, 1975, 1978) has been a valuable source of written data, in connection with adverbials. Illustrations due to this author are referred to by the initial J, followed by the year of publication of the relevant work, together with the appropriate page references, e.g. (J 1964: 286). (Jacobson's work is discussed in some detail in section 1.4.)

Occasional reference is also made to Hartvigson (1969) who offers an intonational, positional and semantic description of sentence adverbials, focusing primarily on their prosodic features. A serious drawback of the study, however, is its reliance on the 'analyst's own or someone else's correct [sic] rendering of a speech sequence' (1969: 26) where the texts used are drawn from samples of written rather than spoken language! Material drawn from this source is therefore treated as written data, and is identified by the initial H, followed by the year of publication, 1969, and the appropriate page reference, e.g. (H 1969: 135).

15   Even very large corpora such as the 200 million word Bank of English (BoE) which, at the time of writing, is the largest computer corpus

in existence, '*is still too small*', according to de Beaugrande (1996: §67; 529f): 'It confronts us with a fresh version of the complex ratios between what *has been said* versus what *can be said*, and between what people *can understand* versus what they *have occasion to say*.' His comments highlight the problems of skewing immanent to the compilation of any corpus: there will always be an imbalance with regard to the range of sample texts collected, the discourse topics involved ('murder', 'shooting', 'robbery' are amongst those de Beaugrande cites in connection with the BoE), and the ratio of spoken to written texts. His remarks also point to the value of elicitation testing, so central to the SEU, as a means of obtaining additional data to compensate for the inadequacies of a corpus. See also note 11.

16   In their discussion of the aims of elicitation experiments, Greenbaum and Quirk (1970: 7) point out that

> we cannot escape from the artificiality of the test situation, though with continuing refinement we can hope to remove some of the worst effects of bias that the test situation introduces. Meantime, we can be sure that the alternatives are considerably less promising: reliance upon corpus alone and reliance upon introspection alone. Both need supplementation by experimental evidence.

17   Corpus linguistics may ultimately be most influential in the domain of language teaching and specifically in the preparation of reference works such as dictionaries, which are increasingly compiled on the basis of large electronic collections of spoken and written texts. (See, for instance, the range of learners' dictionaries produced by Longman that are based on a mix of spoken and written databases, running into several million words, or the Collins COBUILD range of ELT reference publications.) As de Beaugrande (1996: §77; 532) remarks: 'Wide access [to corpora] would at least enable influential groups, such as language teachers, to get accurate data about usage.' In addition to revealing the contexts of use, the data display words in combination with 'the company they keep', to reformulate the quotation from Firth (1957: 195). This includes not only idioms and lexical phrases (see 5.2) but other combinations of words, collocations, where the association between the items may be less fixed. De Beaugrande (1996: §77; 532) suggests that 'If the chief unit of language use and language learning is recognised to be the *collocation*, then learning words would be systematically correlated with learning the company they keep.' The evidence provided by our description of co-occurrence and the subsequent informant tests indicates that awareness of the modals' adverb collocates results in a better

understanding of the complex workings of the English modal system as a whole.

Mindt, in Thomas and Short (1996: 232–47), argues that, notwithstanding the use of corpora in the preparation of dictionaries and other linguistic works of reference, corpus-based studies should play a much bigger role in the preparation of teaching materials, especially in the design of textbooks for teaching English as a foreign language. He suggests, for instance, that the order of presentation of modal verb forms should take into account their frequencies of use and, referring to the practice observed in two textbooks widely used in German secondary schools, remarks that:

> Both textbooks postpone *will* in favour of the [relatively] infrequent modal verbs *must* and *may*. It is very difficult to see why *will* should be introduced only in the middle or at the end of the second year when it is so frequently used by native speakers in spoken conversation. (1996; 236)

See also Stubbs (1996: ch. 8) on the relevance of corpus analysis for applied linguistics. In a short case study, the author explores the different ways in which modality can be expressed in English, as attested in various corpora; the resulting description is then offered as the basis of a (preliminary) 'modal grammar of English'. He argues that such a grammar has a wide range of applications, particularly in the area of language teaching:

> The sociolinguistic competence to make tentative or tactful statements, about controversial subjects about which one has reservations, is a problem for foreign learners ... And it is well known that non-native speakers of English can sound rude, brusque or tactless if they make mistakes in this area. (1996: 227)

18 We do investigate, however, the constraints on co-occurrence that are due to the specific association of modality with pragmatic notions of 'power' (see 2.7) and 'politeness' (see 3.5). Both are manifest across a broad range of discourse contexts. The concept of power involves various kinds of institutional authority, such as government, the judiciary, or the military. On the other hand, politeness, defined as appropriate language use (see 3.5.2), offers a highly generalized interpretative framework for the assessment of co-occurrence.

19 See Klinge (1995) for an investigation into the role of the (primarily unmodified) modal auxiliaries in the discourse context of legal contracts. Using as his empirical basis a corpus of ten British English household insurance policies, the author aims to establish a framework for assessing the semantic and pragmatic factors involved in the

interpretation of contractual modalities.

He suggests (1995: 670) that 'the most interesting modal in legal language is *shall*', noting that this modal 'is very frequent in legal and other formal contexts'.

20   The particular value of authenticated language samples is forcefully articulated by de Beaugrande (1996: §25; 512) who condemns the facile and decontextualized inventions of (particularly) generative linguists. Hence, 'beloved evergreens' like 'The man hit the ball' or 'The cat sat on the mat'

> do not appear [in the Bank of English corpus], not because they aren't properly grammatical or well-formed English but because they aren't *natural*: typical contexts of real discourse require less simple-minded and peremptory utterances.... We shouldn't regard the grainy details of the real data as a mere obstruction to be filtered out by rarefying and decontextualizing.... Instead, we should respect the naturalness of real data because, unlike the grammaticalness or well-formedness of the formalists, *it has been decided for us by real users of the language....*

21   In his revised and updated introduction to functional grammar, Halliday (1994) discusses what he refers to as the 'mood element' in the clause within a functional rather than a formal perspective. As is the case in his earlier work, he recognizes that 'There is in fact a wide range of variants for the expression of modality in the clause ...' (1994: 354). These variants he now refers to as 'metaphors of modality' which would, presumably, encompass modal–adverb realizations of modality: 'It is not always possible to say exactly what is and what is not a metaphorical representation of a modality. But speakers have indefinitely many ways of expressing their opinions – or rather, perhaps, of dissimulating the fact that they *are* expressing their opinions ...' (1994: 355). Adverbial carriers of modal meanings are referred to variously as 'modal adjuncts' (1994: 49) or 'mood adjuncts' (1994: 83).

It should be noted, however, that Halliday adopts a rather idiosyncratic view of mood and modality which differs from the more traditional approach used in this study.

22   See Coates (1980b) for a detailed review of Palmer (1979). Palmer's approach to the use of spoken data in the later edition of this work (1990) remains basically unchanged.

23   See Quirk and Svartvik (1966), Greenbaum and Quirk (1970), Greenbaum (1988) and Quirk (1995) for detailed information on the various test techniques devised for investigating linguistic acceptability.

24 Jacobson's earlier work has been severely criticized for its empiricism. A reviewer of his 1964 study remarks: 'He [Jacobson] is concerned with the presentation of data rather than with the presentation of evidence, the distinction being that evidence requires a theory whereas data do not. In this distinction lie the successes and failures of the present work' (Keyser 1968: 359). The reviewer's own commitment to universal grammar, however, coincides with a tendency to undervalue the benefits of studying the material evidence provided by a data-based study of a single language.

Two

Mood and modality

Le propre du réel est de pouvoir être toujours
regardé à un autre point de vue . . . être interprété
encore d'une autre façon – représenté autrement, et
ceci sans limite, sans dérivée.

(Paul Valéry)[1]

When we speak or write, we are often vague,
indirect and unclear about just what we are
committed to. This might appear, superficially, to
be an inadequacy of human language: but only to
those who hold a rather crude view of the purposes
of communication. Vagueness and indirection have
many uses [. . .] Whenever speakers or writers say
anything, they encode their point of view towards
it: whether they think it is a reasonable thing to
say, or might be found to be obvious, questionable,
tentative, provisional, controversial, contradictory,
irrelevant, impolite or whatever. The expression of
such speaker's attitudes is pervasive in all uses of
language. All utterances encode such a point of
view, and the description of the markers of such
points of view and their meanings is a central topic
in linguistics.

(Michael Stubbs, 1996: 202)

2.1 INTRODUCTION

The two concepts whose explication is central to the present study
are those of mood and modality. Confusion may arise out of the use
of these terms because the terminological distinction between
them is not always rigorously observed when modal concepts are
being discussed. Thus Palmer (1979: 4) argues that 'Modality . . . is
a semantic term . . .' only to propose in a later work (1986: 1) that
'. . . it is possible to recognize a grammatical category, that of
modality, which is similar to aspect, tense, number, gender, etc.'.

Elsewhere, Palmer (1994: 2536) suggests that modality be used to refer to the grammatical category even though 'traditional studies talk of mood'. The terminological problem mirrors peculiarities in the way modal contrasts are expressed in English; but in this book we endorse traditional approaches and use mood to refer to the grammatical category, and modality to refer to the entire semantic field of modal contrasts whether these be realized lexically, grammatically or prosodically.

After making some preliminary observations on the grammatical role of the modal auxiliaries in relation to the system of mood in English, we examine the concept of modality in accordance with a range of semantic and pragmatic criteria which are considered relevant to its definition. The discussion is based on the fundamental distinction which is drawn between epistemic and deontic modality and the characterization of modality in terms of a series of contrasts between subjectivity and non-factuality and objectivity, proposition and event, and possibility and necessity. The pragmatics of modality is related to Speech Act Theory and the notion of 'utterance', where the epistemic and deontic dimensions are examined according to the notions of authority, knowledge and power. Treatment of modality and politeness strategies is postponed until the end of Chapter 3 (3.5.2), following a detailed description of the modals and their adverb satellites.

2.2 MOOD

There are many languages other than English where modal concepts are signalled by inflecting the verb; in other words, inflection is used as the formal marker of mood. Mood may thus be formally defined as a morphosyntactic category akin to tense and aspect. Jespersen (1924: 313) states that mood is an inherent verbal category: '... it is very important that we speak of mood only if the attitude of mind [of the speaker] is shown in the form of the verb: mood is thus a syntactic, not a notional category'. Lyons (1977: 848) also maintains that 'mood is a grammatical category that is found in some, but not all languages'.

In describing the mood system of English, grammars typically refer to the indicative, subjunctive and imperative.[2] In general terms, the indicative mood (also referred to as the 'unmarked' category of mood) and its characteristic verbal inflections are associated with factual assertions ('Gertrude is on holiday'); the imperative is used to inflect the verb when making requests or demands ('Kindly refrain from smoking'); and the subjunctive is used for the verb form in subordinate clauses involving non-factuality ('The coroner demanded that the remains be returned for further examination'). Here, it is clearly not a factual assertion that is being reported but that the coroner was concerned to bring about a certain event. In English the subjunctive occurs in subordinate clauses in association with a very small class of verbs like DEMAND, INSIST, REQUIRE; and in main clauses it is restricted to archaic or formulaic utterances such as 'So be it!'. Originally, the subjunctive was used to convey a wide range of attitudes on the part of the speaker towards the factual content of his utterance, such as doubt, certainty, vagueness, and possibility, which over time have come to be conveyed by modal expressions, including the modal auxiliaries. In this respect, English contrasts with inflected languages, such as German, French, Romanian or Spanish which, in addition to modal verbs, deploy the subjunctive widely in expressing modality. Where mood is expressed through verbal inflection, it can be described as 'synthetic'. But mood is just one way in which modality can be expressed. In English there remain only vestiges of these modal functions expressed through contrasts in verbal inflection. 'There is no need to be much concerned with the subjunctive in English. . . . This has largely disappeared . . . and it can well be argued that it has been replaced by the modal verbs . . .' (Palmer 1986: 43).

For this reason, Huddleston (1984: 164) proposes 'an analytic mood system' as distinct from 'a synthetic mood system'[3] when auxiliaries, rather than inflection, are the exponents of the grammatical mood system, used to express differences between factual assertion and various kinds of non-factuality:

> We are taking the view that there is no inflectional system of mood in modern English, but the contrast between *He is downstairs, He may be downstairs, He must be downstairs,* and so on, also falls within this semantic area and we will accordingly regard the VPs *is, may be* and *must be* as differing in mood; since the terms in the VP system are differentiated not inflectionally but by means of auxiliaries, we will talk of an analytic mood system.

The initial distinction is between non-modal and modal VPs, with the latter being then subdivided into more specific mood categories according to which modal auxiliary they contain.

(Huddleston 1984: 164)

In order to be consistent with the terminological distinction we have drawn between mood and modality and to avoid any ambiguity, we refer to 'modalities' or 'categories of modality' rather than 'mood categories', where the focus is on meaning rather than form.

The terminological convenience of referring to the modal auxiliaries as 'an analytic mood system' is of obvious appeal where English is concerned, even if this is to extend the traditional definition of mood to incorporate syntactic as well as morphological realizations of modality. As Palmer (1986: 21f) points out, if the term mood is restricted to verbal morphology 'there will be no general term for all the grammatical systems that are exponents of (semantic) modality...'. Huddleston offers an attractive solution to the terminological issue, although it is worth noting that the traditional characterization of mood as a uniquely inflectional category is still widely preferred.

2.3 MODALITY

Discussion of what is now generally known as modality and the modal concepts of possibility, probability and necessity goes back to Aristotle and classical Greek philosophy. These notions seem to derive from the fact that human beings often categorize their attitudes and experience in terms of the way things might or must be, or might have been or must have been, other than they actually are or were. This capacity to envisage things other than they are or were ('things being otherwise'), to hold competing and incompatible world views, is fundamental to our everyday thinking. When a speaker utters 'They may well have left' he expresses a state of affairs which is conceivably real even if it is not in fact the case. By contrast, in producing the unmodalized utterance 'They have left', he makes a factual assertion about a state of affairs which he considers to be the case.

Philosophers and logicians have frequently attempted to analyse and categorize modal notions through recourse to the idea of 'possible worlds' where 'things being otherwise' can be described in terms of what is true or real in another 'possible world'. Rather than say 'such and such may be the case', they argue that 'a possible world exists where such and such is the case'. There certainly seems to be one possible world and that is the actual one in which we are living but there may also be others which constitute alternatives to the real world. Of course the issue of whether possible worlds are as real as the actual one or just abstract alternatives to the real world they may represent – modes of expression as it were – is a matter for philosophy and logical semantics rather than linguistics. In any case, most people would find it reasonable to maintain that there are many ways in which things might have been. In producing the modalized utterances 'Josephine evidently must have forgotten the appointment' or 'Josephine might perhaps have forgotten the appointment', the speaker operates with alternative worlds or scenarios in mind in which Josephine has forgotten the appointment. Similarly, in an utterance like 'Josephine really should have remembered the appointment', the speaker envisions a possible world in which things are as he would want them to be, namely a world where Josephine did not forget her appointment! To conceive of things being otherwise is to hold that they are real or true in a world other than the actual one we are living in or that they are real or true in the actual world but at a moment in time other than the present.

By construing talk about possible worlds as talk about ways in which the world can be conceived to be different helps explain the conceptual dimension of modality. Possible worlds are significant because they contrast with the current actual world and exist in a particular abstract relation to it. Clearly there are different types of possible world, each type corresponding to a particular modality. The nature of the modality involved reflects the conceptual framework within which a particular world-view or state of affairs is qualified.

There have been several proposals concerning the number and type of modalities that need to be recognized. For example, Jespersen (1924: 320f) distinguishes twenty subcategories of modality (which he calls 'moods') involved in expressing 'certain attitudes of the mind of the speaker towards the content of the sentence' (1924: 313). He acknowledges that there is some overlap between the different categories and that their number is open to dispute. However, his classification is significant because the recognition of two fundamental types of modality: the one 'containing an element of will', the other 'containing no element of will' correlates with the fundamental distinction to be made between deontic and epistemic modality which we discuss below. Rescher (1968: 24f) also offers a comprehensive typology of modalities, although his extended system is advanced on philo-sophical rather than linguistic grounds. Of the eight major categories he discusses, the two most important for natural language are the epistemic and deontic modalities, relating to knowledge and belief, and to duties respectively. Von Wright (1951a) who distinguishes four 'modes' (our 'modalities') also includes epistemic and deontic types in his account. As Perkins (1983: 10) observes, 'the number of modalities one decides upon is to some extent a matter of different ways of slicing the same cake'. In terms of natural language, there seems to be a consensus among interested parties that at least two modalities are primitive; namely, deontic and epistemic.

2.4 THE CHARACTERISTICS OF EPISTEMIC AND DEONTIC MODALITY

A pair of sentences such as:

(1)   You may have a car

(2)   You must be very patient

may mean at least two different things. Both sentences can be paraphrased: 'Perhaps you have a car' and 'I confidently infer/am forced to conclude that you are very patient' in which case they express the speaker's beliefs and different degrees of conviction concerning the state of affairs 'You have a car' and 'You are very patient'. But they may also be paraphrased by 'You are permitted to have a car' and 'You are required to be very patient' when they express the speaker's permission or injunction that such and such an act be performed or obligation fulfilled. The first reading is referred to as 'epistemic modality', and the second as 'deontic modality'. Epistemic modality is concerned with matters of knowledge or belief on which basis speakers express their judge-ments about states of affairs, events or actions. In the epistemic interpretations of (1) and (2), the speaker is clearly not making statements of fact or categorical assertions but conveying his subjective view of the world. Deontic modality is concerned with the possibility or necessity of acts in terms of which the speaker gives permission or lays an obligation for the performance of actions at some point in the future. The deontic interpretations of (1) and (2) are also non-factual and the speaker's stance subjective (although subjectivity is not a defining characteristic of deontic modality).

In the following three sections, we explore in further detail the contrasts and similarities between epistemic and deontic modality in terms of subjectivity and non-factuality, and the modal notions of proposition and event, and possibility and necessity.

2.4.1 Subjectivity and non-factuality

Two features associated with epistemic and deontic modality in different measure are subjectivity and non-factuality. Palmer (1986: 16) argues that modality in languages is essentially subjective:

> Modality . . . is . . . concerned with subjective characteristics of an utterance, and it could even be further argued that subjectivity is an essential criterion for modality. Modality could, that is to say, be defined as the grammaticalization of speaker's (subjective) attitudes and opinions.

Subjectivity can certainly be regarded as an essential feature of epistemic modality since the speaker is expressing judgements in accordance with his own (subjective) set of beliefs. Since what is at issue is the view of the speaker, his qualified assertion, epistemic utterances are non-factual. There are problems, however, with subjectivity when it comes to an analysis of deontic modality, for here there are varying degrees of speaker involvement:

(3)   Can I just try some more cake?

clearly involves the speaker but the source of permission or obligation may be external where there is no degree of speaker involvement whatsoever unless the speaker is identified as a member of the society or institution instigating the action:

(4)   Will lecturers kindly refrain from missing classes?

(5)   Under no circumstances must students arrive late for class.

Even when the modality is clearly subject-oriented, the non-factual status of the utterance can be questioned as in

(6)   Sebastian can sing in Romanian;

which conveys the speaker's assertion that Sebastian has the ability to perform a particular action, namely to sing in Romanian. In this use, Palmer (1986: 102) argues that CAN is used 'to express what seems to be a factual non-modal statement'.[4]

Again, where one is concerned with the willingness as opposed to the ability of the subject and not the speaker's attitude or opinion, the utterance can be considered non-modal:

(7)   She'll fetch the car, if you ask her.

For this reason linguists often recognize a third type of modality, known as 'dynamic' (Palmer 1979, 1990). Unlike epistemic and deontic modality, dynamic modality is not subjective and is subject-rather than speaker-oriented: the subject's ability or willingness is at issue, not the speaker's attitudes or opinions.[5]

In the past the problem has been avoided by making a binary dictinction between epistemic and what is referred to as 'root' modality where the question of indeterminacy between deontic and dynamic modality does not arise.[6] Root is an unfortunate term for it implies that this type of modality is the more basic. For this reason, the umbrella term 'nonepistemic' is to be preferred because, in the main, epistemic modality can more clearly be defined than other types of modality. The CGEL (219f) separates deontic modality from other types by distinguishing between what it refers to as 'intrinsic' and 'extrinsic' modality. Intrinsic modality is characterized by meanings that relate to permission, obligation and volition and which involve some kind of human control over events. Extrinsic modality involves no such human intervention and associates meanings to do with possibility, necessity and prediction with human judgement of what is or is not likely to happen. Intrinsic modality largely correlates with what is under-stood by deontic; extrinsic modality subsumes epistemic and dynamic. We emphasize the contrast between epistemic and nonepistemic modal–adverb expressions, although we distinguish the two nonepistemic types of modality, dynamic and deontic, where appropriate.[7]

2.4.2 Proposition and event

A further dichotomy between epistemic and deontic modality concerns the nature of what it is the speaker qualifies when he modalizes his utterance. Put simply, a distinction can be drawn between what is said and how it is said. According to this view an utterance can be seen to consist of two elements; one modal, the other non-modal. Lyons (1977: 452), for example, talks of how the speaker can 'express, parenthetically, his opinion or attitude towards the proposition that the sentence expresses or the proposition that the sentence describes', on the assumption that the sentence comprises a modal element and a propositional element.[8] The propositional element roughly corresponds with the 'what is said' and the modal element with the attitudinal, non-factual component. The term 'proposition' is often used in a restricted sense to refer to something that is either true or false and is thus usually associated with epistemic rather than deontic modality. For this reason, Huddleston (1984: 167) departs from standard practice and coins the neutral term 'residue' to refer to what is left of the meaning expressed in a sentence once the modality is abstracted away, regardless of the type of modality involved. The residue may thus subsume the proposition but is not to be conflated with it. The modalities which operate in sentences (1) and (2) above arise out of the different conceptual frameworks within which the speaker is making a judgement or seeking to bring about a particular action. The nature of the residue is intuitively different in each case.

In epistemic modality, the residue has the status of a proposition; the proposition itself is a somewhat abstract claim that things are a certain way and this enables the speaker to draw a conclusion that may be true or false. We have already suggested that propositions can be equated roughly with 'what is said', yet propositions are relative to an individual speaker's set of beliefs, they are not facts or states of affairs. This point is crucial for it underlines the essentially subjective nature of epistemic modality in natural language. If Bill utters in response to a knock on the door 'That may be the milkman' whereas Catherine urges 'It must be the milkman', the modalizations are different because the proposition 'It is the milkman' is construed according to each speaker's individual set of beliefs and world view.

Where modality involves considerations of truth-value, use of the term proposition is apposite because what is said is measurable in terms of whether it is true or false. However, it is less appropriate where the modality involves not truth conditions but the occurrence of some event and the expression of ability or permission. In contrast to epistemic modality, the residue in deontic modality has the status of an action. The point at issue is not whether something is true but whether something is going to be done by others, or by the speaker. Hence Palmer (1979: 25) refers to epistemic modality as 'the modality of propositions' and deontic modality as 'the modality of events'. In the latter case, the speaker typically (but not necessarily) gives permission or lays an obligation for an action to be performed:

(8)   Certainly you may have a car.

(9)   You really must be more patient.

2.4.3 Possibility and necessity

The notions of possibility and necessity, traditionally associated with modal logic, are also central to the discussion of modality. Epistemic MAY and MUST express assessments that it is possible or necessary that a particular state of affairs exists, while deontic MAY and MUST express the possibility or necessity for a state of affairs to come into being. In the first instance, a state, event or action is specified; in the second, it is the situation itself:

(10)   I think that actually may be his name. (CG/248)

(11)   The alternative is for a collapse of formal political institutions as corruption must inevitably erode political legitimacy. Under these conditions everybody must suffer. (THES/04.06.93/12)

(12)   "may I 'just 'answer this quéstion# (S.5.6.655)

(13)   But now we really must get down to business. (CG/167)

We are dealing with two types of possibility and necessity,

construed in terms of different sets of possible worlds. In (10) the speaker envisages a possible world where the state of affairs he envisages, the name in question, is in fact the case; in (12) the speaker envisions a world where things are as he wants them to be, in which he is allowed to answer the question. In (11) the speaker considers a possible world where the state of affairs referred to is considered highly likely or probable, while in (13) the speaker has in mind a possible world in which the circumstances are as he wants them to be. Common to all these examples and different modalities is the notion of 'things being otherwise'. Necessity may seem less obviously related to 'possible worlds' but in neither (11) nor (13) are we dealing with matters of fact or categorical assertions. Once modalized, both utterances convey the speaker's intervention and assert his presence: 'The postman must be late' differs significantly from the factual statement 'The postman is late'.[9]

Two systems of possibility and necessity can be recognized, the one epistemic and the other deontic. In both systems they operate as complementary notions, as can be shown in terms of how the modals behave in relation to negation. In 2.4.2 we distinguished between the modal element and the non-modal element, Huddleston's 'residue', realized by either a proposition or an event, according to whether the modality is epistemic or deontic. Either the modality or the residue can be negated in both systems; (14) and (15) are epistemic, (16) and (17) deontic:

(14)   He can't possibly have left;
        'It is not possible that he has left.'

(15)   He may not have finished yet;
        'It is possible that he has not finished yet.'

(16)   You may not enter that room unaccompanied;
        'It is not possible/permitted for you to enter that room unaccompanied.'

(17)   They mustn't come before Thursday;
        'It is necessary for them not to come before Thursday.'

In (14) and (16) the modality is negated, whereas in (15) and (17) it is the residue. In (14) the speaker makes a negative judgement about a positive proposition; in (15) a positive judgement about a negative proposition. In (16) the speaker lays a negative obligation about a positive course of action; in (17) a positive obligation about a negative course of action. The formal parallel between the two systems becomes apparent when it is noted that with epistemic modality the tendency is to formulate negation in terms of possibility, as (14) and (15) demonstrate. Utterances such as:

(18)   It mustn't be finished yet.

are of marginal acceptability at best; the negation of epistemic MUST by CAN'T is more natural. With deontic modality, the reverse is true, and necessity is more basic than possibility. To replace MUSTN'T by CAN'T in (17) gives the sentence a dynamic rather that a deontic reading. Likewise it sounds more natural to utter:

(19)   You needn't go if you don't wish to.

than to say:

(20)   You can/may nót go, if you don't wish to.

either of which sounds decidedly odd, if not unacceptable.[10]

2.5 OTHER MODALITIES: SUBJECTIVITY AND OBJECTIVITY

Subjectivity is widely seen as a defining characteristic of epistemic and deontic modality in everyday language, notwithstanding the different degrees of speaker involvement which may affect the subjective status of the latter. In this respect, linguistic treatments of modality have differed from those of traditional modal logic with its focus on objective modality and, in particular, 'alethic' modality, concerned with the necessary or contingent truth of propositions. Von Wright (1951a) in his seminal treatise on modal logic, distinguishes the alethic 'modes' or 'modes of truth' and Rescher (1968), in his detailed account of the conceptual domain of modality, refers to the 'alethic modalities' in terms of the notion of truth itself. Some linguists, however, argue that the objectivity associated with alethic modality is also a feature of epistemic modality and everyday language. Lyons (1977: 791) comments that there is an intuitively closer relationship between alethic and epistemic necessity than between either and deontic necessity; this can be demonstrated by reference to an adaptation of one of his examples:

(21)   Alfred is a bachelor, so he must be unmarried.

The meaning of MUST to express necessity can be interpreted in three ways (the glosses are Lyons' own); 'Alfred is obliged to be unmarried' (deontic); 'I (confidently) infer that Alfred is unmarried' (epistemic); and 'In the light of what is known, it is necessarily the case that Alfred is unmarried' (alethic). The last two modalities conform to rational laws of deduction and inference, although the alethic interpretation involves what is logically necessary while the epistemic interpretation involves what the speaker believes to be true; the one is a matter of logical argument, the other an expression of human opinion. As in the case of epistemic versus deontic modality (see 2.4), there is no formal grammatical distinction between epistemic and alethic modality. Palmer (1986: 11) argues that the alethic interpretation is on a par with a categorical assertion of what the speaker believes, as a matter of fact, to be true:

(22)   Alfred is a bachelor so he is unmarried.

How plausible is an alethic interpretation and its implicit objectivity in the context of everyday language? Lyons (1977: 792) argues that the alethic interpretation of (21) involves 'no reference to the speaker or to the actual drawing of inferences, but only to the evidence which determines the epistemic necessity of the proposition in question; and this evidence would be treated as something objective. The subjectivity of epistemic modality ... is not represented at all in standard systems of epistemic logic.'

In practice, where linguists refer to objectivity, they usually do so in terms of epistemic rather than alethic modality. Matthews (1992: 33), for instance, describes such sentences as 'I know John is ill' and 'I think John is ill' as epistemic expressions where the speaker's knowledge with regard to the truth or probability of the proposition is 'absolute' and objective in the first instance, or 'relative' and subjective in the second. However, 'I know' is in fact an overt qualification of the speaker's commitment to the proposition; this is clearly absent in the categorical non-modal statement 'John is ill' (see 2.5.1). 'I know' is an indication of belief rather than knowledge in any absolute sense; the expression in no way affects the truth-value of the proposition 'John is ill' but merely conveys the strength of the speaker's commitment. As Palmer (1986: 84) remarks: 'Hearers do not expect the truth, or what is known to be true, but only what the speaker believes to be true.'

There is, however, a sense in which objectivity may be involved in the conceptual domain of epistemic modality; these examples are due to Lyons (1977: 797):

(23)   Alfred may be unmarried.

(24)   Alfred must be unmarried.

In each case, the speaker's commitment to the possibility or necessity of Alfred's being unmarried can be seen as subjective where the relative weakness or strength of the judgement expressed simply reflects different degrees of uncertainty in the speaker's mind. In terms of our discussion of modality so far, with its focus on the everyday use of language, this would be the natural interpretation and both utterances accounted for in terms of subjective epistemic modality. However, where the unverifiability of Alfred's being unmarried is contingent upon the very nature of the state of affairs itself, it could be argued that objective epistemic modality is involved. In (23) it can be argued that in using MAY the speaker is presenting the possibility of Alfred's being unmarried as an objective fact, quite independent of its truth and the degree of likelihood involved: 'It is possible that Alfred is unmarried.' In (24) MUST can be interpreted in a sense which relates it to alethic necessity, because the evidence available allows for no alternative conclusion and the speaker's attitude is quite simply not involved: 'It follows from what is known (for example, Alfred is a bachelor) that Alfred is unmarried'. Lyons (1977: 798) suggests that objective epistemic modality, as illustrated here, lies somewhere between alethic and subjective epistemic modality and 'might be assimilated to either'.

In similar vein, Perkins (1983: 68) argues that 'all modal expressions which incorporate the verb BE express objective modality, the objectivity being a function of the fact that the modality itself is actually asserted'. He suggests that in:

(25)   She may be unmarried.

(26)   It is possible that she is unmarried.

(27)   There's a possibility that she is married.

the possibility each expresses is of a different kind; in (25) it relates simply to what the speaker believes to be the case, 'a figment of the speaker's own imagination', whereas in (26) and (27) it is not related to the speaker's belief at all but presented as an independent and objective statement of fact. Perkins (1983: ch. 5) maintains that adjectival modal expressions such as IT IS POSSIBLE in (26), or its nominal modal equivalent THERE'S A POSSIBILITY THAT in (27), are 'explicitly objective epistemic modal assertions' which represent the objectification of the modal value expressed by their modal counterpart, in this case, MAY. A system of correspondences between periphrastic modal expressions and their modal equivalents is elaborated on this basis.

Perkins (1983: ch. 6) also cites modal adverbs as exponents of objective epistemic modality on the grounds that they chiefly express epistemic modality and can be related to equivalent adjectival expressions. In an utterance like:

(28)   Possibly she is unmarried.

it is argued that the adverb is inherently objective, placing the utterance on a par with (26) and (27). Equivalence with adjectival forms is the syntactic criterion by which Perkins distinguishes the objectivity of modal adverbs; hence PERHAPS and MAYBE, which lack this correspondence, are not 'unambiguously objective'. Semantically, modal adverbs are treated as objective exponents of epistemic modality because they assert the modality expressed by focalizing it.[11]

There are problems, however, with linguistic approaches to modality which are predicated on such notions of objectivity. While it can be demonstrated that the distinction between subjective and objective epistemic modality is defensible on theoretical grounds, as in the potential interpretations of examples (23), (24), (26), (27) and (28), objectivity is not a viable concept in everyday language. This is acknowledged by Lyons (1977: 805): '... few linguists have ever considered the possibility that epistemic modality could be anything other than a matter of the speaker's attitude towards the propositional content of his utterance'.

The problem seems to lie with the terms objective and

objectivity, since they imply that the modality involved is not related to any particular conceptual framework or set of empirical circumstances and is independent of human reason and therefore judgement. Thus Halliday (1970: 337) uses the term 'objectification' in connection with examples like (26) and (27); the expression of the modal notion, in this instance possibility, is treated as a detachable element of meaning which is actually 'removed from the realm of modality'. He restricts the term 'modality' to what has been referred to here as subjective epistemic modality, and the domain of ordinary language.

The fact, however, that in ordinary language the speaker has a variety of means at his disposal for expressing similar modal notions is significant because it indicates that, even though subjectivity is a defining characteristic of epistemic modality, it is present in varying degrees (as we have seen in our discussion of deontic modality). The modal notions of possibility, probability and necessity can be asserted and focalized in accordance with the speaker's need to be formal, indirect, tentative, or whatever the pragmatic constraint happens to be, and the process can be described in terms of objectification but a different kind of 'objectification' to that referred to by Halliday or Perkins or Matthews in their use of the terms objective and objectivity. In the case of ordinary language, 'objectification' can be redefined as a relative rather than an absolute concept and one which, as Lyons (*op. cit.*) suggests, can be assimilated to (subjective) epistemic modality. So, within the conceptual domain of epistemic modality, possibility or necessity may be highlighted and therefore objectified but without precluding subjectivity. We shall continue to base our exposition on discussion of the notion of possibility (the relationship between MUST and necessity and the combination of MUST with NECESSARILY is examined in 3.4.3). A group of expressions like:

(29)   It may be snowing (for all I know).

(30)   It may possibly be snowing (we had best take precautions to be on the safe side).

(31)   It's possible that it's snowing (I agree, but somehow I doubt it).

(32) There's a possibility that it's snowing (and we can't afford to take any risk by assuming it isn't).

all highlight possibility in different ways, in contexts which we have tried to capture and illustrate by tagging on what the speaker might have appropriately added in each case. In comparison with the equivalent, non-modal, objective statement:

(33) It is snowing (we'll just have to wait until it stops).

these examples all clearly indicate the speaker's subjective commitment, yet they indicate different degrees of objectification. We shall focus on the modal–adverb expression, MAY POSSIBLY in (30), where the adverb POSSIBLY iterates the state of possibility expressed by MAY by focusing upon it. The objectification of the modal is a direct reflection of the speaker's epistemic warrant; the possibility expressed is not 'independent of the speaker' precisely because it is a function of the speaker's inference; on the basis of the evidence available to the speaker and his more or less limited knowledge, the tentative assessment offered is considered to be the appropriate one in the circumstances.

The modal–adverb combinations described in this study are considered to be inherently subjective; the adverb alone is a signal of speaker presence and an indicator of his commitment or attitude to propositional content. Objectification, as we have defined it, is a process whereby the speaker asserts and highlights a particular modal meaning, possibility, necessity or an intermediate value, but within a modal framework which is fundamentally subjective.

2.6 MODALITY AND LANGUAGE USE (UTTERANCE FUNCTIONS)

The account so far has focused on a number of conceptual features associated with modality; we now examine modality in relation to language use. Our main focus is on certain categories of utterance function which derive from Speech Act Theory (SAT henceforth) and which a number of linguists have cited as a basic framework for the discussion of mood and modality.[12] SAT is concerned with meaning and more specifically with the relation between the speaker and what he says; Lyons (1977: 725) notes its particular relevance:

To produce an utterance is to engage in a certain kind of social interaction. . . . One of the most attractive features of the theory of speech-acts . . . is that it gives explicit recognition to the social or interpersonal dimension of language behaviour and provides a general framework . . . for the discussion of the syntactic and semantic distinctions that linguists have traditionally described in terms of mood and modality.

Whereas traditional grammar focuses on the formal-syntactic properties of language, the formal classification of sentence types into declarative, interrogative, imperative and exclamative, independently of the context in which they occur, SAT takes as its point of departure the discourse functions with which these major types of sentence can be broadly associated at a semantic level: statements (mainly used to present information), questions (primarily used to elicit information or a response), directives (chiefly used to issue commands, requests, etc.) and exclamations (vehement expressions of the speaker's emotions). In general, there is a correspondence between the syntactic and the semantic class of an utterance – for instance, the association of the imperative mood with orders or commands – but, as the following examples demonstrate, this is not always the case:

(34)   You can't possibly do it?

(35)   Why the bloody hell should I pay the fine?

(36)   Perhaps you would come to my office for a moment.

(37)   How could she possibly jeopardize the operation!

(34) is what the CGEL (814) refers to as a 'declarative question'; syntactically it is declarative but semantically it is a question ('What do you mean you can't do it?). (35) is an interrogative but semantically a statement ('I have no intention of paying the fine'). (36) has the form of a declarative but is semantically a directive ('Please come into my office'). (37), however, is syntactically an exclamative and semantically an exclamation ('What on earth does she think she is up to!').

The classification of discourse functions can be further refined by reference to how actual utterances are used in practice. SAT aims to characterize utterances in relation to the speaker and hearer in interpersonal communication. For example, a statement, the

semantic realization of a declarative, is principally an expression of
the speaker's belief about how the world was, is or will be, and can
be used to make an assertion, where the speaker tells (truly or
falsely) the addressee how things are, as he perceives them:

(38)   This vessel is decorated with masks, projecting spiked
         triangles, and reticulated rectangles which might possibly
         represent fishing nets. (W.13.3.123/4)

It may also be used to make a prediction:

(39)   No doubt Mr Tellaby will want a full statement from you
         in due course. (HB/91)

or to make a promise:

(40)   I shall certainly apologize to the Chairman, Captain.
         (W.16.4.218)

The linguistic form of an utterance does not necessarily reflect or
even hint at the speaker's communicative intention. Assertions,
predictions, promises represent instances of language as action; they
are pragmatic categories which indicate how the different semantic
classes of utterance are actually used and they lie at the heart of
SAT.

   The theory of speech acts derives from the work of J.L. Austin
(1962) and was subsequently developed by, among others, J.R.
Searle (1979, 1983).[13] The underlying tenet of the theory is that
language is a pratical means of communication whose purpose is to
cause an effect on our audience; this, of course, involves more than
just the transmission of descriptive statements. We want our
opinions recognized, if not endorsed, our assertions to be supported, our requests, orders or commands to be complied with, our
advice taken, our apologies accepted, our questions answered and
so on. Whatever the motivation for a communicative act may be,
the goal is frequently to influence the beliefs, attitudes or behaviour
of our interlocutor(s). We actually do things with words; we
perform 'acts' when we produce an utterance.[14]

   Initially, Austin distinguished between 'constative' ('non-
performative') and 'performative' utterances; the first being
descriptive statements analyzable in terms of truth-values, the
second expressions of activity not held to be truth-bearing. While
the basis on which the distinction was drawn has been challenged

from the outset, it nevertheless makes it possible to identify two fundamental uses of language which are of particular relevance to this study: language as an instrument for commenting on or asserting our interpretation of the world, and language as a tool for effecting some change in it. These two uses Perkins (1983: 14) refers to as the 'representational' and 'instrumental', respectively. The former, an essentially static view of the world, involving the degree or nature of the speaker's commitment to what he says, is the domain of epistemic modality; by contrast, the latter, a dynamic world view, involving the speaker's expression of his attitude towards potential actions by himself and others, lies within the scope of nonepistemic modality. The selection of modal–adverb expressions mirrors this diversity in the way language is used:

(41)   In the right circumstances, maybe, just maybe, by moon, or surf, or candlelight, she could warm to him. (AA/304)

(42)   "Will you just 'come this wày# per"haps you'd 'like to 'tell us 'what you wànt# (S.2.3.288/9)

Originally, (41) would have been characterized as a 'non-performative' utterance, yet it involves, as does (42), the speaker in an act of verbal behaviour, literally a 'speech act'. Saying or asserting that such and such is the case is itself a kind of doing; stating a fact or expressing an opinion are all utterances which can be considered performances of an 'act' precisely because, in making them, we are attempting to get the addressee to react to the truth of what is asserted, to act in accordance with our world view.

Austin went on to develop his theory in terms of a threefold distinction between 'locutionary' 'illocutionary' and 'perlocutionary' acts, where each act represents a stage in the hierarchy of speaking. We offer only an outline here to serve as a backdrop for our pragmatic treatment of modal–adverb expressions in the next chapter.[15]

The first act in the hierarchy of speaking, the locutionary act, is an instance of saying, the actual production of a language expression as a meaningful utterance:

(43)   They must have been delayed and may well be on the next flight.

In making this utterance, however, we perform a speech act; in this particular instance, we are making a statement; to all appearances we are not asking a question, issuing a command or making a request. The declarative dimension of this utterance is referred to as its 'illocutionary force'. Lastly, if in making this utterance we achieve additional effects on the addressee, say, as here, the offer or undertaking on his part to go and meet the delayed travellers at the airport, or the request to postpone meeting them until later, we are referring to the perlocutionary effects of the utterance. There is a crucial distinction between the illocutionary force of a particular utterance, its status as a promise, threat, request and its actual or intended perlocutionary effect on the attitudes, beliefs, behaviour of the addressee.

Speakers can mark the illocutionary force of an utterance explicitly by using a 'performative verb'; these denote the performance of an action by virtue of the utterance being made. Prototypical examples include 'apologize', 'baptize', 'promise' and similar verbs which denote the realization of the illocutionary act:

(44)   I must hereby apologize for my conduct.

is an explicit performative utterance. However, in general, performative verbs are not present in speech acts and the illocutionary force of the utterance is implied rather than stated explicitly. In these cases, the speech act performed is referred to as 'indirect'. Thus:

(45)   I just couldn't stand there without doing anything . . .

will have different illocutionary force in different contexts and could be interpreted as an apology, an admission of guilt, or a plea, accordingly. The addressee will interpret how the utterance is to be understood in accordance with the context in which it is produced. In fact, the relation between form and use here is arbitrary.

It is therefore misleading to argue that a given utterance is to be equated with a speech act where there is a single illocutionary point. In:

(46)   Perhaps you will kindly make arrangements to call and discuss with me the question as to reductions in the loan. (W.7.9.65)

the status of the illocution is a request or an invitation but there is the hint of a warning, and the implication of a command. The categorization of the illocutionary act as a request does not allow for the apparent indeterminacy between these different illocutionary points, precisely because it does not allow for the particular context in which the utterance is made. The illocutionary point of an utterance is understood by an inferential process which takes cognisance of the total context: its linguistic, societal and psychological dimensions. The wider perspective, with its focus on the perlocutionary effect(s) of an utterance, is typically the province of pragmatics. The pragmatic argument is that it is the perlocutionary effect of an utterance on the addressee which provides the key to understanding a speaker's underlying motivation for performing a particular illocutionary speech act; pragmatics seeks to explain how speakers use contextual information to select a particular illocutionary force from those potentially associated with the production of an utterance.[16] The categorization of utterances within a speech act framework, however, focuses on their potential or 'naked' illocutionary force. The potential use of the conjoined declarative statements in (43) to make a request and therefore to be understood as what Searle refers to as a 'directive' (see below) is not determined by the linguistic context alone; other, non-linguistic factors come into play. We do not attempt to explain how speakers actually use non-linguistic context to select a particular illocutionary force from the potential illocutionary forces associated with the utterance − an approach considered by some to be the essential focus of pragmatics (see Mey 1993: 256f). This study is concerned with the linguistic aspects of the context and the relations between language and context which are grammaticalized. It is the potential illocutionary force of modal–adverb combinations which informs our approach in the sections on common uses of modal–adverb combinations found in the next chapter. These uses are still regarded as pragmatic acts because they are viewed from the user's point of view (see Mey 1994b: 3269), except that our attention is restricted to the linguistically relevant aspects of the overall context.

One of the problems SAT has to contend with is the question of how many speech acts there are. Differences in approach and the criteria used have produced competing taxonomies where the number of speech acts identified may approach several thousand, as suggested by Austin or, by comparison, a diminutive five, as proposed by Searle. Searle's basic categories of illocutionary speech acts – 'assertives', 'directives', 'commissives', 'declarations' and 'expressives' – are cited in Palmer (1986: 13), who rightly stresses their value as a semantic framework for the discussion of modality. Of these five categories, the most relevant for this study are assertives, directives and commissives. Declarations, which correspond to Austin's explicit performatives, where the utterance itself brings about a new state of affairs in the world ('I would hereby like to resign'), rarely involve modal expressions, notwithstanding our illustrative concoction! Expressives involve the conveyance of feelings such as apology, sympathy, regret but the category is vague and of dubious status.

2.6.1 Assertives (factuality and non-factuality)

Assertives represent the speaker's subjective state of mind; in asserting a particular proposition to be true, the speaker does so on the basis of his belief, which in turn influences the relative strength of his commitment:

(47)   Yes. I may be wrong. I hope I am, but I know I'm not. (SB/136)

(48)   You think maybe there must have been maybe a mistake somewhere?
        I consider it extremely probable, Mr Aaronson. (DM/217)

Assertives are representational instances of language use; the words are made to 'fit' the world as it is perceived. However, not only does this category embrace the whole of epistemic modality, it also includes statements of fact. We indicated in 2.4.1 above that non-factuality is considered a defining characteristic of modality. Indeed, Lyons (1977: 797) comments that 'Straightforward statements of fact (i.e. categorical assertions) may be described as epistemically non-modal ... the speaker ... is not explicitly laying claim to knowledge in the utterance itself'. Where the assertive utterance is subject to modal qualification, it does function epistemically.

Later, Lyons (1977: 809) makes the apparently contradictory observation that 'there is no epistemically stronger statement than a categorical assertion'; he suggests that in saying, for instance, 'Louise is singing' rather than 'Louise must be singing', the speaker is more strongly committed to the factuality of the utterance, because of the (visual?) nature of the evidence available to him. He adduces (1977: 808) the introduction of such modal markers as MUST, NECESSARILY and CERTAINLY into the utterance as support for his claim that the speaker's commitment to the factuality (verifiability) of the proposition is thereby weakened. Thus:

(49)   He may well have resigned,

betrays limitations in the speaker's 'knowledge', whereas:

(50)   He has resigned.

is epistemically stronger. In (49) the speaker clearly has evidence available to him which enables him to signal his commitment, whereas in (50) the nature of the evidence is such that no indication is required. The purpose of the communication is that the speaker believes it to be optimally relevant and hopefully true, for as Palmer (1986: 87) remarks, 'Why, otherwise, would he, normally at least, say anything at all?' SAT supports this view; it maintains that, when communicating, participants 'co-operate' by attempting to be informative, truthful, relevant and clear.

At an abstract level and as an exercise of ingenuity both of Lyons' points can be accommodated if we accept that even when making a modally unqualified assertion the speaker is signalling his maximum commitment to the truth of the proposition precisely by not qualifying it, by, in other words, not making his utterance explicitly dependent on or relative to an epistemic or modal conceptual framework. But this argument has only a remote relationship to experience. What is at issue is the status of the speaker's 'informed' judgement rather than 'knowledge', in any epistemological or objective sense of the term. The inclusion of modal markers in an assertive utterance formally, semantically and pragmatically distinguishes that utterance from its unmarked coun-terpart where the nature or even degree of the speaker's commit-ment to the truth of the proposition is simply not at issue: 'The point is that the declarative does not indicate commitment at all, even if generally it is assumed that the speaker is telling the truth as he sees it' (Palmer 1986: 87). For the purposes of the present discussion, we consider explicit reference to speaker commitment a defining characteristic of assertives used epistemically. In all other cases, the assertive is epistemically neutral.

Furthermore, Lyons' suggestion that the inclusion of modal markers in an utterance heralds a weaker commitment on the part of the speaker is counter-intuitive: expressions of the speaker's commitment do not necessarily weaken it; CERTAINLY, for instance, among other adverbs denoting a high degree of probability, is regularly used for reasons of emphasis:

(51)   Cézanne himself would certainly have been puzzled had he lived to see the fruits of his life's work. (J 1964: 240)

And as Palmer points out, even where the adverb occurs in an otherwise unmodalized assertive, the effect may be to strengthen rather than weaken the 'declarative statement':

(52)   John is at home
         I don't think so
         Oh yes he certainly is/He must be

                                                        (Palmer 1986: 87)

There are, however, problems with Searle's category of assertives when it comes to interpreting deviant utterances such as those involving figurative meaning. For instance, the statement:

(53)   She must be very clever

may be open to the 'standard' epistemic interpretation based on the principle of 'literalness'; that is, the speaker is committed to the truth of the proposition the statement expresses. But if the speaker is making an ironic observation to imply the opposite of what is asserted – that 'she is far from clever' – it cannot be argued that the speaker is committed to the proposition expressed. What determines the appropriate interpretation, of course, is the context and the extralinguistic clues this provides. In our example, the speaker is not performing an assertive speech act according to Searle's definition because he does not want his assertion to be accepted at face value, as being true in any literal sense. The actual illocutionary force is recoverable because the contextual effects facilitate the appropriate interpretation.[17]

The notion of truth-value, central to epistemic modality, is a further issue here. If the speaker in (53) intends the utterance to be understood as an interpretation rather than as an assertion whose proposition he believes to be true, the truth-value of the proposition is no longer involved and the utterance itself no longer describes a particular state of affairs. Hence Blakemore (1992: 105) refers to the notion of 'faithfulness' according to which the speaker creates expectations relevant in the context and in accordance with 'pragmatic principles'. In this connection, the co-occurrence of, say, EVIDENTLY with MUST as in:

(54)   She must evidently have forgotten the appointment.

makes explicit that the information referred to by the speaker derives not from himself but from another source and should be interpreted accordingly.

It should now be clear that it is not always the speaker's intention to have his assessment of a state of affairs interpreted in terms of truth-value, in a literal sense. As Blakemore argues (1992: 108): 'Sometimes his aim is to express his attitude towards an opinion that a particular person or people in general hold. And the optimally relevant means of doing this will often be to echo the opinion and indicate ... that he is dissociating himself from it.' Seen in this perspective, the role of evidential adverbs in harness with the modals is crucial (see 3.3).[18]

2.6.2 Directives and commissives

Directives, 'where we try to get our hearers to do things', and commissives, 'where we commit ourselves to do things', (Searle 1983: 166) obviously correspond to deontic modality; in each case the speaker effectively tries to make reality conform to his requirements, the world is made to fit the words:

(55)   Could you possibly find out who really did do it?

(56)   That I shall certainly do.

The essential difference between the two types of speech act is illocutionary force: directives can be associated with the making of requests, creating an obligation in the person addressed, or 'requestee', and commissives with the making of a promise, creating an obligation in the speaker or 'promiser'. Both types of act are performative since both initiate action by the speaker or by others. They share with 'assertives' the feature of non-factuality and subjectivity according to the nature of the deontic source. Finally, unlike assertives which can involve past, present or future, directives and commissives refer only to the future: 'At the time of speaking a speaker can get others to act or commit himself to action only in the future' (Palmer 1986: 97).

2.7 MODALITY AND POWER

In 2.4 we saw that there are two dimensions to modality, the deontic (relating to instrumental uses) and the epistemic (relating to representational uses). In general, modality is concerned with speaker or writer authority, irrespective of the particular dimension involved. This allows for two possible interpretations. Authority may be associated quite literally with the power which an individual or collectivity can exert over another individual or collectivity. Alternatively, it may be defined in terms of the claim to 'knowledge' the speaker implies when voicing a judgement or an opinion. The uses of MAY in the sense of permission or of MUST in the sense of obligation, represent claims to power; their parallel uses to denote possibility or necessity represent claims to knowledge. The potential ambiguity between the deontic and epistemic readings is mirrored in the relation between power on the one hand and knowledge on the other:

> Firstly, if it is a matter of the authority of one participant in relation to others, we have *relational modality*. Secondly, if it is a matter of the speaker or writer's authority with respect to the truth or probability of a representation of reality, we have *expressive modality*, i.e. the modality of the speaker/writer's evaluation of truth.
>
> (Fairclough 1989: 126f)

The connection, therefore, between modality and power and modality and knowledge is an entirely natural one, given that the speaker/writer (henceforth speaker should be taken to subsume writer) mediates the two types of authority.

In the main, linguistic research into the concept of power has dwelt on its repressive or negative characteristics, focusing on how language is used by individuals, groups and society at large to exert power *over* others. An obvious example is the way the modals (and language in general, for that matter) can be used to police or mobilize people. Fairclough (1989: 127) cites this routine example:

(57)   Your library books are overdue and your library card may not be used until they are returned. If the books are not returned within a fortnight, you must pay the cost of replacing them before you borrow more.

Here, negated MAY and MUST are operating deontically; permission is being withheld until an obligation is fulfilled. Of significance is what Fairclough (1989: 112) refers to as the 'relational' value of the text; in the present instance, what cues do the modals provide to the power relations enacted in the discourse, discourse here being equated with language as a societal activity determined by social structures? The point is that the authority or power by which the originators of the text withdraw permission or impose their will are nowhere explicitly stated, but the reader of the text is left in no doubt as to the force of the admonition and the course of action required. The discourse associated with official notices, where again the particpants are separated by time and place, typically exploits relational modal values:

(58)   You must check in your rearview mirror before reversing.

(59)   Applicants must have spent at least one year abroad.

(60)   To gain a licence you must spend 40 hours in the air.

(61)   Candidates may not consult dictionaries in the exam.

In the case of 'expressive' modality, where epistemic senses are involved, the relationship between speaker authority and knowledge, the latter a potential source of power, can also be indeterminate. The speaker's claim to knowledge as evidenced by the use of the modal forms is implicit:

(62)   If cooperation is impossible there must be conflict.

(63)   It would be disastrous to offer him the appointment.

Whitaker's article on MAY and MIGHT (1987: 35f) quotes the following official announcement where, ostensibly, the selection of MAY HAVE rather than MIGHT HAVE is at issue:

Most certainly it is also true that the circumstances leading to the sinking [of the ship] inevitably resulted in the suppression of information where such information may have jeopardised the Task Force then or compromised national security thereafter.

MAY HAVE implies that possibly the information would have jeopardized the Task Force or, possibly, it would not have done so. In the event, the prospect of either possibility occurring did not arise as the information was suppressed. Although there is now no room for speculation, MAY HAVE nevertheless invests the final clause with the ambiguous implication that there had existed two potential outcomes. The ambiguity is exploited by the authority to defend, even justify, the course of action taken, namely the sinking of the ship. This analysis of institutional motive calls to mind observations made by Kress and Hodge (1979: 127) about the value of modal indeterminacy:

> The speaker translates uncertainty about status in the power situation into uncertainty about the status of his utterances. We see vividly in this instance the relationship between power and knowledge, or claims to knowledge and claims to power. A speaker uses modalities to protect his utterances from criticism.

The implied status of authority and the power relations expressed in terms of either relational or expressive values are matters of ideology and this, Fairclough suggests (1989: 2), embraces 'common-sense assumptions which are implicit in the conventions according to which people interact linguistically, and of which people are generally not consciously aware'. Language, be it spoken or written, is ideologically loaded, or weighted. The deliberate selection of, say, one modal form in preference to another characterizes the utterance in terms of the speaker's authority. The basis of that authority may be due to any number of factors: differences in social status, age, gender, cultural identity and so on.

So far we have only considered the unmodified modals, which encode the authority of the speaker without necessarily identifying the source from which his power or knowledge ultimately derives. A command or an injunction may be depersonalized and consequently more difficult to challenge, as in examples (57) or (61); or an assessment, judgement or opinion can be advanced with a dissimulating detachment that distinguishes it from categorical commitment, as in examples (62) and (63). The unmodified modals may be used to convey a certain vagueness or indeterminacy which is clearly functional, whatever the speaker's underlying motive may be.

It is significant that when the modals are modified by adverbs, identification of the speaker with, or as, the source of authority becomes more explicit. The modal–adverb expression actually points to the speaker in such a way that the modal operation itself becomes the focus of attention rather than the ostensible content of the utterance (see Kress and Hodge 1979: 127f). In other words, our attention is drawn to the speaker as the probable instrument of command or the source of opinion:

(64)   You really oughtn't to have turned up just yet. Mr. Mulligan was just going to tell me what a thrilling speech he's preparing for the Bazaar, when you came and interrupted us. (SB/117)

(65)   Perhaps you would like to reconsider or provide some justification for your statement. (W.7.11.144)

It is for this reason that official pronouncements of the institutional kind exemplified by (57) contain no adverbial modification of the modal verb head; in fact, the co-occurrence of an adverb would sound distinctly odd in such contexts:

(66)   ? Withdrawals must certainly not exceed £200.

(67   ? Smoking may well damage your health.

The potential ambiguity between the two types of authority inherent in the unmodified modals may be neutralized when the modal is accompanied by an adverb collocate. The adverb signals the overt intrusion of the speaker, making it possible to distinguish between power and knowledge. For instance, the modification of MAY by POSSIBLY or WELL in 'He may possibly/well go' places these utterances firmly within the realm of speaker knowledge; the deontic interpretation possible when the modal is unmodified is now out of the question. However, even with modal–adverb expressions there can still be a tendency for the modals to conflate the two dimensions of authority:

(68)   The shop really/definitely ought to be open at this hour

could imply that the speaker insists that this should be so, or that he is making a not unreasonable deduction in claiming that it is so. A detailed investigation of modality in terms of how modal meanings embody and, in turn, reinforce social processes would no doubt help explain the interrelation between speaker authority and power, and the exploitation of modal meanings for manipulative and other purposes. Modal expressions, perhaps more than other linguistic forms, are particularly susceptible to such an approach precisely because they characterize and promote the speaker's version of the world which is then offered to or imposed on others. Practitioners of so-called 'Critical Linguistics' (Kress and Hodge 1979; Fairclough 1989) have undertaken preliminary studies of modality in this respect, but their focus has been on modal verbs rather than on the realizations of modality in general. Detailed investigation of this area requires more than a consideration of the prototypical cases discussed here; it would necessitate cross-disciplinary research into the nature of power itself, and discussion and analysis of the issues involved would go well beyond the prerogatives of language study and hence the scope of this book.

NOTES

1   Paul Valéry, *Cahiers*, I, p. 533, Éditions de le Pléiade, Paris: 1973. In my own translation, this reads: 'It is characteristic of reality that it can always be looked at from another point of view, interpreted in yet another way, depicted otherwise, and this in limitless, equally original ways.'
2   In English the imperative requires no modal verb and is thus as unmarked modally as the declarative. See Palmer (1986: 23f).
3   Davidsen-Nielsen (1990: 46) also argues that mood in English is implemented syntactically by means of the modal auxiliaries or 'grammatical verbs' which constitute an 'analytic mood system' (after Huddleston 1984: 164): 'Grammatically expressed' modality is termed *mood*. If mood is expressed *morphologically*, we shall refer to it as *synthetic* [inflected].'
4   Views differ widely on the true modal status of CAN. Steele (1975: 38) argues that CAN only expresses modality where it functions with its root sense of permission. Thus CAN in 'Elephants can kills crocodiles' cannot be considered as expressing modality because it does not

'indicate the possibility of the situation which the sentence describes, but rather the potential . . . of the subject of the sentence'. Boyd and Thorne (1969: 71f) hold a similar view, maintaining that CAN 'is only to be regarded as a modal when it is an alternative form of MAY' in its permission sense. Other uses are explicitly non-modal. In contrast, Antinucci and Parisi (1971: 38) claim that these so-called non-modal uses – CAN of ability ('He CAN play tennis'), CAN as marker of progressive aspect ('They CAN hear music'), CAN as marker of sporadic aspect ('Receptions CAN be boring') – are in fact special cases of epistemic modality where the speaker expresses a deduction on properties internal to the sentence. See Perkins (1983: 29f) for discussion of these conflicting assessments.

5   See Palmer (1986: 102f) for further discussion.

6   The term 'root' was first used by Hoffmann (1966).

7   Halliday (1985, 1994) discusses epistemic and deontic modality in terms of 'modalization' and 'modulation', respectively.

8   The distinction between propositional and modal elements, or proposition and modality, closely resembles the distinction between locutionary act and illocutionary act as proposed by Austin (1962: 98) in his theory of speech acts. In the locutionary act we are 'saying something', while in the illocutionary act we are 'doing something', such as giving an opinion, answering a question, making a request or giving an undertaking. Speech Act Theory and its relevance to modality is discussed in 2.6. See also Palmer (1986: 14f).

9   The paraphrase of epistemic MUST by 'It is necessary that . . .' is less appropriate than the use of 'It is possible that . . .' for MAY because, as Palmer notes (1990: 50): 'necessary and necessity are not words used in ordinary speech to indicate epistemic judgements (unlike possible and possibly)'. For this reason, some scholars prefer use of the term 'certainty'. This is misleading because certainty indicates the way the speaker feels and the strength of his belief rather than his actual judgement. 'Epistemic necessity' is also the traditional term used to cover the epistemic meaning of MUST. See Palmer (1990: 53), and White (1975: 75f) for further discussion.

10 A logical relation can be established in terms of negation for the two types of possibility and necessity in order to demonstrate the connection between the epistemic and deontic systems. Thus 'They can't have left' (where the modality is negated: 'It is not possible that they left') is construed as logically equivalent to 'They mustn't have left' (where the proposition or residue is negated: 'It must be the case that they have not left') and 'You may not leave' (negated modality: 'It is not possible/permitted for you to leave') as logically equivalent to 'You mustn't leave' (negated event: 'It is necessary for you not to

leave'). The logical relation between possibility and necessity is usually expressed as follows: to say that something is 'not possible' is equivalent to saying that something is 'necessary not'; to say that something is 'not necessary' is equivalent to saying that something is 'possibly not'.

11 Halliday (1994: 354f) also describes modal adverbs such as PROBABLY or CERTAINLY and adjectival modal expressions such as IT'S LIKELY or IT'S CERTAIN as 'objective' expressions of modality. Again, his use of the term 'objective' is potentially misleading since it seems merely to correlate with the extent to which a speaker chooses to associate with or dissociate himself from the content of a given proposition. Halliday argues that the expression of probability may be subjective or objective and stated explicitly or implicitly: 'I'm certain Mary knows' and 'Mary must know' are explicit and implicit subjective statements of probability and contrast with their 'objective' counterparts 'Mary certainly knows' and 'It's certain Mary knows'. What is at issue is *how* the modality is encoded: 'Speakers being what we are . . . we like to give prominence to our own point of view; and the most effective way of doing that is to dress it up as if it was this that constituted the assertion ("explicit [subjective]" *I think* . . .) – with the further possibility of making it appear as if it was not our point of view at all ("explicit objective" *It's likely that* . . .).' Halliday does therefore recognize that all such statements are ultimately subjective:

> The importance of modal features in the grammar of interpersonal exchanges lies in an apparent paradox on which the entire system rests – the fact that we only say we are certain when we are not. If unconsciously I consider it certain that Mary has left, I say, simply, *Mary's left*. If I add a high value probability, of whatever orientation [subjective or objective, implicit or explicit], such as *Mary's certainly left*, *I'm certain Mary's left*, *Mary must have left*, this means that I am admitting an element of doubt – which I may then try to conceal by objectifying the expression of certainty. (1994: 362f)

Halliday goes on to claim that whereas the subjective modal metaphors, such as 'I'm sure' or 'I believe' cover all values in the modal spectrum, their objectifying counterparts are mostly concerned with the expression of a relatively high value probability or obligation. The implication is that speakers only tend to resort to the process of 'objectification' when they are 'claiming objective certainty or necessity for something that is in fact a matter of opinion' (1994: 363). However, a number of modal expressions indicate that, to use Halliday's terminology, speakers also 'objectify' possibility: 'She's possibly already left', 'It's possible she's already left.' And, frequently, as modal–adverb combinations demonstrate, 'subjectification' and 'objectification' may combine: 'She may just possibly have forgotten.'

12   The term 'utterance' is a pragmatic notion which refers to speaker meaning and the production of spoken and written stretches of language in a given context. The term contrasts with the traditional notion of sentence, which refers to syntactic structure and the grammatical relations between words and what these mean independent of context. A sentence is a theoretical unit of language description and an utterance represents its production and interpretation within a context of use. See Crystal (1991: 313f), Levinson (1983: 16f), Blakemore (1992: 39f) and Mey (1993: 182f).

13   See Searle (1989, 1995) for details of recent modifications in his approach towards SAT.

14   In Austin's theory, a speech act cannot be performed successfully unless certain requirements, known as 'felicity conditions', are met. Various felicity conditions have been proposed but the main principle is that violation of any of these renders the act null and void. Thus, for instance, 'Could you possibly lend me a fiver?' is invalid as a request if the speaker knows the addressee is a bankrupt. The utterance could also lend itself to a different interpretation and be seen as a joke or sarcastic remark where both parties to the communication are aware of its inappropriateness. See Blakemore (1992: 102f) and Mey (1993: 118f).

15   See Searle (1969, 1979), and for a general appraisal of Speech Act Theory, Mey (1993: 109f).

16   Mey (1993: 256f) refers to the concept of 'pragmatic act' rather than 'speech act'. He takes the societal context as paramount and rejects approaches which ignore sociolinguistic and psycholinguistic factors on the grounds that they isolate linguistic elements from their contexts of use. He underlines the significance of context with this example: 'What does an individual utterance end up meaning, when considered in its total context? For example, is a particular request (e.g. asking for a match) really a speech act of asking, or maybe a come-on remark, a plea for human understanding and sympathy or a prelude to armed robbery?' Mey is preoccupied with a context-oriented pragmatics where acts of speech are not necessarily or even exclusively involved.
    Emphasis on the broader interpretation of pragmatics and the wide range of psychological, biological or sociological variables this implies, hampers perfectly valid attempts to restrict attention to

linguistically relevant aspects of context. Although speech acts are ultimately dependent for their interpretation on the sociopragmatic factors of the situation, and although they resist definition in any absolute terms, they clearly embody what is frequently an obvious association between the structural resources available in language and the conventionalized uses to which these are put. (See 5.2.)

There can be no doubt that the societal pragmatics advocated by Mey, with its attention focused on the 'total context', has tremendous vitality and that it extends the narrower Anglo-Saxon interpretation, as represented by Leech (1983) and Levinson (1983), beyond purely linguistic considerations. But such an approach would prove insatiable within the framework of this book and, if pursued recklessly, could well obfuscate the association between modal–adverb combinations and their regular and attested pragmatic functions.

17 Klinge (1995) maintains a distinction between meaning which is linguistically encoded or semantic meaning, and meaning which is contextually determined or pragmatic meaning. His main thesis is that although there exists an intuitive connection between the modals and the meanings they are traditionally assigned, such as permission and obligation – which is done on the basis of sentence meaning – their ultimate interpretation is to be derived at 'the level of the utterance', which involves 'a full pragmatic interpretation'. This can be achieved by making the distinction between the 'situation representation conveyed by a sentence and the world situation it is taken to represent in an instance of utterance' (1995: 674). Elsewhere (1995: 650), he argues that:

> The majority of traditional approaches to modality leave us with linguistic data arranged according to a predetermined set of modal meanings, but they tell us little as to how those meanings were arrived at. In terms of the interpretive step from linguistic form to communicated meanings we are left with a gap. I suggest that it is a fundamental task of linguistics to bridge this gap by identifying and isolating the communicative levels and variables that determine interpretation [in a given context]. Once this goal has been achieved, it will be possible to account for the synergetic effect of the combination of vague linguistic semantic input and situational, pragmatic factors contributing to communicated meaning. *As a result, many, if not all, of the ambiguities and indeterminacies traditionally predicted by linguistic theory will be superfluous.* (My italics)

In view of this emphasis on 'utterance meaning' (see note 12) it is perhaps surprising that the author (1993: 316) warns against relying on corpus-derived data where the 'unique features of individual data

rather than the general rules that generated the data in the first place'
are what tend to be described. Certainly, unprincipled dependence
on corpus-derived material runs the risk of promoting ad hoc
investigations, and clearly introspection and intuition have a valuable
role to play in assessing any linguistic phenomenon, but investigating
language data that have been isolated from their contexts of utterance
is at best artificial and at worst misleading:

> Most of what passes for generality, vagueness, or ambiguity in the
> meaning of language and impels semanticists to build finicky sets
> of rules to eliminate it, evaporates when we look at suitably sorted
> real data. . . . Quite plausibly, the ambiguity is largely an artefact of
> using isolated and invented data.
>
> (de Beaugrande 1996: §39; 518f)

See the discussion in 1.3.

18 The potential ambivalence of expressions, such as (53), is sometimes
accounted for according to the Principle of Relevance Theory (after
Sperber and Wilson 1986), whereby all communicative acts are
considered to be optimally relevant in their proper context. As (53)
demonstrates, an interpretation that is optimally relevant does not
necessarily coincide with the proposition when this amounts to a
literal representation of the speaker's views. The theory becomes too
much of a catch-all and loses in explanatory force what it gains in
scope. And, as Mey (1993: 81f) points out, it has little to say about
everyday communicative interaction and actually omits reference to
the social dimensions of language. But, see Blakemore (1992) for a
comprehensive defence of the overall merits of Relevance Theory.

Three

The modals and their adverb satellites: an overview

An analysis of the modals will constitute a first step in a much broader analysis of a wide range of expressions and other linguistic devices which are also available for the expression of modality in English.

(M.R. Perkins, 1983: 25)

3.1 THE FORMAL CLASSIFICATION OF THE MODAL AUXILIARIES

The modal auxiliaries constitute a reasonably well-defined word class which can be identified according to long-established, familiar criteria. On syntactic grounds, it is possible to restrict membership of this subset of auxiliary verbs to nine items (see Table 3.1), sometimes referred to as the central modal auxiliaries, and their associated range of forms.

Table 3.1 The modal auxiliaries

Positive forms	Negative forms	Enclitic negative
CAN	+ NOT / CANNOT	+ N'T
COULD	+ NOT	+ N'T
MAY	+ NOT	+ N'T
MIGHT	+ NOT	+ N'T
SHALL / 'LL	+ NOT	SHAN'T
SHOULD / 'D	+ NOT	+ N'T
WILL / 'LL	+ NOT	WON'T
WOULD / 'D	+ NOT	+ N'T
MUST	+ NOT	+ N'T

In practice, grammars often also include in their treatment of the modals, the so-called 'marginals': DARE, NEED, USED TO, OUGHT TO, as these satisfy most of the criteria which identify the central modal auxiliaries. The incidence of modal auxiliary occurrence varies considerably from CAN (four times per thousand words in spoken British English) to MIGHT (once per two thousand words in written British English). Marginals such as OUGHT TO and DARE are rare (seven times per fifty thousand words and once per 50,000 words in written British English, respectively). Modals tend to be more common in spoken discourse where co-occurrence with adverbs is correspondingly more frequent.[1]

We do not consider DARE, NEED, USED TO or HAVE (GOT) TO in the present study: DARE and NEED as modals are extremely rare; USED TO, while satisfying the criteria of the marginal modal set, often functions semantically as an auxiliary of tense and aspect. OUGHT TO is the most common of the marginals and in its semantic functions can be a suppletive form for SHOULD. It is thus included in this study. HAVE (GOT) TO can be substituted for MUST, particularly in past time contexts, but is unremarkable from the point of view of co-occurrence and is not treated here.

The criteria for establishing the modals are well known and need only be summarized here.[2, 3] (For a more detailed account, see Palmer 1987, 1990.) Firstly, the modals may be distinguished from main verbs and are similar to the other primary auxiliary verbs BE, HAVE, and DO in their occurrence with negation, inversion, 'code' and emphatic affirmation; often referred to as the NICE properties, after Huddleston (1976: 333). When contracted for negation they may take the enclitic negative N'T as in 'She couldn't come'; they function as the operator when inverted with the subject without requiring 'do-support' as in 'Can I'; they may function as the operator in a reduced clause as in 'Frank should come and so should Mike'; and they may carry nuclear stress for reasons of emphasis as in 'Alun cán solve the problem'. In addition there are a number of criteria which apply specifically to the modal auxiliaries which further sets them apart as a discrete word class. The modals are followed by the bare infinitive: 'She will arrive soon' not *'She will to arrive soon'. They cannot occur in non-finite functions as infinitives or present and past participles and as a result occur always as the first element of the verb phrase in which they occur: *'To may eat is essential for survival'; *'The French loathe musting';

★'We have could spoken of it.' They are not inflected in the third person singular of the present tense: ★'He cans go later'; they do not take direct objects: ★'He must it' or ★'They might so', and, with the exception of some Scottish dialects (see Brown 1991: 74f), they do not normally co-occur: ★'You should will come.' Finally, both the present and the past tense forms of the modals share abnormal frames of time reference and may be used to refer to the present and the future: 'They could well be leaving on the next ferry'; 'Perhaps you might like to get in touch with the committee now.'

There are also formal criteria which largely corroborate the distinction between the epistemic and nonepistemic functions of the modals.[4] It is generally the case that only the epistemic as opposed to the deontic modals combine freely with the perfective and progressive aspects: 'She may/might have already left', ★'You may have left'; 'You must be going mad!', ★'You must be singing now'.[5, 6] Although epistemic combinations with the progressive and the perfective may make reference to the future and the past, respectively, the modality itself is unaffected and remains in the present, since the judgements are made through the act of speaking.[7] It is perfectly natural to pass judgements on future as well as past events: 'They may well be getting in touch with you this afternoon'; 'Well, they certainly must have been in a hurry to leave last night since they forgot their passports'; 'This would probably have happened about two or three months ago.' The combination of both perfective and progressive constructions with the epistemic modals is also possible: 'You couldn't possibly have been waiting for that long!'[8]

Three exceptions to the progressive/perfective diagnostic include the deontic (obligational) uses of SHOULD and OUGHT TO and the dynamic use of COULD, where no such restrictions apply: 'She ought to be revising the script now' ['but she isn't']; 'She should have finished it' ['but she hasn't']; 'They could have been rehearsing now, if the script had been ready on time.'[9]

The patterns of association between the modals and their adverb satellites further characterize this class of auxiliary verb as a distinct set, especially in the case of the epistemic modals, where collocational trends most clearly emerge. For instance, strict collocational restrictions come into play at the 'extremes' of the modal spectrum, where the epistemic modals of possibility and necessity, MAY and MUST, may normally combine only with adverbs expressing similar modal meanings, such as POSSIBLY or CERTAINLY: 'She MAY

POSSIBLY have forgotten', *She MAY CERTAINLY have forgotten';
'They MUST CERTAINLY have taken the later train', *'They MUST
POSSIBLY have taken the later train.' Further discussion of the issues
raised here is postponed until Chapter 5, where the status of both
epistemic and nonepistemic modal–adverb combinations is examined in detail and then summarized in the data profile of modal–
adverb co-occurrence provided in section 5.4.

Compared with other languages, such as German, French,
Romanian or Spanish, to take an arbitrary selection, the modal
auxiliaries in English can be more readily identified as members of
a distinct grammatical system. Palmer (1990: 5) argues that it is
plausible to suggest that the complex set of formal characteristics
which sets the modals apart from other categories of auxiliary or
verb 'have been retained in the language because native speakers are
aware of the modals as a set . . .'. A corollary of this observation is
that recognition of the grammaticalized modal system entails
awareness of the range of adverb collocates the modals generally
attract. This is especially true of those adverb modifiers which have
become closely integrated members of the system because of their
idiomatic association with particular modal verb heads: 'They MAY
+ WELL be late' [probability], 'She CAN'T POSSIBLY have left'
[impossibility].

3.2   THE SEMANTICS OF THE MODALS: SOME APPROACHES

The semantics of the modals is an extremely complex area which
has already been treated in considerable depth elsewhere (see
Chapter 1, section 1.4, in which we review seminal works in the
field). In his survey of modality in English, Nagle (1989: 95) sees
fit to comment that: 'Even a brief review of the ongoing debates
regarding the semantics of the modals (and modal expressions in
general) reveals the resistance of this area to succinct exposition . . .'. Extensive exploration of this most complex area of
meaning is beyond the scope of the present study. We do not
propose a radically new approach here and our debt to previous
work in the field is evident throughout. Our aim is to provide an
adequate backdrop against which meaningful discussion of co-
occurrence can take place. We largely adopt the practice followed

by the CGEL which acknowledges that the modals rarely exhibit discrete meanings and that there are often areas of overlap in the senses they are used to convey: there is a gradient between epistemic and nonepistemic modality.[10] To this extent, the CGEL classification of modal meanings differs from most of the competition which either treats the semantics of the modals in terms of core-meanings (the monosemantic approach), or indulges their semantic ambiguity and allows for a range of apparently discreet or distinguishable meanings (the polysemantic approach).

Neither approach is entirely satisfactory. Probably the majority of scholars favour a monosemantic approach where a basic meaning for each modal is identified and departures from the core meaning measured in terms of variables or interpreted as subsidiary meanings or overtones. The problem here is deciding which meaning is primitive or is the base literal one. The relatively abstract nature of the meanings the modals are used to convey does not favour the precise identification of any such basic sense, even when the constraining factors of the epistemic versus nonepistemic distinction are taken into account. Context also plays a role in determining the nature of what we might call the modal hue. The modals convey varied and often related meanings, and as Palmer (1990: 15) says '. . . there is no a priori reason why there should be a single meaning; it is more likely that there is a conglomeration of vaguely related meanings . . .'.

Polysemantic approaches on the other hand tend to veer towards the opposite extreme equating each difference of use with a difference in meaning, even where the meanings distinguished are related and to some extent overlap. In support of a core-meaning approach, Perkins (1983: 28) criticizes proposals in terms of six distinct meanings for MAY (Huddleston 1971: 297f) or ten for CAN (Kenny 1975: 131), arguing that this would imply the modal system of English tends towards 'semantic anarchy'. Insofar as it is possible to distinguish between epistemic and nonepistemic uses and to talk of complementary semantic systems, the strong version of the polysemantic approach seems as untenable as its monosemantic counterpart.[11]

For these reasons, an approach such as the CGEL's, which recognizes the indeterminate nature of the modals but which also seeks to establish a basic framework where the modals are assigned major (but not necessarily 'core') meanings, gains in plausibility.

Thus, for instance, CAN is described in terms of possibility, ability and permission, and WILL / 'LL treated under the headings of prediction and volition. Their classification avoids the danger of oversimplification by recognizing uses of the modals which depart from but are yet still related to the major meanings already outlined. In the case of WILL, for example, three related uses of the modal are described in terms of prediction and a similar number of subsenses are identified in relation to volition. The various uses are given equivalent status: continua of meaning are established but the need to identify core and peripheral meanings is obviated. In her treatment of CAN, Coates (1983) regards ability as the core meaning, extending towards possibility at its periphery. But one could equally well take possibility as primitive and establish a cline of ability-oriented meanings as one moves towards the periphery. Why should ability be more basic than possibility? The identification of core and peripheral meanings is far from convincing; as Palmer (1990: 21) notes in his discussion of indeterminacy, '. . . the meanings of the modals cannot be described in terms of wholly discrete categories, . . . categories merge or fade into one another, so that in some cases it is not possible in principle to decide between two possible categorizations'.

We differ from the CGEL in connection with the terminological issue of 'intrinsic' versus 'extrinsic' modality. As pointed out in 2.4.1, we maintain the distinction between the epistemic and nonepistemic senses of the modals; the latter, broad category embracing the so-called 'root' meanings or meanings ascribed to the deontic and dynamic uses of the modals. The CGEL (220f), however, regards the root/epistemic distinction as a subcategorisation of extrinsic modality and so in its treatment of CAN it is now argued that even though ability typically involves human control over events (which is how intrinsic modality is characterized earlier), 'Ability is best considered a special case of possibility'. We need to distinguish the epistemic from the nonepistemic uses of the modals since the distinction is central to an account of co-occurrence.

3.3   EPISTEMIC AND NONEPISTEMIC MEANINGS

The basic distinction between the epistemic and nonepistemic senses of the modals has already been discussed (2.4). Most of the modals can function epistemically or nonepistemically, but vary considerably in the senses they most commonly convey. This has implications for the type of adverb satellite with which they typically co-occur.

For example, MIGHT is widely used as a modal of epistemic possibility but only occasionally as a permission auxiliary. Our examination of the SEU data reveals that an overwhelming proportion (92 per cent) of all combinations of MIGHT with an adverb are used in the expression of epistemic modality. The combination of WILL with the adverbs PROBABLY and PRESUMABLY highlights its use to make modalized predictions in the present about some future state of affairs, and marks out these modal expressions as potential co-ordinates of epistemic probability. However, unmodified WILL is frequently used to make a relatively straightforward prediction about some future state of affairs and, even though the future is unknown or at best not fully known, it is less clear that in these cases WILL can carry the speaker's epistemic judgement of probability. Here, it is unusual, if not inappropriate, for the modal to co-occur with an adverb: ?'Oil will probably float on water' or even ?'Oil will certainly float on water' (unless this latter is uttered in contradiction of an opposing, and from our knowledge of the world, incorrect assertion). When operating nonepistemically, WILL regularly co-occurs with the adverbial request markers KINDLY and PLEASE in such pragmatic functions as the making of polite requests or offers.

At times there is a natural ambivalence between the epistemic and nonepistemic meanings of the modals and where the final reading is decided by the co-occurrence of an adverb satellite. A poignant example comes to light in Jacobson:

(1)   Any history of art written for the consumption of twentieth-century Europeans must necessarily regard the Giotto–Cézanne period as the most important section of art history. (J 1964: 298)

The occurrence of NECESSARILY unambiguously conveys the speaker's epistemic judgement with regard to what constitutes the history of art in question. MUST alone, however, hovers tantalizingly between its epistemic and deontic (a subcategory of nonepistemic) senses; for just as the speaker may be conveying the strength of his conviction ('It is not possible that a history of art written for the twentieth-century reader does not have as its main focus the section of art history associated with the Giotto–Cézanne period'), he may equally well be claiming that it is incumbent on the writer of such a work to concentrate on the period in question. The nature of the latter constraint is deontic. It could also be argued that the modal expression MUST NECESSARILY not only conveys the speaker's conviction but actually specifies that the assertion is based on a conclusion drawn from all the available evidence. The action or process of inferring is thereby made explicit. This would imply that epistemic modality involves a dual process, one which includes both inference and confidence; each may be present in different or equal measure according to the modal–adverb combination in question.

Palmer (1986: 64) argues that the inference–confidence axis represents two different but closely related types of epistemic modality: 'In one the speaker indicates that he is inferring from available information, in the other he indicates the degree of confidence he has in what he is saying.' Surely, what we are dealing with is two sides of the one coin rather than separate denominations of the same currency. The selection of MUST implies that the speaker not only has sufficient epistemic warrant to make a particular judgement but that the evidence available to him is sufficient for him to be able to do so with confidence. If the speaker's confidence is limited, this must reflect a degree of uncertainty incompatible with the epistemic value of MUST. This is attested by the grammatical unacceptability of utterances such as: *'They must possibly have left' or *'She may definitely be there'. Inference and confidence go 'hand-in-hand' and are directly tied to the status of the speaker's 'knowledge'; the stronger the evidence, the more forceful can be the expression of the speaker's resolve. Both strands – inference and confidence – are inherent in MUST and either may be enhanced by an appropriate adverb collocate:

(2)   It must certainly bring him to grief sooner or later. (CG/228)

(3)   The need is for controls, accountable government and an independent mechanism to make life impossible for the corrupt official. The alternative is for a collapse of formal political institutions as corruption must inevitably erode political legitimacy. Under these conditions, everybody must suffer. (THES/04.06.93/12)

It is clear that in (2) the adverb conveys the speaker's confidence; in (3), however, the adverb marries inference with conviction; it is the perfect match for epistemic MUST.

WILL and its adverb collocates behave in a similar way where the modal is used to make a prediction:

(4)   The disintegration will inevitably continue. Faith in Christ is the only thing to save you from despair at that point: and out of Faith in Him good actions must inevitably come. (J 1964: 282)

The inference–confidence distinction is also susceptible to the effects of tense. Combinations with the past tense modal forms COULD, MIGHT and WOULD are modally more marked; again, the type of epistemic modality given prominence is ultimately determined by the co-occurring adverbial satellite, be this speaker confidence as in (5) or (7) or inference as in (6) or (8):

(5)   She certainly could have polished the bag before setting out. (CG/92)

(6)   The insurers . . . might just possibly check that the name on the policy was the name of the registered owner. (FC/145)

(7)   In Manila . . . the Constabulary by now would surely have a file on him. (AA/340)

(8)   Christian had a way with euphemisms and doublespeak and would inevitably go far in the Company. (AA/361)

In nonepistemic contexts, modal–adverb synergy is less clearly marked; the adverbial may directly enhance the overtones of tentativeness or indirectness conveyed by the modal itself (again, the past tense modal forms are more marked for tentativeness or indirectness than their present tense counterparts) in accordance with its pragmatic function, or act as an independent but complementary marker of courtesy:

(9)   so per"haps you could 'telephone me to ar'range an'other appóintment# (S.9.3.676)

(10)   He gestured . . . to the bartender that the small glass might kindly be replenished. (AA/86)

(11)   per"haps you would 'give me a telephone call at 'three or five# (S.5.12.423)

That there is indeterminacy between epistemic and non-epistemic readings and within the categories themselves should come as no surprise, given how indeterminate the modal system is. Sometimes, it is hard if not impossible to decide which of the two readings – epistemic or nonepistemic – is the most appropriate, irrespective of whether the modal is accompanied by one or more of its adverb collocates.

(12)   The chemist (really) must/should/ought to be open (by this time)

allows for either interpretation: is the speaker being (deontically) judgemental about the chemist's opening hours, or offering an (epistemically) informed assessment about expected normal hours of business?

It is also striking how much overlap in meaning there is among the modals themselves. SHOULD and OUGHT TO are largely interchangeable in their meanings of tentative inference (epistemic) and obligation (deontic). The idiomatic MAY WELL collocation rivals WILL and PROBABLY in the expression of epistemic probability. CAN and MAY overlap in their permission (deontic) senses. Rarely, however, is it a matter of free variation; any treatment of the grammar and semantics of the modals and their adverb satellites should be mindful of the related principles of gradience and indeterminacy. The semantic category of modality does not lend itself to rigid discreteness.

3.4 THE MODALS AND THEIR ADVERB SATELLITES

The epistemic and nonepistemic status of the modals influences the nature and range of adverbials with which they collocate, although the adverbials themselves may determine status in cases of ambiguity. This reflects the synergetic relationship that exists between the two word classes and further points to the significance of co-occurrence. In this section we review each of the central modals: CAN, COULD, MAY, MIGHT, MUST, SHOULD, WILL, WOULD, SHALL, and the marginal auxiliary OUGHT TO, which is contrasted with SHOULD. This is not intended to be an exhaustive account of the meanings of the modal verbs but rather an appraisal of their semantic status in relation to epistemic versus nonepistemic modality and how this influences trends in co-occurrence. A detailed examination of the adverb collocates involved and the different semantic processes that can be associated with co-occurrence is postponed until Chapter 4.

Epistemic modality is generally distinct from other kinds and constitutes a relatively well-defined modal system in English. Yet there is ambivalence between epistemic and other modalities; indeterminacy is a pervasive feature of modality, compounded by the fact that the same modal forms are used in both epistemic and deontic modality:

(13)   They may leave tomorrow.

(14)   The shops ought to be open.

(15)   She must be there.

There is a marked tendency for the epistemic modals to attract adverb satellites, *pace* Palmer (1990: 68) who remarks that 'In general, epistemic modals cannot be modified by adverbs'. Co-occurrence allows for greater refinement in the way the speaker's judgement is expressed in terms of the inference–confidence axis discussed in 3.3. It may additionally resolve any inherent ambiguity:

(16)   They may well leave tomorrow.

With other types of adverb, however, the modal status remains indeterminate and can only be resolved through recourse to the context:

(17)   She definitely must be there.

When operating deontically, the modals also display affinities with particular adverb modifiers, be this to give emphasis:

(18)   You simply must see the new baby.

or to otherwise enhance the modals' deonticity:

(19)   Could you possibly take a look at the new plans?

Indeterminacy is not confined to the epistemic/nonepistemic divide; there is also considerable indeterminacy within the domain of nonepistemic modality itself, where it is not always easy or indeed possible to distinguish between deontic and dynamic uses of the modals. Palmer (1986: 17), for instance, observes that in:

(20)   You must leave at once.

the modal 'might indicate either the speaker's insistence or a general (objective) necessity for leaving, or it could well be indeterminate between the two readings'. In nonepistemic environments, adverbial modification is normally associated with deontic uses, as the adverbs involved typically indicate the speaker's intrusion:

(21)   You really must leave at once.

is thus a matter of the speaker's insistence.

Dynamic modality may be taken to subsume those uses of the modals, in particular CAN and WILL, where subjectivity and factuality are at issue (see 2.4.1). The dynamic uses of the modals are sometimes held to lie outside the scope of modality proper (see Palmer 1986: *passim*); it is therefore significant that co-occurrence in dynamic contexts is exceptional.

For ease of presentation, the present and past forms of the modals are reviewed together, and appropriate reference made to similarities and differences in use. This is not to imply that present and past forms exist in free variation or that the latter are simply past tense forms of their present tense counterparts; this is only true where they serve as past time equivalents in indirect speech constructions.

Our review of the modals and modal–adverb combinations is mostly confined to an examination of their behaviour in positive declarative clauses (assertive contexts),[12] although reference is also made to combinations in negative and interrogative environments (non-assertive contexts) where this is felt to illuminate an important aspect of co-occurrence.

First, the status of each modal is assessed in terms of the epistemic and nonepistemic distinction, and then the basic meanings associated with the different types of modality involved are illustrated with reference to co-occurrence. Modal–adverb combinations fulfill a range of pragmatic uses and are typically involved in such illocutionary acts as making requests, offers, recommendations, commands and so forth. These aspects of modal–adverb usage are treated separately in section 3.5, followed by more detailed discussion of the relationship between modality and politeness (see 3.5.2).

3.4.1 CAN/COULD

3.4.1.1 *Status*

Other than in non-assertive contexts where CAN has such rhetorical uses as in:

(22)   Can it possibly be a case of love at first sight?

or, and this is more frequent, where it is negated:

(23)   They can't possibly be playing tennis.

the epistemic status of CAN is exceptionable, if not questionable. Our examination of the Survey indicates that as little as 2 per cent of adverbial combinations with CAN may involve the expression of epistemic modality and these all occur in non-assertive contexts with one possible exception which we consider below (26). COULD is another matter; although not as frequent as CAN, it seems that as many as 14 per cent of all co-occurrences in the Survey can be accounted for epistemically. As the most frequent modals in both the spoken and written language, CAN and COULD serve a wide variety of functions; they also provoke more controversy than any other members of the modal set. There is wide disagreement over their epistemic credentials outside non-assertive contexts, and accounts of their nonepistemic uses are notably divergent.[13]

Perkins (1983: 35) argues that there are cases where CAN might be regarded as having an epistemic sense, as in:

(24)   Cigarettes can seriously damage your health.

where it is felt one is dealing with evidence from which the truth status of the proposition ('Cigarettes damage your health') may be inferred. Pullum and Wilson (1977: 784) promote a similar view, arguing that in:

(25)   Elephants CAN kill crocodiles.

there are two possible readings: 'Elephants have the ability to kill crocodiles' (nonepistemic), or 'It can happen that an elephant kills a crocodile' (epistemic). Yet it seems more plausible that in both (24) and (25) CAN is operating dynamically (Palmer 1979: 155f; 1990: 107f) where the point at issue is not the verifiability of whether cigarettes damage your health, or whether elephants kill crocodiles, but that in certain circumstances smoking is damaging to your health and elephants do kill crocodiles. In neither example is CAN directly concerned with the truth of the proposition, but rather with the disposition of circumstances to the occurrence of some event. It is possible to say: 'She can bake, but never will because she's too idle' but not: 'She may bake, but never will ...' precisely because CAN focuses on the current state of circumstances in contrast to MAY, which focuses on the current truth status of a proposition.

But are there instances of epistemic CAN? The Survey offers a tantalizing example:

(26)   Rubbish! You can only be about fifty. (S.1.10.568)

It seems that an epistemic interpretation is possible, but as a result of CAN co-occurring with the semi-negative adverb ONLY. This gives the utterance negative import and thus establishes a non-assertive context, in which CAN may operate epistemically. Remove the adverb and the acceptability of the utterance is in doubt: '*/?You can be about fifty.' The CAN ONLY expression is almost on a par with MUST: 'You must be about fifty'; there is evidence available to the speaker such that the proposition expressed has a very strong likelihood of being true. It could be paraphrased: 'It is scarcely possible that you are older than fifty.' At the same time it could also be argued that CAN is functioning dynamically and the possibility involved is circumstantial; the appropriate paraphrase is: 'It is possible for you to be about fifty'. Certainly CAN lacks the inherent epistemic quality of MAY or MUST, typically associated with epistemic judgement but it regularly replaces MUST in non-assertive contexts:

(27)   When you hear a strident voice in your head telling you that you can't possibly be an alcoholic, don't pay attention. (AA/517)

In 3.4.3 it is suggested that epistemic MUST may constitute an epistemic subsystem in which the speaker's judgement is related to and based upon available evidence. This is especially true when the modal co-occurs with evidential adverbs such as: APPARENTLY, EVIDENTLY, INEVITABLY, OBVIOUSLY. In non-assertive contexts, where CAN'T or CANNOT are used in place of negated MUST, evidentials occasionally combine with the negated modal:

(28)   She was not in England, apparently she cannot have stolen the film. (DM/132)

The adverb collocate implies that the speaker's judgement is based on physical or mental perception of the available evidence; the modal adverb combination produces a distinct epistemic flavour. However, there remains ambiguity between the epistemic and a potential nonepistemic dynamic reading, because (28) can be glossed as: 'Apparently it was possible that she did not steal the film', or 'Apparently it was not possible for her to steal the film'. It would be incautious to be dogmatic where there is obvious indeterminacy. Where the adverb collocate has no inherent modal or evidential characteristics, CANNOT behaves in the same way as positive CAN and has a dynamic sense:

(29)   Although you may begin by regarding it as ideal if every opera performance causes a sensation, what this means is that people start to make demands that simply cannot be met. (EK/87)

COULD more readily lends itself to epistemic interpretations than CAN. Even though its epistemic status is sometimes called into question, there do seem to be genuine cases of epistemic use:

(30)   Could Madeleine really have retired in her prime, become a country woman on her own, her days plotted by the seasons, evenings alone with books and wireless, or writing letters to her children; a friend occasionally for weekends perhaps? (W.16.1.16)

This seems especially true where the modal combines with adverbs which focalize the idea of possibility:

(31)   In the right circumstances, maybe, just maybe, by moon, or surf or candlelight, she could warm to him, but this was all speculation since he was about to split. (AA/304)

The adverb's relationship to truth-value is contextually significant if not decisive in establishing an epistemic environment; the occurrence of the noun SPECULATION underlines the association. Collocations with such adverbs as POSSIBLY and WELL, which again focus on the concept of possibility, may prompt an epistemic reading:

(32)   If you are looking for someone with imagination and intelligence, backed up by experience and determination, then she could well be the person you require. (W.17.1.256)

(33)   I thought I'd write before I got the chance to forget: not, of course, that I could possibly do so. (W.7.31.4)

Palmer (1990: 185) also quotes the following example from the Survey:

(34)   Well, now we're coming to this big fight of the evening described in the programme right here in front of me as 'Eliminating World Heavyweight Contest'. Well, it could well be that, and probably is. (S.10.3.1)[14]

A nonepistemic interpretation is implausible in the context; the modal expression and the adverb point to likelihood and clearly involve the speaker's subjective judgement. Palmer argues that, since MIGHT is a potential suppletive for COULD in these cases and the modal expressions refer to what is conceptually possible, such assertive uses of COULD appear to be epistemic. But he also suggests that a dynamic interpretation is equally possible, where COULD is taken to indicate 'what would be (or would have been) experientially possible'. Palmer equivocates over the issue and concludes that either interpretation is admissible. Certainly, COULD is largely indeterminate in this respect, but the idiomatic combination with WELL is perhaps best accounted for epistemically. In comparison with MIGHT and MAY, Coates (1983: 165) argues that COULD is the more tentative co-ordinate of epistemic possibility: 'While MIGHT and MAY cover the gamut of likelihood from probable (*might well*), through a 50/50 assessment of possibility (*may or may not, might or might not*), to tentative possibility, COULD seems . . . to express only tentative possibility.' Coates goes on to suggest that as MIGHT has become the chief exponent of epistemic modality in everyday spoken language, and in this usage is virtually synonymous with

MAY, the expression of tentative epistemic possibility has now fallen to COULD. However, the evidence of co-occurrence suggests that COULD is not central to the epistemic system and that when it does co-occur with an adverb, the expression often connotes a higher modal value than possibility as with COULD WELL in (32) and (34) above. In other cases, the adverb collocate is an evidential which focalizes the inferential process as with COULD PRESUMABLY in (53) below. There is little evidence in the data to indicate that COULD is making any significant inroads into the epistemic territory of MIGHT. Certainly, as we have noted, MIGHT and MAY are frequently interchangeable in their epistemic uses but the role of MIGHT in expressing tentative epistemic possibility remains intact; see example (72) below.

COULD and CAN therefore differ considerably in the extent to which they allow for an epistemic interpretation, especially in assertive contexts, where it can be argued that COULD clearly does have epistemic uses, as in combinations with WELL. This non-equivalence is neutralized, however, in nonepistemic contexts where both modals share similar basic meanings, even though COULD is marked for tentativeness.

There is not always a clear distinction between the three basic nonepistemic meanings of possibility, ability and permission, which can be attributed to CAN and COULD. It can be argued that possibility is primitive. Perkins (1983: 33) who, it should be remembered, adopts a core-meaning approach (see 3.2), argues in favour of this view on the grounds that the meaning of CAN 'is clearly related to the notion of possibility' and represented 'as a transitive relationship between circumstances and an event'. Of all the modals, CAN and COULD are the most plausible candidates for such an approach. Whilst adverb satellites tend to clarify distinctions in meaning, it is significant that, in combinations with CAN and COULD, they primarily focalize the notion of possibility. The evidence of co-occurrence would thus support the view that CAN and COULD are primarily possibility-based:

(35)   We'll send a car as soon as we possibly can. (CG/251)

(36)   What purpose could he possibly have had for visiting this dreary place? (AA/53)

(37)   True, if he had been thinking clearly the man from X

could easily have unlocked the coffer. (CG/236)

Palmer (1990: 85) also comments that 'there are only a few examples in the Survey where ability seems clearly indicated' but, even then, his chosen examples remain ambivalent. In the following instance, which Palmer also quotes, although it is unclear whether the ability of the subject to perform the action is indicated or not:

(38)   oh "one thing 'you want to a'void if you 'possibly cán# is a "present from my mòther# (S.2.10.265/6)

the primary characterization relates to possibility: 'If it is at all possible, avoid ...'. The indeterminacy between the dynamic possibility and ability senses makes it all but impossible to distinguish between them and it seems pointless to argue which of the two senses prevails:

(39)   Some folk just can't stand to see a fella like yourself move ahead of the pack. (AA/64)

(40)   I frankly can't talk to Greg for more than five minutes without rigor mortis. (FC/207)

(41)   I can't believe Ella's dead. I just can't believe it. (AA/110)

The CGEL (222) states that 'the *ability* meaning of CAN and COULD can be considered as a special case of the *possibility* meaning, *viz* one in which the possibility of an action is due to some skill or capability on the part of the subject referent'. In a sentence such as:

(42)   He still couldn't read the man's face. (AA/382)

either the construction BE ABLE TO or BE POSSIBLE can be used in paraphrase and still convey a similar meaning: 'He was still unable to read the man's face' or 'It still wasn't possible for him to read the man's face'.

Although there are few instances attested in the Survey of adverb combinations with CAN and COULD used to express deontic possibility or permission, their deontic status is beyond doubt; both contrast with MAY in terms of formality. Even here, indeterminacy may arise: where CAN is used in the context of rules and regulations, as a less formal variant of MAY, there is ambivalence between a dynamic and deontic reading:

(43)   A maximum of ten books can be borrowed at any one time.

Jacobson (1978: 53) also acknowledges that specification of the meaning a modal conveys may involve adverbial co-occurrence where there would otherwise be ambiguity. He selects four modals – CAN, COULD, MAY, and WILL – to illustrate his point and it is significant that only in the case of CAN and COULD are adverbs cited which have no inherent connotations of modality or degree but whose meaning, it is suggested, disambiguates which of the modal senses is involved. He argues that in a sentence like:

(44)   You can't lawfully drive without a driver's licence.

disambiguation between the meanings or 'states' as he refers to them, of permission, possibility and ability 'is achieved by ascription of the quality of lawfulness to the driving, since it is only in the sense of permission that *can* can co-occur with a preverb denoting the norm according to which permission is granted'. Here, however, Jacobson is describing a possible environment of CAN rather than what the modal itself actually contributes to the meaning of the sentence; there is still potential ambiguity between the possibility and permission readings, even though the adverb LAWFULLY invokes the kind of institutional (deontic) authority discussed in 2.6. CAN and COULD have a more obvious affinity with adverbs which also have an inherent modal value and connote possibility-related senses. The strength of attraction is demonstrated by the proximity of the modifier to the modified and the invariant syntactic relation between them:

(45)   You can't possibly lawfully drive without a driver's licence.

(46)   You could certainly lawfully drive without a driver's licence before the war.

If, however, the order of the adverbs is reversed, and the non-modal meaning given precedence, the sequence is on the borderline of acceptability:

(45a)   */?You can't lawfully possibly drive without a driver's licence;

(46b) */?You could lawfully certainly drive without a driver's licence before the war.

With regard to subjectivity, there are frequent uses of CAN and COULD where neither the attitude nor the opinion of the speaker is involved. Combinations with perception verbs (such as SEE, HEAR SMELL) or mental-state verbs (such as REMEMBER, UNDERSTAND) are best accounted for as idiomatic use:

(47)   She can hear the birds singing;

(48)   They could understand everything.

There were no instances of adverb modification occurring in such contexts in the Survey, although both modal verbs are in principle open to emphasis by such adverbs as CERTAINLY or DEFINITELY.

CAN is nearly twice as frequent in the corpus as COULD (with a relative frequency of 19 per cent as opposed to 10 per cent). COULD has a wider range of modal functions, and operates epistemically in both assertive and non-assertive contexts and this may be why it is more susceptible to adverb modification than CAN. Given their indeterminate status, it is often impossible to distinguish clearly between their various meanings but, in terms of co-occurrence, it is the modals' inherent characteristic of possibility which is most regularly focalized, be this epistemic or otherwise: the over-whelming number of adverbial expressions with CAN and COULD (91 per cent and 82 per cent respectively in the Survey) connote nonepistemic (dynamic) possibility or ability.

3.4.1.2 *Epistemic meanings: possibility and necessity*

Save for its occasional rhetorical use, CAN basically only operates with an epistemic meaning in non-assertive contexts where it is used for the negation of epistemic necessity as expressed by MUST. In this use, CAN is often partnered by POSSIBLY, and less frequently by CONCEIVABLY, where both adverbs function as intensifiers (see 4.3.3), highlighting the notion of possibility:

(49)   I'm talking too much. You can't possibly be interested. (BB/111)

(50)   They can't conceivably be travelling on the early train.

COULD is the more common form and, unlike CAN, is free to occur both in assertive and non-assertive contexts:

(51)   That she could quite possibly identify him was something he didn't stop to consider. (AA/337-8)

(52)   But what could Galloway conceivably know? (AA/302)

The idiomatic expression COULD WELL, although not as frequent as MAY WELL and MIGHT WELL (see 3.4.2.2), is also used to convey probability as in (34) above.[15]

Occasionally, epistemic COULD co-occurs with adverbs which signal the actual process by which a conclusion is drawn or an inference made:

(53)   If he'd wanted tea, he could presumably have asked for it. (CG/151)

This feature recalls the inference–confidence axis discussed in 3.3; however, COULD is much less susceptible to this type of modification than MIGHT, MAY or MUST (see 3.4.2.2 and 3.4.3.2) and the relative infrequency of co-occurrence indicates the peripherality of this modal to the epistemic system.

3.4.1.3 Nonepistemic meanings: possibility, ability, permission

The use of CAN and COULD to express nonepistemic possibility (of which ability may be considered a special case) is well attested in the data:

(54)   Oxygen can readily be detected in the presence of tungsten, gold, or lead. (W.9.8.4)

(55)   Shaving was immediately made more comfortable because the blade, with its coating, could now slice cleanly through the facial hair. (W.15.4.30)

(56)   I can "honestly săy that# "I'm 'no eco'nomic gênius# (S.13.871/2)

(57)   I don't know how you cope – I did a part-time teaching thing for a bit but honestly could not carry on. (W.7.3.44)

Occasionally there are cases where ability is more clearly indicated:

(58)   my "father cèrtainly couldn't speak German#
         (S.2.13.470)

But, in the main, the distinction is hard to make. There is less blending between the deontic and other nonepistemic senses, although there are few examples in the Survey of permission CAN and COULD:

(59)   A: "can I 'pinch a cǐggie#

         B: "còurse you 'can#

         A: "would you like a ménthol# or a "plàin#
             (S.2.11.284/5/6/7)

(60)   "could I 'just get 'all this dǒwn# (S.9.2.145)

3.4.2 MAY/MIGHT

3.4.2.1 *Status*

According to the Survey, the overwhelming majority of adverbial combinations with MIGHT and MAY relate to the expression of epistemic modality (92 per cent and 76 per cent respectively). Both modals are basic to the epistemic system and serve as co-ordinates of epistemic possibility. They are used to convey 'weaker' judgements than expressions involving MUST (3.4.3). The evidence of co-occurrence and the relative frequency of the unmodified modal to express possibility, suggest that MIGHT is the principal co-ordinate; the CGEL (223) notes that it is often used in preference to MAY. Coates (1983: 147) suggests that MIGHT and MAY in their epistemic usage are interchangeable, although she concedes that the evidence of research into child language (Wells 1979; Perkins 1981) and regional dialects (Strang 1968; McDonald 1981) supports the view that 'MIGHT is superseding MAY as the main exponent of Epistemic Possibility'. Of course, MAY is also regularly used as a permission auxiliary (accounting for 19 per cent of all combinations), whereas MIGHT with this sense is extremely rare. There were no examples found in the Corpus, prompting the authors of the CGEL (224) to observe that 'It is rare and apparently obsolescent in this usage'. In the deontic system, MAY contrasts with MUST; the distinction between them parallels their epistemic roles as MAY is now the co-ordinate of deontic possibility, used for giving permission.

Although usage shows that MIGHT and MAY are interchangeable in many epistemic contexts, MIGHT generally indicates a more remote possibility than MAY.[16] It does not normally contrast with deontic MAY, other than in very polite or formulaic expressions where again the meaning is more tentative:

(61)   Might I be so bold as to suggest . . .

(62)   Might I just/possibly have a word with you?

In fact, deontic MIGHT is virtually restricted to such contexts, when it may also co-occur with the negative particle NOT and/or an intensifier like JUST or POSSIBLY, thereby increasing the degree of tentativeness expressed:

(63)   I was wondering if I might not just/possibly have a word
         in your ear in private.

There has been a tendency by some linguists to pair MAY (but not MIGHT) and CAN, the implication being that not only is there an overlap in their possibility/permission guises (especially the latter), but that there is an element of free variation between them. Palmer (1990: 103f), for example, talks of the frequent interchangeability of the two forms, and Perkins (1983: 36f) represents MAY as having the same core meaning as CAN. The evidence of our research into co-occurrence supports Coates' (1980a: 209) observations that rarely in everyday usage is there an overlap in meaning between the two modals and, where there is overlap (in the permission and nonepistemic possibility usages), they are not in free variation, because MAY is more loaded for the expression of modal meanings.

MAY and CAN are central to the expression of possibility, although each characterizes possibility of a distinct kind. In:

(64)   they're "all 'very Kèntish# they "may be in Sùssex
         áctually# (S.7.3.588)

the speaker conveys his assessment of the possibility of the proposition being true: 'it is possible that they are in Sussex'. The possibility expressed is inferential. By contrast, in:

(65)   Well, if you get the sack, you can always come and work
         for me. (W.5.1.36)

the possibility expressed is theoretical: an interpretation made all
the more poignant by the co-occurring adverb's suggestion of
timelessness. There is no assessment at all as to the likelihood or
otherwise of the possibility expressed actually coming about,
precisely because the writer's attitude to the truth of the proposition is not involved in the meaning of the modal, which can be
paraphrased by 'it is possible for'. While MAY is susceptible to
adverbial modification, CAN generally remains unmodified. (The
obvious exception, as we have seen, is when CAN occurs in non-
assertive contexts.)

A further distinction can be drawn between the two modals on
the basis of the stress patterns with which each typically interacts.
Epistemic MAY is frequently stressed (as in well over two-thirds of
epistemic MAY and adverb combinations in the SEU), whereas
nonepistemic CAN is usually unstressed. Epistemic MAY is also
typically associated with fall–rise intonation as shown in (64)
above.

Occasionally, MAY and MIGHT operate as formal substitutes for
CAN and COULD in the expression of nonepistemic possibility (but
see the discussion in 3.4.1.1 and 3.4.2.3 below). As with permission, there is a shared area of meaning but neither pair is in free
variation, because the former are marked for formality:

(66)   The fat in our diet may/can be reduced by buying low-fat
         products.

The nonepistemic meanings of MIGHT and MAY are treated in
greater detail below.

3.4.2.2 Epistemic possibility

MAY and MIGHT primarily express epistemic possibility; in combination with their adverb collocates they frequently (but not
necessarily) relate to the higher value of probability:

(67)   Sex discrimination can be either direct or indirect. For
         example, if a woman is refused a job in favour of a man
         with inferior qualifications, that may well be a question of
         direct discrimination. (W.13.3.123/4)

(68)   If Dillon does as he did the other night, he may probably visit this bar. (HT/222)

(69)   it "may wèll bé# that "there were faults# (S.12.4.1120/1)

(70)   it may "well have bĕen# that "we'd have been 'able to 'help hèr to sée# (S.6.5.527/8)

(71)   It might well be the kind of thing somebody says in sheer desperation. (AA/325)

(72)   This vessel is decorated with masks, projecting spiked triangles, and reticulated rectangles which might possibly represent fishing nets. (W.1.6.152)

(73)   "well I 'just míght be 'there# "round about 'seven to 'half păst# (S.7.3.223)

(74)   He might just conceivably have something pertinent to tell them. (CG/243)

In speech, epistemic MAY and MIGHT are often associated with a fall-rise nuclear tone, as in (69) and (70). Both modals are subject to intensification where the effect of the adverb modifier can be to diminish or weaken the force of the modal, as in (72), (73) and (74) or to strengthen it, as in (67), (68), (69), (70) and (71). Of the modals, MAY and MIGHT are among the most susceptible to adverbial modification; certain combinations, such as those with WELL, are idiomatic. Idiomaticity and collocation are discussed in Chapter 5.

In non-assertive contexts, CAN and COULD replace epistemic MAY and MIGHT (see 3.4.1.1):

(75)   I'm talking too much. You can't possibly be interested. (BB/111)

(76)   How could she possibly jeopardise her own little world? (AA/321)

(77)   "could I 'possibly af'ford twò húmbugs# (S.6.4.843)

The idiomatic association with POSSIBLY heightens the modality expressed.

Epistemic MIGHT and MAY attract a similar range of adverbial collocates, and combinations mostly involve the semantic process of intensification (see 4.3.2.2, and 4.3.3). In this respect, both contrast significantly with MUST whose association with evidential collocates such as EVIDENTLY, INEVITABLY, OBVIOUSLY marks it out as the potential coordinate of an evidential epistemic subsystem, unique in terms of the epistemic system in English (see 3.4.3.2). In contrast to MUST, MIGHT and MAY convey the speaker's relative lack of confidence in the truth of what he is saying and neither additionally conveys to any great extent the notion of inference which so strongly characterizes uses of epistemic MUST.

In 3.3 it was suggested that the inference–confidence axis represents two kinds of interrelated epistemic modality, con-spicuous in the use of MUST where the strength of the judgement conveyed is informed by the nature and reliability of the evidence available to the speaker. In the case of MIGHT and MAY, the theoretical distinction between inference and confidence is diluted to an extent that the two aspects are all but impossible to distinguish. It can be argued that MIGHT and MAY are essentially conjectural and are used where there are few or no 'known facts'; the speaker hazards a guess about the state of things according to his intuitions, there is little reasoning on the basis of information available. This is clearly suggested in the comments of Perkins (1983: 38): 'The epistemic use of MAY indicates that evidence available to the speaker is such that the proposition expressed by the sentence cannot currently be inferred to be true, but nor can it currently be inferred to be false.' The lack of evidence inhibits deduction but allows for a tentative assessment.[17] By contrast, MUST implies that the speaker makes deductions after assessment of available evidence which empowers him to make an informed opinion as opposed to a speculative observation. The spirit of MUST is captured in Coates' (1983: 41) observation that: 'In its most normal usage, epistemic MUST conveys the speaker's confidence in the truth of what he is saying, based on a deduction from facts known to him (which may or may not be specified).' As a result, MIGHT and MAY favour adverbs which indicate the speaker's degree of confidence, rather than collocates whose function is to highlight the inferential process by which the judgement itself is reached. This distinction in the nature of collocational attraction is not watertight; MIGHT and MAY can co-occur with 'evidentials' but they do not exhibit the marked tendency of MUST or, for that matter, WILL and WOULD (see 3.4.5).

3.4.2.3 *Nonepistemic meanings: possibility and permission*

The nonepistemic uses of MIGHT and MAY are problematical in that, as with MUST, there can be indeterminacy between epistemic and nonepistemic, and deontic and dynamic readings. The nonepistemic uses of MIGHT are largely confined to deontic contexts and rather formulaic use:

(78)   He gestured with his free hand to the bartender that the small glass might kindly be replenished. (AA/86)

Occasionally the modal is used in a similar way to iterative WOULD to refer to an habitual activity in the past:

(79)   At the weekends they might go for long walks.

Even then, it is rare and archaic. But there are cases of indeterminacy between the epistemic and nonepistemic divide. Palmer (1990: 110) quotes an interesting example from the Survey which, he suggests, is amenable to a dynamic or an epistemic reading:

(80)   We operate what might be described as a gigantic tutorial system. (S.6.Ic.8)

In a dynamic reading the use of MIGHT can be acccounted for on the grounds of formality. An epistemic reading is equally plausible, however, where MIGHT simply conveys the speaker's tentative opinion on how the description might be characterized. The interpolation of POSSIBLY or WELL would favour an epistemic interpretation. Probably, however, there is, as Palmer (*op. cit.*) concludes, a blending between 'can be called' ('it is possible for') and 'might be called' ('it is possible that').

There are occasions where MAY substitutes dynamic CAN and the sense conveyed can be paraphrased by: 'It is possible for ...'. Like dynamic MUST (see 3.4.3.3) there is no implication of human control. The CGEL (223) quotes this example:

(81)   During the autumn, many rare birds may be observed on the rocky northern coasts of the island.

MAY here is purely a stylistic variant for the more colloquial CAN; it frequently occurs in written texts when a more elevated style is considered appropriate. Adverbial modification is exceptional.

MAY (like CAN and MUST) is often used to refer to institutional rules and regulations. Palmer (1990: 104) suggests that these uses may be treated as deontic or dynamic according to whether the rule is seen as a report of deontic modality or as a statement about what is dynamically possible:

(82)   Any Director may at any time appoint any person to be an alternate Director of the Co., and may at any time remove any alternate Director so appointed by him from office. (W.14.3.87)

(83)   The smallest investment will be set at a level to ensure that a very large number of people can consider buying shares. In addition payments may well be by instalments, so you would not have to pay the full cost all at once. (W.15.5.318)

In (83), the otherwise epistemic expression MAY WELL is used exceptionally in a nonepistemic sense, although the collocate still functions as an emphasizer. The most appropriate reading would seem to be a deontic one; the speaker is not only reporting a rule but identifying himself with the source of authority and agreeing with the rule. In neither example is MAY unambiguously dynamic, especially (83); with the substitution of CAN, on the other hand, either a deontic or a dynamic interpretation would seem reasonable. Perkins (1983: 37f) comments that:

When MAY, as it were impinges on CAN's dynamic territory . . . either the hypotheticality of its epistemic use or the permission sense of its deontic use never appears to be far away, and this has the effect of differentiating the examples with MAY from the more purely dynamic versions with CAN. . . .'.

MAY is, of course, modally more loaded than CAN.

In non-assertive contexts negated MAY is used and permission is thereby refused; the interdiction can be emphasized:

(84)   You certainly may not borrow the car!

MAY and especially MIGHT combine with (JUST) AS WELL to create an idiomatic expression typically used to make a circumspect or sardonic recommendation:

(85)   "well I'm 'at your mòther's# "so I think I mìght as 'well hang òn a 'little 'bit for you# (S.7.2.212/3)

(86)   "Shakespeare wróte it# we "might just as well 'keep it all
        in# "něarly 'all of it# (S.6.2.807/8/9)

(87)   She might just as well have advertised their affair.
        (CP/140)

Again, it is not altogether clear which type of modality is involved
here; there are distinct epistemic and deontic overtones. Given that
such combinations are idiomatic and invariable, they are perhaps
best considered outside the usual modal categories; there is
blending of the different epistemic and nonepistemic senses but it
is pointless to argue which sense prevails.

3.4.3 MUST

3.4.3.1 *Status*

Adverbial combinations with MUST encode epistemic and nonepistemic modal meanings in roughly equal proportion, according
to the Survey (53 per cent and 47 per cent respectively). Epistemic
MUST is the co-ordinate of epistemic necessity, used in expressions
to make the strongest of all possible judgements; deontic MUST,
with its parallel function in the deontic system as the co-ordinate
of deontic necessity, is used to lay an obligation. The centrality of
MUST to the epistemic and deontic systems of English mirrors that
of MIGHT and MAY except, of course, MUST is situated at opposite
extremes within the two modal dimensions. Although MUST is
formally unpaired, it does contrast for formality, tentativeness, and
remoteness with SHOULD and OUGHT TO (see 3.4.4). The more
even distribution between the epistemic and nonepistemic uses of
MUST additionally sets it apart from MIGHT and MAY given their
weighting towards epistemic uses. Bouma (1975: 324f) suggests that
MUST is mostly restricted in its usage to the written language and
formal contexts. The Survey data contradicts both findings: MUST
is regularly attested in colloquial speech and found in a variety of
written contexts, and not just the formal. Palmer (1990: 116)
concludes that this may reflect a difference in the usage patterns of
British and American English.
    The CGEL (224) treats MUST in terms of logical necessity, which
seems to imply the objectivity characteristic of alethic rather than

epistemic modality. Lyons (1977: 793f) theorizes on the potential distinction between subjective (SEM) and objective (OEM) epistemic modality (the latter approximating to alethic modality which relates to the necessary or contingent truth of propositions: the traditional concern of modal logic). The features of subjectivity and objectivity have been examined in detail (2.5); in essence he argues that with SEM the speaker himself is uncertain about a given state of affairs, whereas with OEM the uncertainty or unverifiability is due to the nature of the state of affairs itself. However, Lyons (1977: 797) observes that 'this is not a distinction that can be drawn sharply in the everyday use of language', acknowledging that 'it may well be that the objectification of epistemic necessity and possibility is a rather sophisticated and impersonal process which plays little part in ordinary non-scientific discourse'. In similar vein, Miller and Johnson-Laird (1976: 495) surmise that in everyday discourse, it is unlikely that a distinction between SEM and OEM need be drawn: 'logical necessity characterizes one domain of discourse, but it is not a domain of pre-eminent concern to the average person.'

MUST is used to convey the speaker's judgement, not that the proposition expressed is necessarily true in any strictly logical sense of the term, but that there is at least a very high likelihood of it being true. We cite again example (1) from 3.3:

(88)   Any history of art written for the consumption of twentieth-century Europeans must necessarily regard the Giotto–Cézanne period as the most important section of art history. (J 1964: 298)

The author is not making an objective assessment, tempting though it might be to think this because of NECESSARILY (even though he may well be invoking the informed appraisal of the art critic establishment) but stating with considerable conviction his personal judgement: the co-occurrence of NECESSARILY emphasizes and reinforces the truth-value of the proposition, reflecting the strength of the writer's epistemic warrant. As discussed in 2.4.1, few linguists have considered the possibility that epistemic modality could be anything other than a matter of the speaker's subjective attitude towards the propositional content of his utterance. In her corpus-based survey of the modals, Coates (1983: 41f) remarks that epistemic MUST is frequently found with hedges. Hedges are not just adverbials but may also be modal lexical verbs like MEAN, SUPPOSE, FANCY, GUESS co-occurring in such frames as: 'I guess he must have forgotten.' Significantly, she notes that hedges 'underline the fact that epistemic modals are essentially subjective' and 'focus on the speaker's attitude to the proposition'.

Deontic MUST sets an obligation or a requirement which demands compliance on the part of the addressee. Speaker involvement in relation to epistemic MUST is constant but (as we have seen in section 2.4 on the epistemic and deontic systems of English) with deontic MUST (as with deontic MAY) there are degrees. The speaker may be totally involved, totally uninvolved or partially involved as the 'representative' of a collective or group:

(89)   We really must get on with the project.

(90)   Withdrawals must not exceed £200.

(91)   Candidates for positions with our organisation must be EC nationals.

The context may make the degree of involvement clear or give only a vague indication of the extent to which the speaker identifies himself as the source of authority. We have also suggested in 2.7 that the speaker may have reason for not wishing to be identified as the source of deontic authority consistent with the use of unmodified modal forms, and any number of underlying motives.

Where the context gives little or no indication of speaker involvement, it is arguable whether deontic modality is involved at all. For this reason, Palmer (1979: 36f) proposed the recognition of dynamic modality as a third modal category. He cites, among others, the following example from the Survey:

(92)   If the ratepayers should be consulted, so too must the council tenants. (W.11.5.32)

Without knowing the wider context, it is impossible to argue the case of speaker involvement either way. Yet it seems hardly possible that MUST here is 'neutral' (see Palmer 1979: 113f; 1986; 102f); there are vestiges or overtones of at least some degree of speaker association with the source of authority for why else would the speaker use MUST in the first place? Palmer (1990: 113) offers as another instance of speaker non-involvement the following example, also drawn from the Survey (the prosodic information is omitted):

(93)   Now I lunched the day before yesterday with one of the leaders of the Labour Party whose name must obviously be kept quiet – I can't repeat it. (S.5.5.53)

But here the interpolation of the adverbial OBVIOUSLY indicates that epistemic and not necessarily deontic or dynamic modality may now be involved. The speaker's involvement is explicit under an epistemic reading: 'It is obviously necessary that the name should be kept quiet'; and arguably more determinate under a deontic: 'It is obviously desirable for the name to be kept quiet.' The presence of the adverbial as an overt marker of speaker presence would seem to rule out the possibility of a dynamic reading.

However, it would be misleading to argue that within the broad area of nonepistemic meanings, MUST does not exhibit some indeterminacy between clear cases of deontic and so-called dynamic modality, where its modal status is open to question. Example (93) also reveals that there can be indeterminacy in relation to the epistemic/nonepistemic divide itself, especially where the modal remains unmodified. Palmer (1986: 103) acknowledges the complexity of the issue:

The status of neutral or circumstantial [dynamic] uses of the modals is . . . problematic, for they are not always clearly distinct from deontic modality, in the strictly subjective sense. There is thus indeterminacy, leaving completely indeterminate the dividing line between what is modal (and subjective) and what is non-modal (and objective, declarative).

MUST enjoys a unique status in both the epistemic and deontic realms; it epitomizes the speaker's hegemony in both domains, however indeterminate his involvement may appear to be. This alone frustrates attempts to identify uses which might ultimately have to be considered non-modal. 'Mighty Must' indeed![18]

3.4.3.2 *Epistemic necessity*

Adverbial expressions involving epistemic MUST often reflect the confidence–inference axis discussed in 3.3. The adverb satellite may focus primarily on the inferential nature of the auxiliary (94), (95) or the speaker's degree of confidence (96), but ultimately both features blend and are reinforced:

(94)   As prices go on rising and the value of money declines (as, it seems to me, must inevitably happen) . . . (W.11.2.147)

(95)   I "certainly did 'not think 'this mèant# that it "must in'evitably 'mean wèlcóming# the "lowering of 'academic stàndards# (S.11.2.935/6/7)

(96)   oh "maps 'must have existed# "cèrtainly# (S.2.3.72/3)

In his typological survey of epistemic modality, Palmer (1986: 51f) suggests that two subsystems can be distinguished, one involving 'Judgements' (which is the only system we have discussed so far) and the other 'Evidentials'.[19] In English, the speaker indicates the degree of his commitment to what he is saying in terms of possibility and necessity, and this involves making relatively weak or strong epistemic judgments. MIGHT/ MAY, and MUST are the formal co-ordinates of the epistemic system in English. But in some languages, speakers have other means of indicating that there is no guarantee to the truth of their statements; the epistemic system is formally based not on judgements but on evidentials, where the type of evidence available to the speaker, be it visual, non-visual, hearsay and so forth, is actually encoded formally by the modal system. In his treatment of modality in English, Palmer (1990: 12) points out that the English epistemic system consists only of judgements. However, he goes on to argue that 'epistemic MUST usually not merely makes a judgement, but also bases that judgement upon the evidence available, and to that extent is evidential'. The range of adverb collocates epistemic MUST attracts, such as APPARENTLY, CLEARLY, EVIDENTLY, INEVITABLY and OBVI-OUSLY, supports Palmer's argument. The evidential quality of these collocates also suggests that, in combination with MUST, the resulting expressions constitute an evidential subsystem which is a refinement of the modal's epistemic potential, even though the nature of the evidence itself is not formally encoded. Swan (1987:

49) argues that, by referring directly to evidence, these adverbs actually trigger the use of MUST. The strength of the association is especially marked in contexts where the speaker signals the illocutionary force of his utterance in an explicit way (see 2.6). The function of the evidentials is to point to the reason for the speaker having to perform the act in question, in other words, to make obvious his motivation for doing so. Swan produces this example:

> Obviously/Apparently/Clearly I must offer my condolences [since I just learned that your parrot died].
> [since I can tell from your face that the expected death of your parrot has occurred].

While the other epistemic modals co-occur with evidential adverbs, they do so less markedly; again this points to the unique status of MUST:

(97)   The need is for controls, accountable government and an independent mechanism to make life impossible for the corrupt official. The alternative is for a collapse of formal political institutions as corruption must inevitably erode political legitimacy. Under these conditions everybody must suffer. (THES/04.06.93/12)

The wider context provided by this example makes the process of reasoning which underpins the speaker's confidence explicit.

Negated MUST is usually replaced by CAN'T in negative epistemic contexts; interestingly, this is a feature of the modal system which often produces one of the strongest collocational bonds represented by any modal–adverb expression:

(98)   It must certainly result in a termination of the project

becomes:

(98a)   It can't possibly result . . .

MUST NOT and MUSTN'T are rarely used although the CGEL (795) notes that there seems to be some encroachment on CAN'T. Perkins (1983: 49) produces this example:

(99)   He must not be Dr. Livingstone after all.

However, for many native speakers, CAN'T would be the more natural choice of expression.

As Palmer (1990: 62f) has observed, epistemic modality is rarely open to question; the use of epistemic MUST in interrogatives is rhetorical, conveying the force of a strong assertion: no answer is generally expected, and the modal tends to co-occur with ALWAYS:

(100)   Why MUST you ALWAYS make such a fuss?

(101)   MUST it ALWAYS end up this way?

3.4.3.3 *Nonepistemic meanings: necessity and obligation*

The use of MUST to express nonepistemic necessity was mentioned in 3.4.3.1. However, there are contexts which have not yet been discussed in which MUST occurs and where there is no or little implication of human control; the sense conveyed is clearly paraphrasable by: 'It is essential/necessary for ...'. The CGEL (225) gives the following example:

(102)   To be healthy, a plant must receive a good supply of both sunshine and moisture.

Here MUST seems to refer to a necessary condition, 'plants need sunshine and moisture in order to be healthy', which applies generally to the class of things referred to. The noun phrase 'a plant' is being used generically, of course. The Survey reveals a number of similar examples, such as this one quoted in Palmer (1990: 129f):

(103)   Protoplasm, the living substance of all plants, contains nitrogen and the rose tree must absorb this nitrogen in the form of nitrates. (W.10.3.3)

In such contexts MUST affirms the intervention of natural not human laws, similar in force and meaning to the use of WILL in such contexts as:

(104)   Oil will float on water.

The use of MUST to refer to defining or necessary characteristics of the subject represents its dynamic use because the deontic source does not in any way derive from the speaker or any entity with which the speaker can be identified (see Palmer 1990: 113f).

It is significant that when MUST operates dynamically it is rarely if ever modified. There are in fact no examples in the Survey of what Palmer (1990: 130f) refers to as 'characteristic' MUST taking an adverbial collocate. The interpolation of an adverbial conveying modal or temporal constraints, CERTAINLY or SOMETIMES for instance, in any of the above examples, is anomalous. Not even the common emphasizer REALLY is comfortable in these contexts.

Where MUST relates to obligation and involves human control of events the picture is clearer. And there is marked tolerance of adverbial modification even though this is mostly restricted to instances of co-occurrence with emphasizers and intensifiers.

(105)   All of us reason about and understand what people necessarily must be; we dream about, are bewildered by, what they accidentally and incomprehensibly are. (J 1975: 205)

(106)   One clear runner must always be left behind shelves. (W.10.4.82)

(107)   we "really must get it conclùded 'mùstn't we# (S.5.11.240)

(108)   you must just "keep on goìng 'at it# (S.5.9.291)

(109)   I "really must be getting 'home in a móment# (S.2 2.831)

In (105) and (106) an external authority is either advocating a certain form of behaviour or imposing some kind of obligation. Even though the source of authority remains unspecified, there is always the implication of human control; this helps distinguish the central deontic use of MUST from its other nonepistemic sense of necessity. Where the subject is 'I' or 'We' as in (109) and (107) the obligation appears to be self-imposed; Palmer (1990: 113) observes that 'Generally speaking we do not lay obligations upon ourselves' and argues that such uses of MUST with first person subjects should be treated rather in terms of 'neutral' or 'dynamic' necessity. Clearly, however, there is speaker involvement and the notion that the speaker can exercise authority over himself is consistent with the meaning of self-admonishment; the speaker is appealing to his own sense of duty or code of conduct (see the CGEL: 225). The force of his moral imperative is regularly captured by the co-occurrence of REALLY as in (107) and (109) above.

3.4.4 SHOULD / OUGHT TO

3.4.4.1 *Status*

Although formally the past tense form of SHALL (see 3.4.6), SHOULD is paired with the marginal auxiliary OUGHT TO on the grounds that both are readily interchangeable in a wide variety of contexts. Palmer (1990: 122) argues that 'it is not at all clear that English makes any distinction between SHOULD and OUGHT TO', and Bîră (1979: 206) also remarks that 'Most native speakers of present-day English do not feel any difference between the two modals and use them interchangeably'.[20] The degree of interchangeability is neatly demonstrated in these two examples drawn from the Survey, where both expressions exist in free variation:

(110)   if "Carol thìnks that we 'ought to 'look at him# per"hăps we should 'look at him# (S.2.6.1130/1)

(111)   Even so no version of history ought to be believed without question. No historian should be trusted implicitly. (W.9.3.126)

SHOULD is, however, much more common in both speech and writing and, stylistically, is perhaps the more felicitous expression of the two.[21]

About a fifth of all adverb combinations with SHOULD and OUGHT TO are used to express epistemic senses, according to the Survey. But co-occurrence is infrequent. In common with COULD, MAY and MIGHT and in contrast to MUST, SHOULD and OUGHT TO express not the speaker's confidence but what the CGEL (227) refers to as the speaker's 'tentative inference'; the 'speaker does not know if his statement is true, but tentatively concludes that it is true, on the basis of whatever he knows'.[22] There is often indeterminacy between epistemic and nonepistemic senses where it is unclear whether a tentative assumption or an obligation is at issue:

(112)   They really should/ought to be home by now.

SHOULD and OUGHT TO interact very differently from MUST in relation to the future and, in the case of the latter, the sense becomes deontic rather than epistemic:

(113)   We should/ought to be in Nice by this time next week.

(114)   We must be in Nice by this time next week.

In their nonepistemic uses, SHOULD and OUGHT TO are mostly concerned with senses related to obligation and duty but they are weaker in force than MUST and there is frequently the implication that the recommended course of action will not actually be carried out. The CGEL (227) contains this example:

(115)   They should/ought to have met her at the station.

This implies that they did not, whereas:

(116)   They must have met her at the station.

implies that they almost certainly did but now, of course, the modality has shifted into the epistemic domain.

Occasionally, there seem to be cases of nonepistemic use which are difficult to treat in terms of deontic modality, although the suggestion of obligation is not altogether absent. Palmer (1990: 123) quotes these examples from the Survey and suggests that they are dynamic, but others might well disagree:

(117)   You should read, my dear, more. You don't read enough, my darling. (S.2.10.47)

(118)   I ought to be ashamed to say so, but I can't. (S.8.3e.5)

Again, the problem is one of indeterminacy.

The Survey revealed very few instances of co-occurrence with SHOULD and only one with nonepistemic OUGHT TO. With regard to their epistemic status, both are inherently tentative like MIGHT but, unlike that modal, are relatively peripheral to the epistemic system and never fully divested of their more common deontic roles. Often, it seems that they simultaneously express both epistemic and deontic senses as in (117), where the speaker concludes that the addressee does not read enough and that it would be beneficial to read more. The effect of such indeterminacy, which Coates (1983: 17) refers to as 'merger', is to militate against co-occurrence, but it does not preclude it.

3.4.4.2 *Epistemic meaning: tentative inference*

There are relatively few instances of co-occurrence found in the Survey (or other corpus material consulted) where the modal–adverb combination could be considered unambiguously epistemic:

(119) and "he lost 'four pints of blòod# and he "bloody well 'shouldn't have púlled through# (S.2.12.186/7)

(120) In fact, the shadow chancellor and the party leader should probably be taken at their word – vague as it is. If they make promises now and break them after polling day, their government will lose its credibility.[23]

Occasionally, where the modal verb alone would seem to convey deontic meaning, the co-occurring adverb lends the utterance an epistemic hue. This is particularly true in the case of combinations involving PROBABLY and PERHAPS:

(121) If this does not produce a remission inside a month the dose of Distamine should probably be reduced again as the incidence of side-effects seems to increase with dosage. (W.7.13.75)

(122) Today, 37 years later, with India still suffering from political, civil and environmental strife and the world still in crisis, we should perhaps take heart from the ancient proverb 'It is better to light a candle than to curse the darkness.' (W.6.5.117)

In each case, the unmodified modal has an obligational meaning which generally conveys the speaker's deontic authority, but this authority is compromised or weakened through the intercession of the adverb satellite. As a result, there is merger between the epistemic and nonepistemic categories of modality.

No examples of combinations with epistemic OUGHT TO were noted in the Survey, but the following provides an appropriate context (to adapt a well-known example from Coates 1983: 17):

(123) A: Newcastle Brown is a jolly good beer.
       B: Is it?
       A: Well it [certainly/bloody well] ought to be at that price!

Restrictions on adverbial position in relation to OUGHT TO is another factor affecting potential co-occurrence. There are strong stylistic objections to placing adverbials between TO and the infinitive (the so-called 'split infinitive' construction), and there is phonological evidence (/ɔ:tə/), supported by evidence from informal spelling (*'oughta'), that the TO is more closely linked with OUGHT than with the following word. Thus 'The mountains OUGHT TO PROBABLY be in view before long' or 'The mountains OUGHT PROBABLY TO be in view before long' both sound cumbersome in comparison with 'The mountains PROBABLY OUGHT TO be in view before long'. SHOULD is clearly more versatile in this respect as it is equally happy with pre- or post-modification (see the CGEL: 496).

3.4.4.3 Nonepistemic meanings: obligation

In the main, co-occurrence with nonepistemic SHOULD and OUGHT TO is unremarkable and the only noticeable trend at work is the semantic process of emphasis (see 4.3.2), typically involving REALLY:

(124)   "I 'think hŭsbands# "really should be 'made to dò the 'moving actually# (S.9.1.1067/8)

(125)   you know "I 'think nŏw# that you "really 'ought to 'start 'mòurning your 'brother# (S.6.5.296/7/8)

Neither modal expression is central to the deontic system like MUST, even though they function as its tentative counterparts. Deontic modality is essentially performative (see 2.5.2); there is the expectation that an action will be carried out or an event will take place. However, in the case of SHOULD and OUGHT TO, not only does the speaker allow for the possibility that the expectation will remain unfulfilled, but he frequently anticipates this as a matter of course:

(126)   They should/ought to leave this evening, but they won't;

(127)   *They must leave this evening, but they won't.

They are not true 'directives' because they do not necessarily entail action, but in other respects they exhibit deontic behaviour and are best treated in this category.

3.4.5 WILL / WOULD ('LL / 'D)

3.4.5.1 *Status*

The majority of combinations with WILL and WOULD are concerned with prediction (70 and 61 per cent respectively, according to the Survey) and thus also involve the expression of futurity. Where the prediction is a matter of the speaker's judgement, the meaning expressed is obviously epistemic:

(128)   All leave will probably, in the circumstances, be suspended. (GOM/EC/280)

(129)   In Manila ... the Constabulary by now would surely have a file on him. (CA/AD/233)

But where there is no such judgement involved and the prediction is relatively neutral the meaning is clearly not epistemic:

(130)   My babe-in-arms will be fifty-nine on my eighty-ninth birthday ... (S.5.5.11) (Cited in Palmer 1990: 148)

(131)   She felt icy cold and completely desparate. He would have no hesitation about getting rid of the child as well as her. (Lancaster Corpus 16-P) (Cited in Coates 1983: 210)

WILL (and WOULD, where this is used to express future time as seen from a viewpoint in the past) rarely has simple future time reference: 'Futurity is never a purely temporal concept; it necessarily includes an element of prediction or some related notion' (Lyons 1977: 677). Most linguists would now agree that the use of WILL (and SHALL, see 3.4.6) to refer to future time is secondary to a more modal function. Palmer (1986: 217) remarks:

> It is not difficult to see an explanation in terms of a *modal future*, the future expressed by WILL being indicated as a modal judgement by the speaker, in contrast with that expressed by BE GOING TO, which makes an objective statement about current situations relevant to the future.

Certain linguists (for example, see Bîră 1979: 168f) consider all predictive uses of WILL and WOULD epistemic while others, such as Palmer (1979: 119), consider the epistemic use distinct yet acknowledge that 'it is almost certainly true that because of the close relation between modality and futurity it will often be difficult to distinguish clearly at all times between an epistemic future and a "pure" future use'. It is poignant that, in his later study, Palmer (1990: 163) acknowledges that the frequent indeterminacy between the two modes of future expression reflects the fact that 'the two uses of WILL have much in common and they may even be indistinguishable when there is future time reference, but little is gained by identifying them'. The indeterminacy is largely resolved when it comes to co-occurrence as both modals exhibit a marked tendency to co-occur with adverbs connoting various degrees of probability (PROBABLY, PRESUMABLY, UNDOUBTEDLY) and thus express epistemic modality. Like MUST (see 3.4.3), they also co-occur with evidential adverbs, although not to the same extent.

MAY and MUST are associated with epistemic possibility and necessity but WILL is something of a free floater within the epistemic system. Combinations of PROBABLY with WILL and WOULD are potential markers of probability but are rivalled by the more idiomatic and increasingly widespread use of expressions involving WELL (see 3.4.1 and 3.4.2). WILL also approximates to the use of MUST, particularly in combinations with CERTAINLY or DEFINITELY or other adverbs expressing similar degrees of likelihood. In these cases, there is often the implication that the speaker's judgement is based on facts that are somehow 'known' rather than inferred, as these examples drawn from Jacobson (1964, 1975) so clearly illustrate:

(132)   Cézanne himself would certainly have been puzzled had he lived to see the fruits of his life's work. (J 1964: 240)

(133)   She exposed the photograph out of respect for convention, under which heading came what indubitably would have been Tom's feeling. (J 1964: 282)

(134)   Color customs in America (and elsewhere) inevitably will yield to the larger realities of today and tomorrow. (J 1975: 175)

(135)   Regardless of what field you prefer, applying for employment is something you undoubtedly will do several times in finding a suitable place in the world of work. (J 1975: 242)

Matthews (1991: 61) attempts to capture the distinction between WILL and MUST by referring to the two forms in terms of 'predictive certainty' and 'inferential certainty', respectively. The use of 'certainty' is potentially misleading, and it must be remembered that WILL regularly occurs with PROBABLY, where the strength of the prediction is toned down. However, there is an intuitive difference between the behaviour of the two forms, and one which is immediately suggested by the wider range of adverbial collocates that WILL tolerates. Coates (1983: 177) proposes that the usage of WILL contrasts with MUST in that the speaker's confidence in the truth of the proposition 'is not based on a process of logical inference. Instead it is based on common sense, or on repeated experience.' If by 'common sense' it is implied that the speaker's judgement is based on a practical understanding of everyday affairs as this is informed by general experience, then inference is not necessarily precluded, to wit combinations of WILL with PRE-SUMABLY. Furthermore, use of the term 'logical' is misleading for the same reason as talk of objective epistemic modality (see 2.5), in natural language, is misguided. MUST does imply that the speaker's confidence is based on specified or unspecified available evidence but it necessarily entails human judgement and there is nothing logical in any formal sense about the inferential processes by which that judgement is reached. In the case of WILL and WOULD, the speaker's judgement is also the product of experience, be this habitual or not, and similar inferential processes may be involved and marked explicitly, as with PRESUMABLY, or implied through co-occurrence with evidential adverbials like INEVITABLY or NEC-ESSARILY:

(136)   That food is in some way limiting for nestling robins can scarcely be doubted – otherwise the average size of the brood would presumably be increased by natural selection until the food limit was reached. (J 1964: 320)

(137)   American-style deregulation is now spreading to Europe and other parts of the world, which is good news for passengers but will inevitably force more airlines into liquidation.

(138)   To puzzle over each and every sound would necessarily

preoccupy the mind to the exclusion of all else. (CG/231)

The common-sense argument for distinguishing between the epistemic uses of WILL and MUST is vague. It is true that, generally, WILL is less epistemically marked for inference than MUST, and does have a 'matter-of-fact' quality about it, but sometimes collocation may elaborate the inferential dimension, regardless.

Like CAN and COULD (see 3.4.1), WILL and WOULD are sometimes used where there is no implication of the speaker's judgement (epistemic modality) or attitude (deontic modality); in other words, the modality concerned does not refer to truth or likelihood, or social, ethical or moral constraints. This is once again the domain of dynamic modality, involving meanings to do with so-called pure futurity on the one hand, and volition and related senses on the other.

In the case of adverb combinations with WILL and WOULD, where PROBABLY or PRESUMABLY are often involved, it would clearly be misleading to talk of a neutral or pure future or, indeed, of futurity at all; the adverb satellite confers epistemic status on the expression and the time frame is rooted in the present. However, there are uses of WILL and WOULD which are of a dispositional kind; these are 'an expression of the disposition of the world or the situation, but not of individuals, i.e. that in a given world, there is a disposition towards the realization of a particular state-of-affairs' (Matthews 1991: 154). 'He'll be 21 on Tuesday' or the predictive conditional use of WOULD as in 'If you worked today, you wouldn't have to work tomorrow' can be accounted for in this way. WILL and WOULD cannot be adequately described within a dispositional framework and recourse has to be made to the notions of volition and willingness. However, Matthews (1991: 152) objects to this approach on the grounds that it is not the modals themselves which express these notions but the context: 'willingness has nothing directly to do with the semantics of *will*/*'ll*' (Matthews 1991: 152). This is simply untrue:

(139)   No I bloody well won't come and be your valet. (CG/250)

is, if nothing else, a matter of the speaker's will!

The CGEL (229) describes the volitional meanings of WILL and

WOULD in terms of three subsenses: intention, willingness and insistence. Intention and willingness can be related to the deontic system where the speaker either undertakes to perform an action or, by making a request, initiate an action, since deontic modality is essentially performative (see 2.4). Hence, the following can be accounted for deontically:

(140)   "I'll definitely come òver at lúnch-tìme# (S.7.2.1257)

(141)   Perhaps you will kindly make arrangements to call and discuss with me the question as to reductions in the loan. (W.7.9.65)

(140) corresponds to Searle's commissives (see 2.5.2) 'where we commit ourselves to do things'.

Other than in cases of the first or second person, however, a dynamic interpretation seems more plausible; Palmer (1990: 134) quotes a very clear example from the Survey:

(142)   Would he not agree that recent congressional hearings have shown the length to which some American aircraft manufacturers will go to promote and defend the rights of their companies. (S.11.4.82)

The volitional meaning, as Palmer suggests, can be paraphrased by 'are prepared to'. Adverbial modification is all but ruled out in dynamic environments as is the case with CAN and COULD (but see below).

3.4.5.2 Epistemic meanings: prediction

The epistemic uses of WILL and WOULD are made explicit by their adverb satellites. As with the nonepistemic uses of possibility MAY and necessity MUST, the nonepistemic future predictive sense of WILL and WOULD is only retained where the modal itself remains unmodified. Although both modals favour adverbs expressing probability or certainty, they are not immune to modification of a tentative nature:

(143)   well "maybe 'you'll have hèard 'next wèek# (S.7.2.883)

(144)   Maybe with somebody else it would be a piece of cake, but not with him. (AA/340)

They tend to be more flexible in the range of their adverbial associations than other modals:

(145)   By the time you come back from honeymoon, Probate will probably be granted. (W.7.10.25)

(146)   They would very likely hear from them before they heard from Bill. (W.16.7.369)

(147)   I "don't know what I'd 'do if she lĕft# she "will of 'course# (S.1.8.294/5)

(148)   No doubt, Mr Tellaby will want a full statement from you in due course. (HB/91)

This is also demonstrated by their tolerance of multiple modification:

(149)   There's only one thing – if you come next week, on the 26th, she will probably almost definitely be here, so I leave it to you. (W.7.1.259)

Furthermore, Coates (1983: 183) notes that 'Epistemic WILL co-occurs with a whole gamut of modal expressions, from those expressing certainty to those expressing less confidence.' Since any utterance referring to the future will contain some element of doubt, WILL permits of a much wider range of adverb collocates than any other epistemic modal: WILL + POSSIBLY, WILL + PROBABLY, and WILL + DEFINITELY are all modally harmonic combinations.

Combinations with WILL and WOULD further exemplify the inference–confidence distinction which we discussed in 3.3, where the modal expresses inference and the adverb confidence. WILL and WOULD behave in a similar way to MUST (see 3.3), regularly combining with adverbs which indicate that a judgement is being made on the basis of strong evidence; the function of the adverb is also to emphasize the truth-value of what is said:

(150)   They certainly wouldn't be on the watch for as small a bulge as that. (CG/284)

(151)   Christian had a way with euphemisms and doublespeak and would inevitably go far in the Company. (AA/361)

(152)   To puzzle over each and every sound would necessarily

preoccupy the mind to the exclusion of all else. (CG/231)

(153)   The half-point rise in base rates last week will undoubt-edly feed through to an increase in mortgage rates.

Jacobson (1978: 23) states that adverbs such as CERTAINLY, INEVITA-BLY, NECESSARILY, UNDOUBTEDLY 'denote a probability of 100 per cent'. It is true that these adverbs represent the highest point on the scale of likelihood; as markers of the speaker's confidence and a signal of his intervention, they indicate to a very high degree his belief in the truth of the proposition.

There are also habitual uses of WILL and WOULD which may involve combinations with time adverbials:

(154)   Sometimes a bud will break quite early, even before the stock is headed back. (W.10.3.166)

(155)   he would "always tàlk# he "wouldn't stòp 'talking# (S.2.7.746/7)

But timeless statements of predictability, which are instances of dynamic use, do not otherwise normally permit modification. To adapt an example from the CGEL (228):

(156) ?/*Oil will certainly/probably float on water.

3.4.5.3 *Nonepistemic meanings: volition, willingness*

Co-occurrence is restricted to deontic contexts as defined in 3.4.5.1. Where it is a matter of the speaker's intention, WILL and WOULD may receive emphasis:

(157)   I "will of cöurse# "find a mòment if nécessary# (S.7.2.1357/8)

But it is mostly when they have the meaning of willingness, and are used to make requests and offers, that adverb combinations are significant, and particularly in formulaic expressions with PLEASE or KINDLY, which mark the utterance as a request:

(158)   As I would like to get the paper ready as quickly as

> possible perhaps you would kindly telephone me ...
> (W. 7.10.29)

(159)   It would be appreciated if you WILL KINDLY let me have
your observations on this matter as soon as possible ...
(W.7.9.9)

The use of modal–adverb combinations in making requests and
performing other pragmatic functions is discussed in more detail
below (see 3.5.1).

3.4.6 SHALL

3.4.6.1 *Status*

After OUGHT TO, SHALL is the least frequent of all modal expressions
(3 per cent relative frequency) and the least susceptible to adverbial
modification. Its two current uses relate to prediction and volition
and in both it operates as a formal suppletive of WILL.

There is indeterminacy between the two uses, for as Palmer
(1990: 75) suggests, 'making statements about one's future actions
can be taken as a promise'. In practice it is frequently hard to make
a distinction and there is a degree of neutralization between the two
senses.

3.4.6.2 *Epistemic meaning: prediction*

SHALL is not normally considered to be interpretable epistemically
but, when modified, there is a case to be argued, and the adverbs
involved indicate relatively high degrees of probability:

(160)   We shall "have the 'four 'day 'working wèek# of còurse
we shall# (S.5.5.304/5)

(161)   I shall most probably be gone by then. (W.7.2.11)

In both examples, there is the clear implication that an assessment
has been made.

3.4.6.3   *Nonepistemic meaning: volition*

With first person subjects, volitional or intentional SHALL indicates the speaker's undertaking to pursue a course of action and may be treated deontically:

(162)   'Will you find out who really did it?'
        'That I shall certainly do', Bassett promised. (BB/70)

(163)   I shall certainly apologize to the Chairman, Captain. (W.16.4.218)

(164)   I "shall of 'course 'take ac'count of ǎll 'relevant 'factors# (S.11.4.305)

The adverbs focalize and emphasize the strength of the speaker's commitment to action. In questions, SHALL assumes an obligational meaning:

(165)   Shall we replace the carpets, too?

but even in this usage, it is losing ground. The CGEL (231) comments that 'it is frequently replaced by more common verbal constructions'; in our example, the modal could be replaced by 'Would you like us to . . .', which is more idiomatic.
    The use of deontic SHALL with second and third person subjects is archaic and unremarkable from the point of view of co-occurrence; Palmer (1990: 74) cites this example taken from the Survey:

(166)   It is a demand that the Civil Service shall once again return to those traditions of service which have made it so respected. (W.16.6.171–3)

However, a not unrelated, if also restricted use, is the co-occurrence of SHALL with compound adverbs like HENCEFORTH, HEREUPON, THEREAFTER in legal discourse:[24]

(167)   . . . it shall hereafter grant a lease of any flat comprised in the building . . . (W. 14.3.11)

3.5 PRAGMATIC FUNCTIONS OF MODAL–ADVERB COMBINATIONS

In section 2.6 we examined Speech Act Theory as a general framework for the semantic discussion of modality and related the notion of the speech act to the basic distinction which can be drawn between the representational (epistemic) and instrumental (deontic) uses of the modals. These two fundamental uses of language correspond to Searle's speech act categories of assertives on the one hand and directives and commissives on the other, discussed in 2.6.1 and 2.6.2; they mirror the use of language either to comment on or to assert our interpretation of the world, a 'static' use, or else to effect some change in it, a 'dynamic' use. Modal–adverb combinations, no less than the unmodified modals, reflect this basic dichotomy in the way language is used. In this section, we examine a range of pragmatic functions with which the modals and their adverb satellites can be associated.

3.5.1 Overview of pragmatic functions

As a supplement to its treatment of the morphosyntactic criteria which distinguish the modals from main verbs, the CGEL (147) singles out two additional characteristics which the modals all share. Firstly, they are more or less invariable, and even the past tense forms, such as WOULD, are best viewed as independent forms: 'Thus modals might without too much simplification be regarded as modal particles.' Our examination of the status of the modal verbs in 3.4 supports this view of independency. Secondly, from a semantic point of view, the modals are regularly used in the performance of particular types of speech act. The strength of the association between modal forms and their use in indirect speech acts prompts the CGEL to conclude that 'we may go so far as to see in modals a tendency to develop into pragmatic particles'. Modal expressions, including modal–adverb combinations, share these attributes in various degrees and, as Perkins (1983: 161) observes, they are the most prominent linguistic device used in indirect speech acts.

Modal–adverb combinations can be associated with a range of indirect speech acts, such as making requests, offers, suggestions, invitations, all of which frequently involve formulaic or idiomatic expressions of politeness. They are well suited to this role since they effectively mitigate the impositive force of the utterances in which they occur:

(168)   Perhaps you could kindly let me have this information so that I can reply. (W.7.10.193)

is an indirect way of expressing the request 'Let me have this information so that I can reply' and represents an almost formulaic concatenation of modal elements, conjured together in a prefabricated politeness routine. PERHAPS, COULD and KINDLY are here essential components of an effective polite requestive strategy. An otherwise oblique command can be invested with an appropriate measure of indirectness to render it inoffensive:

(169)   Perhaps you will kindly make arrangements to call and discuss with me the question as to reductions in the loan. (W.7.9.65)

Modal–adverb expressions are most commonly used in the making of requests and co-occurrence involves a few adverbs which either mark courtesy in an explicit way, such as KINDLY and PLEASE, or make it implicit by having the general effect of making the utterances in which they occur sound more indirect or tentative. Adverbs like PERHAPS, POSSIBLY, JUST and the courtesy markers KINDLY and PLEASE typically combine with the modals as part of the conventional linguistic implementation of politeness. The most frequent combinations involve CAN, COULD, WILL and WOULD, where the speaker questions the addressee's ability or willingness with respect to a future action:

(170)   Can/Could you (possibly/please) pass the wine?

(171)   Will/Would you (kindly/please) pass the wine?

Although framed as questions, formulaic expressions such as these are not generally used to elicit answers (BE ABLE TO or BE WILLING TO would then be the appropriate expressions to use); the addressee does not interpret them literally as enquiries about his ability (170) or willingness (171) to act, although a condition for satisfying a request is clearly an ability and a willingness to do so. As Kasper (1994: 3209) notes: 'It is part of the pragmalinguistic knowledge shared by members of a speech community to recognize the contextual distribution of such frozen forms. . . . Such formulae encapsulate events which require routinely conveyed politeness.' Uttering a question which addresses these conditions, enables the speaker to make the request for action in an indirect and conventionalized way. The expressions in (170) and (171) are among the most polite requestive strategies available. They are typically, though not invariably, more polite than the use of an imperative:

(172)   Pass the wine.

However, contextual factors such as the social relation between the speakers and the nature of the request itself, for example, if it is beneficial to the addressee, will determine politeness and then the imperative form could well be considered appropriate:

(173)   Get some more wine! (there's a good chap.)

In the context of a family gathering, the directness of an imperative might well reflect the intimacy of the occasion, where the use of an elaborate, modalized request would possibly be considered standoffish if not ironical:

(174)   I don't suppose you could possibly see your way to getting
         some more wine . . .

The danger of overlooking context altogether can lead to misleading generalisations. Levinson (1983: 264), for instance, maintains that 'the imperative is very rarely used to issue requests in English; instead we tend to employ sentences that only indirectly do requesting'. The evidence provided by certain, not unusual contexts (family gatherings, officer–subordinate interaction) offers no basis for this assertion.[25]

Frequently, in polite usage MAY (rarely MIGHT), CAN and COULD occur with first person subjects where the speaker in effect seeks permission from the addressee. It is unlikely that the permission would be witheld, but seeking it is a matter of form:

(175)   "could I 'just get 'all this down# (S.9.2.145)

(176)   mi "lórd# "may I 'very re'spectfully at this stàge# ex"plain
         'what this màn dìd# (S.12.3.798/9)

Expressions involving these modals and intensifiers like JUST or, to a lesser extent, POSSIBLY, can be associated with turn-taking in conversation where one of the participants wishes to signal his 'turn' at speaking:

(177)   "can I just come báck# (S.5.1.702)

(178)   "may I 'just 'answer this quéstion# "you 'raised anòther 'point# (S.5.6.655/6)

Palmer (1990: 78) suggests that while 'MAY is much less common than CAN in the assertive form to give permission, it frequently occurs in this kind of request. It does not appear to be restricted to a formal style, except in the sense that, when making a polite request, it is natural for a speaker to use formal language.' This, too, points to the highly conventionalized and partly fossilized nature of these expressions.

Examples (171) to (174) serve as question initiations which anticipate some form of verbal or non-verbal confirmatory response. The initiating pattern of polite requests could be taken to imply an imbalance of power or authority between the participants; this seems true in the case of (176) where the speaker, legal counsel, is seeking permission from the judge to elaborate his case. The adverb RESPECTFULLY and title of address MI LORD characterize the deferential quality of the request.

In view of the complex relationship between sentence type and speech act, it is not surprising that utterances with the illocutionary directive force of a request are often formally declaratives rather than interrogatives and conveyed by statements instead of questions:

(179)   an "urgent 'message 'to Mìster Ládner# "if you 'possibly càn# the "message is thìs# (S.9.3.971/2/3)

(180)   so per"haps you could 'telephone me to ar'range an'other appóintment# (S.9.3.676)

(181)   It would be appreciated if you will kindly let me have your observations on this matter as soon as possible. (W.7.9.9)

(182)   per"haps you would 'give me a telephone call at 'three or five# (S.5.12.423)

In (179) and (181), the if-clauses function hypostatically in that they mark an essential condition, ability in the one and willingness in the other, on the illocutionary act actually being performed. They also serve as formal markers of the interaction between syntax and indirect illocutionary force (see Levinson 1983: 267). PLEASE has a similar function in signalling request force and, like the two if-clauses illustrated above, occurs with all the basic sentence types.

CAN, COULD, MAY and MIGHT are also closely associated with the speech act category of suggestion:

(183)   per"haps you can have a 'word with hìm# (S.7.2.1323)

(184)   if there was "something 'nice coming ŭp# you could "always 'ring us ŭp you know# (S.2.5.1188/9)

(185)   you "máy possibly prefer thàt one# (S.8.2.590)

(186)   Perhaps your friend – the fat one – might give some useful leads if subtly approached? (W.7.32.228)

Utterances (183), (184) and (186) demonstrate that there is no clear-cut distinction between request and suggestion. With MIGHT (182) there is the implication of a quite forceful suggestion; COULD behaves in a similar way. Likewise, there is blending between these pragmatic categories and the category of advice or recommendation:

(187)   oh "one thing 'you wănt to 'avoid if you 'possibly can# is a "present from my mòther# (S.2.10.265/6)

Given an appropriate context, (187) could be interpreted in terms of any of the speech act categories mentioned above or, for that matter, be taken as a warning. This apparent blending of pragmatic functions also occurs with SHOULD and OUGHT TO where the association of form with a particular kind of speech act, advice or recommendation in the present instance, is generally felt to be quite strong, chiefly because these modals primarily express deontic modality and involve meanings of duty and obligation:

(188)   well you "certainly shouldn't put it in the màttress# (S.2.2.427)

(189)   You do not need to cover the whole of the floor, but there

should at least be a way from the trapdoor into the loft. (W.10.1.179)

(190)   "maybe we 'ought to 'keep her in mìnd Carol# "I 'think she's a strong cándidate# (S.2.6.710/11)

(191)   Perhaps we ought to teach each other restraint. (W.7.4.37)

There is, of course, no invariant relationship between an utterance and its ultimate interpretation; context not only determines what counts as a speech act but also the type of speech act involved. This begs the question of how a speech act can be identified; is it possible or even desirable to try to distinguish between the categories of suggestion, recommendation, advice discussed here? What degree of specificity is desirable? The problem of classification was alluded to in section 2.6 and there is clearly a risk of an undesirable proliferation of categories if any serious attempt is made to uphold rigorous distinctions between such closely related categories as those mentioned here. However, this is not to argue against prototypical uses of modal–adverb combinations; as many of the illustrations in this section have shown, there is, for example, an obvious correlation between the use of PERHAPS in conjunction with the past tense modal forms COULD, MIGHT, WOULD, SHOULD and OUGHT TO and the tentative expression of a request and related speech acts. There are also specific modal–adverb combinations such as WOULD (you) KINDLY/PLEASE which are invariant and idiomatic.

The account so far has focused on the use of modal–adverb combinations as realization strategies to make polite requests, suggestions, recommendations; each represents a speech act where the modal expression is the primary exponent of illocutionary force. The prominence of modal–adverb expressions in the types of speech act illustrated here points to a more general association between modality and different pragmatic domains. These are explored in the next section, with particular focus on politeness and the pragmatic function of the semantic features of indirectness and tentativeness.

3.5.2 Modality and politeness strategy

Modal expressions can be assigned to pragmatic scales where each scale represents a different interpretative domain. There have been a number of proposals for such scales (see Halliday (1970: 334), Horn (1972), Close (1975), Perkins (1983: 50), Matthews (1991: 59), Hoye and Zdrenghea (1995: 31)) which recognize, in the first instance, the distinction that needs to be drawn between the present and past tense forms of the modals. These Perkins (1983: 50f) refers to as the 'primary' and 'secondary' modals, respectively, although the terminological implication that the past tense forms are somehow secondary to their present tense counterparts is misleading, since each modal is, as we have already argued, a largely independent form. The semantic feature common to the past tense forms is that they are more modally marked than their present tense counterparts, and this may convey greater degrees of tentativeness or indirectness, depending on the context. Palmer (1990: 58f), for instance, calls the formally past tense forms 'tentative' forms. Perkins (1983: 50) suggests that all contrasts, regardless of the pragmatic scale involved, can be subsumed under the single scale 'non-conditional – conditional' but, again, this raises a terminological issue, since the concept relates little to the true conditional of hypotheses or conditions.

Perkins' (1983: 50) 'non-conditional – conditional' scale subsumes six scales where each scale represents a different interpretative domain:

non–hypothetical . . . . hypothetical
non–past . . . . past
non–formal . . . . formal
non–polite . . . . polite
non–tentative . . . . tentative
non–indirect . . . . indirect

Within each scale, the modals are used as an 'index of hypothesis, temporal reference, formality, politeness, or tentativeness, and often more than one of these at the same time' according to the context of utterance. The past tense forms are more modally marked for the feature in question than their present tense counterparts. The scales are useful to the extent that they indicate the conceptual domains with which modal expressions can be generally associated. It could be objected that the scales are of a different order, as they seem to imply that formal ('non-past – past'), semantic ('non-tentative – tentative'; 'non-indirect – indirect') and pragmatic ('non-polite – polite') categories are treated as equivalent levels of language function. Indirectness or tentativeness is an inherent semantic feature of the morphologically past tense forms of the modals; by contrast, politeness or formality are interpretative frameworks where indirectness or tentativeness are assigned specific functions. It could be further objected that scales of this kind are vague in their terminology. For instance, as a conditioning environment for the past tense modals, how can indirectness be distinguished from tentativeness? Do these terms differ in their applicability from what Joos (1964: 121) refers to as the feature of 'remoteness'? There is risk, as Palmer (1990: 46) argues, of 'merely explaining the problem by the use of common terminology'. The chief difficulty with so-called pragmatic scales, however, is that they foster the impression that there is a one-to-one association between form, semantic feature and use. We have already argued (see 2.6) that the interrelationship is far more complex. And this is particularly true of politeness, the remaining focus of the present section.

A number of studies on the modals note the association between modality and politeness (Levinson 1983; Perkins 1983; the CGEL 1985; Palmer 1990 are cases in point) and particularly the use of modal expressions to make polite requests, such as those described in the previous section. In linguistic pragmatics, the concept of politeness is used in a technical rather than in an everyday sense, where it tends to be associated with refined manners and courteous behaviour. The pragmatic notion is broader in scope and, of the several competing views that have been advanced so far, the most influential is the 'face-saving' model proposed by Brown and Levinson (1987).

The concept of face (see Goffman 1967) involves the question of human psychological identity and more especially an individual's publicly manifest self-esteem. There are two aspects to face; a positive one which affirms the individual's right to self-determination as an independent agent, and a negative one which stresses the individual's need for approval and freedom from the imposition of others. In interpersonal communication, positive and negative face are constantly at risk; all communication has to be phrased with care, since any kind of linguistic action which has a relational value is potentially face-threatening. To counteract the risk, speakers pursue different politeness strategies to address their positive or negative face wants by lacing their interaction with appropriate doses of politeness. The linguistic strategies associated with positive face emphasize what the participants have in common with each other or refer to desirable attributes in the hearer. With negative face, the strategies suggest distance by emphasizing the individuality and independence of the participants. The terms positive and negative are unfortunate since they imply that politeness may be 'good' or 'bad'. Face, however, is paradoxical in that both aspects are simultaneously present in any communication, but to varying degrees, according to context. Politeness is therefore considered to be a continous phenomenon, where behaving politely can be equated with using language appropriately; 'there is no faceless communication' (Scollon and Scollon 1995). In this respect, Perkins' (*op. cit.*) isolation of politeness as a separate pragmatic phenomenon seems even less appropriate.

Positive politeness, which has also been referred to as 'solidarity' politeness or 'involvement' (Scollon and Scollon 1983, 1995), requires the use of linguistic strategies which express speaker–hearer closeness; there is no feeling of power or social distance between the participants. Typical strategies would entail the use of names or nicknames, the assertion of common opinions, attitudes and knowledge. Negative politeness, on the other hand, sometimes referred to as 'deference' politeness or 'independence' (Scollon and Scollon, *op. cit.*), involves linguistic strategies which reflect distance and respect between the participants. The linguistic strategies associated with this kind of politeness, the use of family names and titles, a dissociative approach to interaction generally, can be characterized as indirect or tentative.

While examples of modal expressions appear in several discussions of politeness and facework (see, for example, Brown and Levinson 1987; House and Kasper 1981; Perkins 1983), the concern is usually with general strategies for protecting face and modal expressions themselves are rarely singled out for special treatment.

Perkins' study on modality is a notable exception; his analysis emphasizes the use of modal expressions to protect negative rather than positive face. He argues that degrees of politeness correlate with the extent to which an utterance is marked for modality, whether this results from the use of the potentially more polite past tense modal forms, the cumulation of different modal expressions, or a combination of both. Thus, he argues:

(192)   could you possibly tell me the way to the library?

is inherently more polite than:

(193)   could you tell me the way to the library?

which in turn is more polite than:

(194)   Can you tell me the way to the library?

Whatever the contextual constraints happen to be, Perkins suggests that 'it is still possible to predict the relative politeness of modal expressions on semantic grounds' (1983: 119). He proposes a number of politeness scales which examine the correlation between degrees of politeness and such features as subjectivity and objectivity, directness and indirectness, and the number of modal expressions a given utterance contains.

The problem with this approach is that it promotes the assumption that politeness is an abstract and independent quality. As Mey (1993: 68) observes, there is the implication that politeness somehow resides 'in individual particular expressions, lexical items or morphemes, without regard for the particular circumstances that govern their use. Being 'inherently' polite implies being always polite, without regard for the contextual factors that may determine politeness in a particular situation.' He cites among other things the importance of social distance or power: the speaker's and addressee's relative positions in institutional hierarchies such as the workplace or family. The impact of such contextual factors is well illustrated in this courtroom example, where the speaker's recognition of the difference in status between himself, legal counsel and the judge automatically accords with courtroom etiquette:

(195)   mi "lórd# "may I 'very re'spectfully at this stàge# ex"plain 'what this màn dìd# (S.12.3.798/9).[26]

The factors of hierarchy and distance and the unequal or asymmetrical relationships they create may also arise due to a motley of differences based on age, gender, education and so forth.

Mey also points to the mitigating effects of what has been referred to as the 'cost-benefit' to the addressee. The use of the imperative in a request may well be appropriate where it involves benefit to the addressee, as in example (173) 'Get some more wine!'. An imperative request also sounds more natural in, say, the context of an intimate family get-together where the use of an elaborate conventionalized indirect expression such as (174) 'I don't suppose you could possibly see your way to getting some more wine ...' would be quite out of place.

Yet generalizations about the relative politeness of a particular expression have a certain intuitive validity, provided that what is considered polite in a given context is seen as ultimately dependent on the constraining factors of the situation, and these are socio-pragmatic.[27] 'Politeness is therefore a relative phenomenon, difficult to define in any absolute terms. What can be measured is the level of directness, and the amount of modification included' (Trosborg 1995: 505, note 93). The linguistically relevant factors can be isolated and the progression from less to more polite seen to correlate with the selection of past tense marking, adverbial signals of mitigation (as expressed by downtoners: see 4.3.3.3) and overt signals of politeness (such as courtesy subjuncts: see 4.3.1).[28]

Brown and Levinson (1987: 70), like Perkins, refer to the use of modal expressions in protecting negative face and in their detailed appraisal of negative politeness, they argue that speakers engage in strategic behaviours or 'facework' to counter or minimize any threat to face:

> Hence negative politeness is characterized by self-effacement, formality and restraint. . . . Face-threatening acts are redressed with apologies for interfering or transgressing, with linguistic and non-linguistic deference, with hedges on the illocutionary force of the act, with impersonalizing mechanisms . . . and with other softening mechanisms that give the addressee an 'out', a face-saving line of escape, permitting him to feel that his response is not coerced.

While speakers have access to a wide repertoire of linguistic strategies to do facework, the linguistic choices they make are not random; there is often a reliance on conventionalized expressions which regularly incorporate modality. For example, many indirect requests in English involve the use of fully conventionalized modal–

adverb expressions which function as mechanisms of indirectness:

(196)   could you possibly book the car in for a service?
         (COULD + POSSIBLY)

(197)   Mr. "Dánby# "may we just try# and "see if we can 'give
         our 'audience a fèw facts 'on thìs# (S 5.6.502/3/4)
         (MAY + JUST)

(198)   You wouldn't perhaps like to chair the meeting this time,
         would you?
         (WOULDN'T + PERHAPS + WOULD)

(199)   per"haps he mìght like to 'take this opportúnity 'to#
         re"emphasize his sup'pòrt# (S.11.4.179/80)
         (PERHAPS + MIGHT)

These utterances would be understood as requests by all participants; only exceptionally would there be a viable alternative
interpretation. Given the institutionalized role of modal expressions to soften impositive force, their role of protecting face in
negative politeness strategies in particular, is crucial.

At the level of linguistic action, Brown and Levinson (1987)
distinguish a wide repertoire of microstrategies available to the
speaker when addressing negative face. While they do not present an
analysis of how modal expressions can be used to perform these
strategies, there are four strategies in particular with which modal
expressions can be closely (but not exclusively) identified: 'hedge',
'be pessimistic', 'minimize the imposition' and 'impersonalize', all of
which soften impositive force. For example, modal adverbs typically
function as hedges in modalized directives, such as POSSIBLY and
PERHAPS in (196), (198) and (199) above, where there is a requirement on the speaker to avoid commitment and mitigate the
directness of his request. 'Be pessimistic' entails the expression of
uncertainty about the likelihood of the face-threatening act being
carried out; the past tense forms of the modals are a typical device
used in this strategy, also illustrated in the above three examples.
'Minimize the imposition' is a means of defusing the potential threat
to face by indicating that the seriousness of the imposition is minimal.
This is regularly achieved through the interpolation of intensifiers,
such as JUST, which has the effect of downgrading the force
of the utterance in which it occurs. This strategy is often deployed,

for instance, in conversational turn-taking:

(200)   May I just add one or two comments before we move to the next item on the agenda?

'Impersonalize' involves phrasing the utterance in such a way that, say, in the case of a request, the agent of the face-threatening act is not directly identified as the speaker or the speaker alone and the hearer is not specifically cited as the person addressed:

(201)   The back door really ought to be locked, if possible.
         (I am telling YOU that YOU should lock the back door.)

On account of the association between modality and indirectness and indirectness and politeness in English, modal expressions are more obviously used in protecting negative rather than positive face. Although the linguistic strategies associated with the latter betoken greater solidarity and closeness between the participants, modal expressions can just as easily be directed to positive face:

(202)   I certainly must agree with you on that point.

(203)   You may well be right.

The function of modal expressions or particles is not to alter pragmatic intent but to mitigate impositive force. They modify the threat to face without entirely removing it. For this reason, House and Kasper (1981) talk of 'modality markers' as devices that modify face-threat, either by increasing it:

(204)   I honestly can't see what you're getting at!

or decreasing it:

(205)   Maybe I can't quite grasp your train of thought.

The conventions of politeness which govern the use of modal expressions suggests that they are pragmatically as well as semantically a coherent class. They are part of the rich arsenal of linguistic strategies available for the realization of politeness, noticeably so in the case of indirect speech acts, such as requests. Both the modals and their adverb satellites can be treated as pragmatic particles to the extent that they operate in tandem as formulaic, language-specific routines. Their communicative value resides in the function they have of matching the politeness value of linguistic action with the context of use: politeness, like modality, pervades everyday human interaction.

NOTES

1 WILL, WOULD, CAN, COULD, and SHOULD are notably more frequent than other modals. See the CGEL (136[d]).

2 An opposing school of thought argues that auxiliary verbs, including the modals, should be treated as main verbs. See Palmer (1990: 200f) for a detailed and articulate rebuff of this position. For the purposes of writing this book, auxiliaries need to be distinguished from main verbs, and the modals from other auxiliaries.

3 Davidsen-Nielsen (1990: 25f) invokes the notion of 'functional dependency' to distinguish between nonepistemic (deontic and dynamic) and epistemic modals, and as a criterion for assessing their status as auxiliary verbs. Where the modal verb alone is subject to adverbial modification, as is the case, he argues, with nonepistemic modals, the latter are functionally independent and may thus be excluded from membership of the category auxiliary verb. Thus, in 'He must definitely offer her a drink' (deontic), 'the adverbial modifies the modal verb alone, i.e. the modification is non-global'. On the other hand, he continues, epistemic modals are mostly functionally dependent as they are not in the main susceptible to direct adverbial modification, and thus achieve auxiliary status. In 'It will definitely happen soon', the epistemic modal WILL 'is not modified by itself' and adverbial modification becomes global to include also the main verb. As a diagnostic for modal (epistemic versus nonepistemic) and auxiliary status, the criterion of 'functional dependency' is seriously flawed: adverbial scope is ultimately deter-mined by a combination of syntactic, semantic and pragmatic considerations and, in the main, does not correlate as closely with the semantic status of the modified modal as Davidsen-Nielsen's com-ments would imply. Furthermore, the author himself notes that: 'In some cases involving this group of [epistemic modal] verbs . . . adverbial modification is not evidently global' (1990: 30). See Davidsen-Nielsen (1990: 25f) for further discussion of the principle of functional dependency. The question of adverbial scope is examined in detail in this book, in Chapter 4.

4 For detailed discussion of the epistemic/nonepistemic dimensions of modality, see sections 2.4 and 3.3.

5 The CGEL (1985: 236) notes that the use of WILL + PROGRESSIVE to express the sense of 'future as a matter of course' is mirrored by the

use of other modals in the same construction: 'He said they MIGHT WELL be callING this evening.'

6   The CGEL (1985: 236) records that MIGHT and COULD combine with the perfective in certain colloquial speech acts, for instance, making a complaint: 'You COULD/MIGHT HAVE told me!'; issuing a rebuke: 'They COULD/MIGHT HAVE been more careful'; expressing irritation: 'We MIGHT HAVE KNÒWN somebody would go and upset her!' In the case of fixed or idiomatic phrases such as these, the modal remains unmodified.

7   Palmer (1990: 65) argues that the modality may be in the past where the epistemic modals occur in past time contexts such as: 'For all I knew he might have done it' ['It was possible that he did it']. Epistemic modality is normally always held to be in the present, but this exceptional 'past' epistemic usage suggests that the epistemic modals are not necessarily performative and, therefore, present. See Palmer (1990: 63f) for further discussion.

8   The auxiliary verb BE frequently co-occurs with both the epistemic and nonepistemic modals: 'They'LL PROBABLY BE there'; 'You SHOULD BE on your way now'. See Perkins (1983: 66f).

9   Complex verb phrases involving the combination of modals with the progressive and/or perfective aspects affect adverbial placement; see section 4.1.2 for further discussion.

10   See Coates and Leech (1980) for further discussions of indeterminacy in terms of 'clines of restriction'. See also Quirk's (1965) proposals on serial relationship.

11   See Klinge (1993, 1995) for a novel approach to the meanings of the modals. The author notes that: 'The recurring problem for linguistic analyses of the modals has been the lack of a principled account of *how* we arrive at an explicit interpretation of an utterance of a sentence containing a modal' (1993: 318). In Klinge's view, the underlying semantic system is relatively straightforward and the differences in meaning which can be assigned to each modal arise from their contexts of use, and are to be accounted for in terms of utterance as opposed to sentence meaning. He favours a monosemic-pragmatic approach and questions the validity of the traditional three modal categories, epistemic, deontic and dynamic, where 'each modal is assigned several semantic interpretations, which give rise to the question whether the interpretations are really of the modals' (1993: 319).

Klinge is rather dismissive of corpus-based studies: 'I will also not be concerned with the multitude of peculiarities of usage that have been noted by scholars over the years, a concern that is more appropriate in corpus investigations. Moreover, peculiarities of usage are just that: peculiarities' (1993: 316). The author underestimates the value of corpus research in this area; certainly, as corpora get larger and better in their coverage of an ever-wider range of language uses and users, the more comprehensive will be our understanding of the contextual variables which affect the diverse uses of the modals and determine their meaning. And, as Stubbs (1996: 233) notes:

> The main topic of analysis for corpus study is recurrent colloca-tions and repeated co-selection of lexis and syntax. It is *inconceivable* [my italics] that such repeated co-occurrences could be the result of performance errors. Quantitative work with large corpora automatically excludes single and possibly idiosyncratic instances, in favour of what is central and typical.

See also Chapter 2, note 17, and de Beaugrande (1996).

12   The CGEL distinguishes between assertion and non-assertion and establishes an interrelated system in which the former is associated with positive and declarative sentences while the latter involves negative or interrogative sentences. Most words can occur in either assertive or non-assertive contexts but some determiners, pronouns and adverbs have specifically assertive or non-assertive use. See CGEL (*passim*); Greenbaum and Quirk(1990: 225f); and Hoye (1984: 118f) for a discussion in relation to modal–adverb co-occurrence.

13   COULD is more frequently used in a rhetorical sense than CAN, and the other past tense modals, WOULD and SHOULD, function in a similar way:

   (a)   COULD we really be meaning to confront critics and audiences with yet another 'Hamlet' without an angle beyond our developing hunches? (BS/50)
   (b)   SHOULD we not have a couple of tricks up our sleeves? (BS/50)
   (c)   Slippers on, putting my chain of office around my neck, symbol of authority, what WOULD I be without it? (BS/124)

14   Palmer excludes all reference to prosodic information, and so it is omitted in all the illustrations quoted from this source; see Palmer (1990: 26f.)

15   Although ambivalent between the two readings 'fully able to do X' and 'able to fully do X', WELL may modify CAN to express probability, but only probability in present time. Bolinger (1972a: 41f) notes that: '*I can well accept that argument* is a possible truth here and now. **He can well break a leg* is not normal because it refers to a necessarily future event.' Either COULD, MIGHT or MAY has to be used instead.

16   The CGEL (233 note), Burchfield (1992: 135), Whitaker (1987: 35f) and others have commented on the tendency of MIGHT and MAY to

become neutralized in epistemic contexts; the CGEL also records that some native speakers perceive little or no difference in their respective tentative values and argue that this is symptomatic of a 'continuing tendency to erode the distinction between real and unreal senses of the modals'.

17 Coates (1983: 19) treats MAY, MIGHT and COULD as non-inferential modals, whose epistemic meanings can be glossed: 'I think it is perhaps possible that ...'. This trio contrasts with MUST ('from the evidence available I confidently infer that ... '), and SHOULD and OUGHT ('from the evidence available I tentatively assume that ...').

18 'Mighty Must' achieved fame in Gilbert and Sullivan's opera 'Princess Ida'; see Whitaker (1966) for an insightful and witty assessment of this modal.

19 The idea that there might be two subsytems of epistemic modality is implied in Givón's (1982: 24) argument that

> a more responsible empirical investigation of the linguistic evidence suggests that at the bottom of propositional/sentential modalities lies the *implicit contract* between speaker and hearer, a contract specifying three types of propositions [the italics are the author's own]:
>
> (a) Propositions which are to be *taken for granted*, via the force of diverse conventions, as *unchallengeable* by the hearer and thus *requiring no evidentiary justifications* by the speaker;
>
> (b) Propositions that are *asserted with relative confidence*, are *open to challenge* by the hearer and thus require – or admit – *evidentiary justification*; and, finally,
>
> (c) Propositions that are *asserted with doubt*, as *hypotheses*, and are thus *beneath* both challenge and evidentiary substantiation. They are, in terms of the implicit communicative contract, 'not worth the trouble'.

The three types correspond to (a) declaratives, (b) evidentials and (c) judgements. Givón's rider in (c) that propositions associated with doubt are based on a degree of speculation that neither anticipates nor warrants objection, suggests that those asserted with certainty (and therefore involving MUST) are evidential in kind. Judgements would therefore be restricted to the dubitative end of the epistemic spectrum while evidentials would necessarily be at the other, indubitative, end. The co-occurrence of MUST with evidential adverbs gives empirical support to Givón's argument and, more significantly, implies that English has an analytic evidential system of modality which complements the more central judgemental system.

20 See Coates (1983: 77f) for a discussion of differences between SHOULD and OUGHT TO.

21 According to the SEU, SHOULD is twenty times more frequent in writing than OUGHT TO. The ratio diminishes in speech, however, where OUGHT TO is more common and SHOULD is only four times as frequent.

22 Palmer (1990: 59) argues that SHOULD should be considered the unreal or tentative marker of epistemic necessity: 'It is, perhaps, conditional – in the sense that it indicates what would be a reasonable conclusion, if circumstances are such as the speaker believes they are.'

23 This example is based on material adapted from *The Economist* (27.04.96/20).

24 See Klinge (1995) for a detailed discussion of the role of modality in legal contracts. The author notes (1995: 670) that, in the data used for his survey, which is based on an examination of ten household insurance policies, SHALL is the second-most frequent modal after WILL.

25 Palmer (1986: 29f) argues that although the imperative is often portrayed as the strongest type of directive (see 2.6.2), the deontic force it conveys varies considerably with its context of use:

> On the one hand, the imperative seems much stronger [than MUST] because it will be used by a person in full authority, e.g. a superior in the army, to ensure that an order is obeyed; MUST would not be used in such circumstances. On the other hand, it seems to be much weaker when used in, for instance, *Come in!*, in reply to a knock at the door. This surely gives permission and the use of MUST would be quite inappropriate; the hearer might well retort 'Who are you to give me orders?' Even MAY or CAN, the modals for permission, *might be less polite than the imperative* [my italics]; the hearer might simply retort 'Who are you to give me permission?' The imperative seems to do no more than express, in the most neutral way, the notion that the speaker is favourably disposed towards the action.

26 This example also reflects the impact of discourse type on politeness strategy. Kasper (1990: 207) suggests that: 'Courtroom discourse is particularly illustrative of the general tenet ... that discourse is not only reflective of social relationships and entitlements but just as much instrumental in constructing them.'

27 See Chapter 2, note 16.

28 Scales of politeness are useful for pedagogical purposes; see Nattinger and DeCarrico (1992: 123) and section 3.5 in this book.

Four

The adverb satellites and their modal verb heads

> *There are very few adverbs that may occur with*
> *epistemic modals (or even modals in general).*
> *They are confined mostly to those that themselves*
> *express judgements or the speaker's confidence,*
> *and so occur largely pleonastically . . .*
>
> (F. R. Palmer, 1990: 67)

4.1 INTRODUCTION: ADVERBIAL CLASSIFICATION

So far we have discussed adverbs primarily in terms of the epistemic and nonepistemic credentials of their modal verb heads and discussed the implications this has for co-occurrence. We have also examined the pragmatics of co-occurrence, especially in the light of speech act theory, and focused on the pragmatic function of modal–adverb expressions in terms of the 'face-saving' view of politeness. In this chapter, we take a much closer look at the adverbs involved, in terms of their syntactic and semantic behaviour in the environment of the modals.

Before examining the various ways in which adverbials can be classified and the significance this has for modal–adverb co-occurrence, a basic distinction needs to be drawn between the terms 'adverb' and 'adverbial', since both are relevant to the present study. Adverbs are a heterogeneous group of items which contrast with the other main word-classes, nouns, verbs and adjectives. They function in a variety of ways, modifying other elements in clause structure, such as adjectives, other adverbs or even the clause as a whole, but their most frequent role is to specify the mode of action of the verb. Syntactically, adverbs can be related to such questions as Where?, When?, How long?, How often?, Why?, How? and, once this is done, the functional equivalence of multi-word units immediately becomes apparent. Thus, the question 'When will you leave?' may elicit any one of the following responses: 'Tomorrow' (adverb of time), 'Very soon' (adverb phrase with 'soon' as its head), 'The day after tomorow' (noun phrase), 'In a couple of hours' (prepositional phrase), 'When I see fit' (finite clause). On the basis of functional analogy with the corresponding part of speech, namely adverbs, these diverse realizations are commonly referred to as adverbials. 'Adverb' is thus a word-class whereas 'adverbial' is a syntactic unit which contrasts with the other elements of clause structure, subject, verb, object and complement.

The adverbial element of clause structure can therefore be realized by a wide variety of linguistic structures, ranging from simple, one-word forms to complex, multi-word units, which may even be clauses themselves. The CGEL (489) distinguishes seven main types: only adverbs or 'adverb phrases' are relevant to this study because, as the CGEL points out and as we shall see in our subsequent discussion, there is a high degree of correspondence between the adverbial element's form of realization, and its semantic, positional and grammatical properties. One final terminological issue: the term 'adverb phrase' (or 'adverb group') refers to a non-clausal structure consisting of two or more words with an adverb as its head: 'quite [dependent] possibly [head]'.

Traditionally, adverbials have characterized any syntactic function which cannot be attributed to the other clause elements. As a word class, adverbs themselves do not have a homogeneous membership and items are sometimes assigned for apparently no better reason than that they appear to relate less to any other class.[1] Their heterogeneity of membership and function makes for considerable semantic and syntactic diversity.

In practice, the syntactic and semantic properties of those adverbials which most regularly co-occur with the modals correspond to a large extent with their realization as single-word items, namely adverbs.[2, 3] It is the single-word, adverb realization of the adverbial function which is the primary focus in this study; the adverbs involved constitute a fairly limited set of items and most share, with their modal verb heads, the expression of modality, or the closely associated notion of degree.[4] For the present, modal adverbs will be taken to subsume the expression of both notions, since they are often similar in their semantic effect. Occasionally in the literature, modal adverbs are referred to as adverbs of mood or modal adjuncts but, to avoid any terminological confusion, the expression modal adverbs is used throughout. As a subcategory, modal adverbs display a certain amount of heterogeneity themselves, in keeping with adverbial behaviour as a whole.

Syntactically, adverbials are the most peripheral element in clause structure, in relation to the subject, verb, object, and complement; they enjoy considerable mobility within the clause, are usually syntactically if not semantically optional, and do not determine what other clause elements occur.[5] They display relative degrees of centrality and peripherality and differ considerably in the scope of their modification which, according to their position and other variables, may involve the whole or part of a clause. These characteristics, together with adverbial realization types, are the basis on which adverbials are generally classified. Traditional classifications therefore take into account four interrelated features: adverbial form or realization; meaning and semantic role; grammatical function, according to the relationship between adverbials and other clause elements; and placement or position in relation to clause structure.

These criteria, while essential to the identification of the concept of adverbial, are not all of equal importance here. It has already been noted that the primary realization type of adverbial which co-occurs with the modals corresponds with single-word items, adverbs. Other realization types, such as adverb phrases, are occasionally involved and reference will be made to these as appropriate. While adverbials have a diversity of semantic roles, it is primarily only those expressing modality or degree which have significance for co-occurrence. This is evident from the range of modal–adverb combinations discussed in Chapter 3. Of course, the modals do occur in the same clause with other semantic categories of adverbial but only exceptionally do these impinge in any way on modal intent, as for instance in the case of time relators (which we examine below). But in the sentence:

(1)   The children must be in the garden.

there is no synergetic relationship between MUST and the obligatory place adverbial IN THE GARDEN that in any way informs our understanding of the verb's modal behaviour, and how it may be semantically modified or complemented. The adverbial signifies semantic relations which are unrelated to modal usage, and co-occurrence is therefore unremarkable in terms of modal–adverb synergy.

The focus in this study is on modal–adverb combinations where the adverb satellite modifies, complements or transforms the meaning carried by its modal verb head, with the result that the modal or the whole clause falls within its scope. For instance, in:

(2)   The children surely must be in the garden.

or:

(3)   Certainly, the children must be in the garden.

there is an intuitive symbiosis between the adverb and the modal verb in each case, since both clearly express modal meanings which are inherently related. The modal specifies that the judgement expressed is based on a conclusion drawn from all the available evidence, and the adverb conveys the strength of the conviction with which that judgement is held; the modal and the adverb satellite have overlapping yet complementary roles. The attraction holds, even where the adverbial is separated from and not adjacent to the auxiliary, as in (3); the bond is so strong that MUST does not permit co-occurrence with an adverb connoting anything less than modalized certainty:

(4)   *The children perhaps must be in the garden.

(5)   *Possibly, the children must be in the garden.

The strength of modal pull the auxiliary exerts over its adverb satellite and the collocational contraints it imposes on its inherent modal content apply even where the adverb occupies a relatively peripheral position in relation to clause structure, as can be seen in (3) and (5). Where the adverb is more integrated in clause structure, as in (2) and (4), even stricter collocational restrictions apply and mostly only adverbs expressing modality or degree are tolerated within the immediate environment of the modal verb head. All modals exhibit similar tendencies, although to varying degrees; the strength of attraction between adverb satellites and their modal verb heads is a matter for collocation, which is discussed in Chapter 5 (section 5.2).

As the most peripheral element of clause structure, adverbials are normally treated as optional clause elements, since they do not determine which other elements occur. There are exceptions, such as the place adverbial in (1) above. However, syntactic optionality does not imply semantic optionality: modal adverbs are more or less central to the modal system, according to how they interact with the modal verb. Their omission has implications for meaning. In:

(6)   He evidently must have forgotten.

as opposed to:

(7)   He must have forgotten.

the adverb additionally specifies circumstantial information available to the speaker on which basis the propositional deduction is made. The presence of the adverb satellite orientates the sentence towards an evidential rather than a purely judgemental epistemic system (see 3.4.3.2), and additionally lends weight to the force of the speaker's argument. In some cases, where the modal–adverb combination has idiomatic status, the invariability of the expression makes discussion of optionality irrelevant. In:

(8)   They may well have left.

MAY WELL conveys a much stronger likelihood (probability) than the unmodified modal, which denotes possibility:

(9)   They may have left.

The semantic processes which can be associated with modal–adverb co-occurrence are also explored in detail later in the chapter.

The remaining two criteria, grammatical function and position, demand closer inspection. Both criteria reflect the degree of integration of the modal adverb in clause structure which naturally affects its behaviour in the environment of a modal verb head. The account given here is based on the adverbial classification proposed in the CGEL: its treatment of the adverbial, the most complex and disorderly area of English grammar, is probably its most innovative contribution to English grammatical description.[6]

4.1.1   The grammatical function of modal adverbs

Most grammars distinguish between adverbials which modify the sentences or clauses in which they occur, referred to as sentence-modifying adverbials, and those adverbials which modify a word or word-group within the sentence or clause, traditionally known as word or word-group modifiers. In some cases, the distinction between the two types of modifier is quite clear, and strikingly so in the case of adverbials which have both functions. For instance, in:

(10)   Honestly, I couldn't swear that he was there.

and

(11)   I couldn't swear that he was there, honestly. [I tell you in all honesty that it is not possible for me to swear that he was there.]

HONESTLY is a sentence modifier; but in

(12)   I honestly couldn't swear that he was there [It is quite impossible for me to swear that he was there.]

HONESTLY is a word-modifier, specifically a modal verb modifier. In practice, it is not always clear how the distinction should be made and grammarians over the past century have noted the difficulty. Sweet (1892-98: II) puts it very succinctly:

> We see ... not only that the same adverb may be sometimes a sentence-modifier, sometimes an ordinary word-modifier, but there is often great difficulty in distinguishing between word-modification and sentence-modification generally. This is especially the case when a verb is the word that seems to be modified. If the verb has no meaning of its own, it cannot of course be logically – though it may be grammatically – modified by the adverb. But if the verb has a distinct meaning of its own, its importance in the sentence makes any modification of it almost logically equivalent to modification of the whole sentence.

The interrelationship between the grammmar and semantics of modal adverbs, their mobility and the diffuse character of the meanings they express leads Perkins (1983: 93) to conclude that, in comparison with other modal expressions, they are 'far less explicit in the way they qualify the meaning of a clause or sentence'. Their peripherality leads him to argue that modal adverbs are 'specifically sentence adverbs' (1983: 90f), and that 'non-sentential uses of modal adverbs are more apparent than real'. The problem with this argument is that it then becomes impossible to distinguish the behaviour of those modal adverbs which, syntactically and semantically, have discernibly different roles in relation to the clause. For example, POSSIBLY has two quite distinct uses in non-assertive clauses according to whether it lies within or outside the scope of clausal negation:

(13)   Possibly, she can't be reached at home.

(14)   She can't possibly be reached at home.

A suitable paraphrase for (13) would be, 'It is possible that she can't be reached at home', where the adverb can be seen to lie outside the verb phrase and thus to modify the entire adjacent clause; it has a peripheral status in relation to other clause elements. By contrast, a paraphrase of (14), 'It is impossible to reach her at home', indicates a much closer integration of the adverb within the structure of the clause and specifically the verb phrase where it directly modifies the negated modal.

Syntactically, modal adverbs may operate both within and outside the clause. The distinction between the two types of grammatical function is upheld in transformational grammar where the POSSI-BLY in (13) would be referred to as an S-adverb (sentence adverb), and the POSSIBLY in (14) as a VP-adverb (verb phrase adverb). Such differences in the syntactic behaviour of adverbials are significant because, as our two examples demonstrate, they correlate with differences in meaning. Semantically, the S-adverb expresses the speaker's comment on the content of the complete utterance and can be seen to modify the sentence as a whole, rendering it a more tentative declaration of the speaker's assessment than its omission would have otherwise allowed. The VP-adverb serves to reinforce or intensify the negated modal, where its scope of modification lies. The sentence adverb is more marked for lexical meaning than its VP counterpart which, by definition, is more integrated in clause structure and thus more syntactically central. This centrality points to the greater integration of modal + VP-adverbs within the English modal system. Lyons suggests that 'the more fully something is grammaticalized rather than lexicalized and integrated with syntax in terms of government and agreement, the more central it is in the system'.[7] Neither type of adverb is structurally obligatory yet both impinge on the nature of the modality expressed. In terms of the adverbial classification adopted by the CGEL (ch. 8), and which forms the basis of the description in this section, S-adverbs, such as POSSIBLY in (13), or VP-adverbs, such as POSSIBLY in (14), are referred to as 'disjuncts' and 'subjuncts' respectively, in recognition of their characteristic syntactic behaviour. The notional category of modal adverbs spans both these formal categories. In addition, two further main types of adverbial are distinguished, 'adjuncts' and 'conjuncts', but these are only minimally involved in terms of modal–adverb synergy (but see 4.2).

While the formal criteria for distinguishing the modals are widely agreed, the basis for the identification and subsequent categorization of adverbials is more controversial. The heterogeneous character of adverbials is reflected in the range of criteria used for their classification, such as their form of realization, their semantic roles, their position in the sentence and scope of modification. The CGEL classification also links the degree of integration (and degrees of obligatoriness) or peripherality (and degrees of optionality) the adverbial exhibits in relation to clause structure with the range of its grammatical functions. Of the four main categories of adverbial identified: adjuncts, subjuncts, disjuncts and conjuncts, only adjuncts share similarities with other elements of clause structure. On the basis of four diagnostic tests, the CGEL demonstrates the affinity between adjuncts and subject, verb, object on the one hand, and the distinction between adjuncts and all other categories of adverbial on the other. Although not watertight, these grammatical diagnostics give greater plausibility to the CGEL classification. The fact remains, however, that few semantic roles are expressed by more than one adverbial category, which would indicate that the degree of integration of an adverb in the clause is often a function of its semantic role. Grammatical function and semantic role are closely interrelated.

A brief examination of the two central criteria, as applied to subjuncts and disjuncts, confirms the validity of the approach. Like other clause elements, adjuncts can be the focus of a cleft sentence (a sentence split into two clauses, each with its own verb): 'It was *in the garden* that they were playing', and they can be elicited by question forms: 'Where were they playing? *In the garden.*' None of the other categories of adverbial shares these criteria. For example, it would be anomalous to say: *'It was *certainly* (subjunct) that they must have realized their mistake', or to reply *'*Certainly*' in answer to a question such as: 'How will they manage?' Likewise, it would be absurd to say: *'It was *frankly* (disjunct) he couldn't remember' or to answer *'*Frankly*' in response to the question cited before. This is not to imply that subjuncts or disjuncts exhibit similar characteristics, even if they share homonymous forms. They can be distinguished according to their subordinate (subjuncts) or super-ordinate (disjuncts) roles in relation to the clause.

4.1.2 Position and transmobility of modal adverbs

It has already been noted that adverbials enjoy considerable mobility in relation to clause structure and that this affects their grammatical and semantic status in relation to other clause elements. The CGEL (490f) distinguishes up to seven different possible positions for the adverbial, the main ones being initial (*I*), medial (*M*), and end (*E*):

I	*(initial)*	*Possibly* they may have been sent to London.
iM	*(initial-medial)*	They *possibly* may have been sent to London.
M	*(medial)*	They may *possibly* have been sent to London.
mM	*(medial-medial)*	They may have *possibly* been sent to London.
eM	*(end-medial)*	They may have been *possibly* sent to London.
iE	*(initial-end)*	They may have been sent *possibly* to London.
E	*(end)*	They may have been sent to London *possibly*.

The syntactic mobility of POSSIBLY generates potentially significant shifts in terms of what it focuses and this does affect the meaning of the sentence.

I is associated with disjuncts (sentential adverbs) which have a theme-setting role; in our example, the possibility expressed by MAY is topicalized by the adverb POSSIBLY. *E* is not typically associated with the expression of modality but a number of disjuncts do occur in this position, especially in spoken rather than written discourse, where it occurs almost as an afterthought and has the effect of strengthening or weakening what has been said before. Certain types may also be inserted at *M* to qualify speaker comment parenthetically.

M position is also the province of subjuncts (word-modifying adverbs) and most readily associated with the expression of modality and degree. *M* is basically that between subject and main verb; the closeness of the association between these two clause elements largely determines the form of adverbial realization. Only for a special effect would a complex adverbial be interpolated; *M* is therefore more usually associated with short adverb phrases, and especially solitary adverbs.

The CGEL (493) notes that because of the semantic association of *M* with modality and degree, even adverbs which purportedly express different sense relations, such as time, take on a hint of these:

(15)   Pupils must at all times wear school uniform.

(16)   You should always remember to bring your key.

Other examples will be considered in the course of our description. The effects transmobility has on meaning is outlined below.

4.1.3 The semantic function of modal adverbs

Disjuncts and subjuncts may be associated with two main categories of modification: approximation[8] and reinforcement.

Approximation involves the thematization, interpolation or tagging of modal values at the level of the clause or the sentence, according to whether the disjunct is positioned initially, parenthetically or finally.

Thematization entails the fronting or topicalization of modal meanings, a process which is enacted when a disjunct occurs in sentence-initial position and is syntactically peripheral to clause structure and sentential in scope. Halliday (1985: 50) suggests that the placement of a modal adverb at the beginning of a clause is a natural theme: 'If the speaker includes within the message some element that expresses his own angle of judgement on the matter, it is natural for him to make this his point of departure':

(17)   Obviously, they must have believed the best part of a bereavement was the wake, for each involved more revelry than the last.

Interpolation of a disjunct within the clause, at some variant of medial position, may have the effect of restricting the focus of the adverbial to the modal verb constituent, although there can be ambivalence as to its precise scope (see 4.5):

(18)   Since everyone in the European Union has now the same rights, they will, presumably, have the same obligations.

Tagging involves the placement of the adverb in final position, where it explicitly invites the addressee's agreement or acquiescence to the truth of what is said:

(19)   Given the circumstances, you could always consider handing in your resignation, of course.

Thematization, interpolation and tagging are interrelated semantic processes: each overtly identifies the speaker as a source of authority and characterizes the utterance in terms of the modal value(s) the adverb and auxiliary convey. The term approximation implies that both modal elements express similar or complementary meanings but, on account of the spatial separation between them, the adverb enjoys a measure of lexical autonomy which it otherwise lacks when modal and adverb are adjoined.

Reinforcement involves the emphasis, intensification or focusing of modal values intrasententially, when the subjunct is contiguous with its modal verb head and occurs in medial position. These semantic processes derive their names from the type of subjuncts involved: emphasizers, intensifiers, and focusing subjuncts. In addition, a fourth type, courtesy subjuncts, combine with the modals in formulaic expressions of politeness and mitigation.

Emphasizers, as their name suggests, give added emphasis to the modality expressed by the modal verb:

(20)   I simply can't speak too highly of him.

(21)   They really must have arrived by now.

Intensifiers convey to a greater or lesser degree the intensity with which the modal attitude is expressed:

(22)   It couldn't possibly happen again.

(23)   She may just have popped out for a minute.

Focusing subjuncts draw special attention to a part of the sentence, restricting the focus of the adverbial on the modal verb:

(24)   You còuld – and indeed shòuld – be more expansive in writing an introductory survey.

Emphasis, intensification and focus give prominence to the modal verb in different ways. Hard-and-fast distinctions can be difficult to make in practice, since the adverbs used for reinforcement tend to be delexicalized and have no meaning independent of the modality expressed by the modal verb head. Subjuncts therefore contrast with disjuncts by reason of their greater lexical redundancy (see the discussion in 4.5.3).

Disjuncts, on the other hand, are more lexically loaded and signal speaker-orientation to a much greater extent: 'the speaker intrudes . . . , and takes up a position' (Halliday 1970: 335). This is particularly noticeable where the adverb conveys the speaker's evaluation towards his utterance and functions as a metacomment on its content:

(25)   Frankly, there must clearly have been a mistake.

FRANKLY and other members of the subcategory style disjunct (see 4.4.1) can be regarded as the equivalent of reduced clauses, 'I tell you in all frankness', and as expressing a separate proposition. Hence Swan (1987: 26) suggests that a sentence containing a sentence adverb 'will be seen as having at least two sets of propositional content'. Other adverbs which function in a similar way are content disjuncts conveying the speaker's value judgement, such as FORTUNATELY or REGRETTABLY (see 4.4.2) and the evidentials, like EVIDENTLY or OBVIOUSLY (see 4.4.2.2) where the speaker actually relates the basis of his judgement and the strength of his conviction to physically or mentally perceived evidence:

(26)   Fortunately, they will probably have forgotten the appointment and we can have the afternoon free.

(27)   Obviously, they really ought to have consulted the operating manual first before switching the machine on.

When these or similar items function as subjuncts in the immediate environment of the modal, and are marked off neither by intonation nor by punctuation, they lose most if not all of their autonomy and serve only to highlight the immanent modal value of the auxiliary with which they co-occur:

(28)   He must frankly/fortunately/obviously have forgotten.

FRANKLY and FORTUNATELY retain something of their meaning as disjuncts but OBVIOUSLY is more tightly integrated because of its widespread use in expressing the speaker's conviction towards the truth-value of his utterance (see 4.4.2).

In the remainder of this chapter, we examine in detail the range of modal adverbs which operate with modal verbs, on the basis of the CGEL classification.

4.2 CO-OCCURRENCE WITH ADJUNCTS AND CONJUNCTS

While adjuncts and conjuncts are minimally involved in terms of the present study, there are some important exceptions and these we attend to now.

4.2.1 Adjuncts

Although adjuncts comprise the largest class of adverbials, including such traditional categories as adverbs of place, manner, time and most closely resemble other clause elements (S, V, O) as regards their relative integration in sentence structure, they do not in their various semantic roles impinge in any obvious way on modal meanings.

However, the subcategory of adjuncts expressing temporal relations, adjuncts of time, interact with the modals in a complex way because of the latter's abnormal time reference. For example, it will have been noted in Chapter 3 that the so-called past tense forms of the modals are regularly used to refer to present and future time rather than to the past. The use of the past tense forms in English to make requests, as in:

(29)   Would you be good enough to pass the salt?

correlates with a pragmatic index of politeness. The morphologically past tense form WOULD is not used here for past time marking; it would be anomalous to say:

(30)   *Would you please pass the salt yesterday?

The nature of the relationship between the modals and tense and the implications this has for co-occurrence with time adjuncts is largely determined by their epistemic or deontic status. We offer an overview below for the sake of descriptive completeness. Palmer (1990) and Lyons (1977) offer more detailed accounts of the relationship between tense and modality.

The most common function of the epistemic modals is to make performative judgements about a particular state of affairs and, since those judgements are made in the act of speaking, the modality is generally in the present only; in such cases, co-occurrence with adjuncts referring to past time is out of the question:

(31)   *They might possibly be there yesterday.

The past tense forms of the modals most usually express a more tentative assessment than their present tense counterparts, but with present time reference. Of course, the proposition (see 2.4.2) rather than the modality may be in the past, because it is clearly possible to make a judgement in the present about a past event. This is accomplished by combining the modal with the perfective aspect:

(32)   it "must have 'been at 'least a 'month àgo nów# it was a "Sunday èvening# (S.2.12.28/9)

There are no restrictions here on co-occurrence with time adjuncts relating to the past. In determining the temporal frame, time adjuncts also reflect the epistemic modals' inherent future reference:

(33)   In a few more years this double relationship may not, I suppose, be so apparent to me; but it is bound to affect what I say. (W.11.1.52)

(34)   They may/might/can/could/should/must leave imme-
         diately/tomorrow.

Deontic modals interact differently. They have no past tense
forms for past time reference. Neither the modality nor the event
(see 2.4.2) can be in the past and so, again, adjuncts with past time
reference are automatically excluded:

(35)   *Could you please go the baker's yesterday?

Deontic modals are performative and initiate action by the speaker
or by others; they are exclusively related to the future: 'At the time
of speaking a speaker can get others to act or commit himself to
action only in the future' (Palmer 1986: 97).

4.2.2 Conjuncts

Of the four major categories of adverbial, conjuncts are the most
peripheral to clause structure and the least remarkable in terms of
modal–adverb interaction. Their function is to relate or conjoin
independent grammatical units ranging from clauses to whole
series of paragraphs. A small subset of this category, contrastive
conjuncts, involve items such as CERTAINLY, INDEED, OF COURSE,
REALLY which in other environments operate as subjuncts or
disjuncts and have a clear modal role. As conjuncts, they encourage
a particular attitude in the addressee as well as expressing the nature
of the connection between the units they conjoin:

(36)   A: She could be waiting at the hairdresser's, I
            suppose . . .
         B: Of course she could but all the same I don't think it
            likely.

In their concessive use, these adverbs are not subject to the same
co-occurrence restrictions which may otherwise apply:

(37)   *She certainly might go.

The use of these adverbs to conjoin independent units is clearly
illustrated in the following:

(38)   He argued last week that by guaranteeing [ethnic]

'diversity' on campus, the university helps the state prepare for the future.

Certainly [cf. 'Furthermore], it will become harder to ensure that California's various racial and ethnic groups are proportionally represented among the university's ... students ... (Ec/260895/42)

(39)   You must learn history. Indeed ['In fact it can be added that ...'], there are many things you must learn. (J 1964: 280)

4.3 CO-OCCURRENCE WITH SUBJUNCTS

The adverbs which most frequently combine with the modals belong to the subjunct class of adverbials. They have, to a greater or lesser extent, a subordinate role in relation to one of the other clause elements or to the clause as a whole. They exhibit considerably less semantic and grammatical independence than disjuncts and are more closely integrated in clause structure and especially the verb phrase. There are four subcategories of subjunct relevant to this study, each consisting of a fairly limited set of items: courtesy subjuncts (considered to have a wide orientation because their scope extends over the entire clause); and emphasizers, intensifiers and focusing subjuncts (each having a narrow orientation in the sense that they are subordinate to an element in clause structure).

These categories are now examined with reference to the grammar and semantics of co-occurrence.

4.3.1 Courtesy subjuncts

The relationship between modality and politeness was explored in 3.5 where it was noted that a number of modal–adverb combinations are represented in more or less formulaic politeness routines associated, for instance, with the making of requests, offers or invitations. Courtesy subjuncts comprise a very limited set of items: PLEASE, KINDLY, CORDIALLY, GRACIOUSLY, HUMBLY. Only PLEASE and KINDLY combine with the modals with any frequency; functioning as overt markers of polite expression, their influence extends over the entire clause:

(40)   I shall be obliged if you will kindly call to see me and in the meantime please do not embarrass us both by using any further cheques. (W.7.9.31)

Frequently, as here, the modal–adverb partnership acts in accord with other markers of politeness present in the context: the rather arthritic locution 'I shall be obliged' and the co-occurrence of another, and, in fact, the most common item in this group, PLEASE. Combinations with the past tense forms of the modals are more common on account of their greater markedness for tentativeness, remoteness or politeness:

(41)   Dear Sir, Could you please send me a copy of the most recent programme details for the BBC World Service. (W.7.15.134)

PLEASE is unique within this category in that it allows no modification *very/*most please (contrast VERY KINDLY, MOST CORDIALLY) and its sole function is to signal politeness or mitigation. Stubbs (1983: 72) remarks that 'it is essentially inter-active: its essential function is to get someone else to do something, and it is, therefore, largely restricted to spoken language'. This is, of course, not strictly true: PLEASE regularly combines with CAN, COULD, WILL, WOULD in contexts requiring (formal) written requests, as illustrated in (41) above.

Courtesy subjuncts are normally restricted to a variant of medial position, occurring either immediately before, or after the modal. PLEASE also occurs in initial and end position:

(42)   Please, may I take a look?

(43)   Could I possibly try it out, please?

Their scope extends to the whole clause, in contrast to all other classes of subjunct, which tend to have a more restricted focus.[9]

4.3.2 Subjunct emphasizers

The modals show a marked propensity to co-occur with this category of subjunct since emphasizers are also concerned with expressing the semantic role of modality. In general, they have a reinforcing effect on the truth-value of the clause or part of the clause to which they apply and, when in the environment of a modal verb, focalize the modality expressed:

(44)   but he "certainly will have 'Tudor and 'Plato commit-ments# (S.5.11.266)

(45)   I simply cannot believe that your discovery of my multiple dalliance alone could lead you to state that I was 'depraved'. (MD/31)

The nature of the reinforcement is slightly different in each case. CERTAINLY, with its inherent modal meaning, gives explicit emphasis to the truth-value of the sentence, as well as focalizing WILL and the degree of confidence with which the speaker is making his prediction. SIMPLY, however, lacks this modal quality: the speaker is commenting on the appropriateness of the negated modal CANNOT, rather than invoking truth-values. In certain environments, the modality expressed by the verb is actually modified in a radical way:

(46)   I know a dinner and a cocktail party may well be on the programme of our four days there. (W.16.4.260)

The possibility expressed by MAY becomes probability in combination with WELL.

There are subtle differences in the ways emphasizers interact with the modals, depending on whether the adverb is inherently modal (CERTAINLY) or has become lexically redundant by virtue of its proximity to the modal verb head (SIMPLY). In addition, there are a few adverbs in the latter category which only function as emphasizers when operating within restricted environments (WELL). It is thus possible to distinguish two basic types of emphasizer.

The first type, A, by far the largest and most important group, consists of items which also function as content disjuncts (see 4.4.2). They are mostly concerned with the affirmation of truth. The most common emphasizers in this group are listed below; items in parentheses only operate as emphasizers within the restricted environments of MIGHT, MAY and COULD. Although in its form OF COURSE is an adverb phrase, it is treated here as a single unit (see entry in 4.4.2.2).

Type A   Emphasizers also functioning as content disjuncts concerned with the speaker's affirmation of truth: ACTUALLY, CERTAINLY,

CLEARLY, DEFINITELY, INDEED, OBVIOUSLY, PLAINLY, REALLY, SURELY, OF COURSE, (WELL, READILY, EASILY)

The second type, B, consists mainly of items which function as style disjuncts (see 4.4.1), conveying the speaker's comment about the style or form of what is being said:

Type B   Emphasizers also functioning as style disjuncts concerned with the speaker's value judgement: FRANKLY, HONESTLY, LITER-ALLY, SIMPLY, FAIRLY, JUST

It is normally assumed that when people make statements they intend them to be accepted as true (unless for reasons of irony, poetic effect or downright deception the speaker is wittingly manipulating the truth-value of what he says). Adding a word like SURELY or FRANKLY does not make them more true, but does emphasize the truth of the sentence.

When emphasizers of either type are positioned immediately before or after the modal, without being separated intonationally or by punctuation, their effect is primarily to focalize the auxiliary, although as the CGEL (584) points out 'there may be ambivalence as to whether the emphasis is on the part or on the whole'. The closeness of the association between the adverb and its modal verb head is apparent in the examples taken from the spoken part of the Corpus. The emphasizer is regularly stressed and thus highlighted, and often its modal verb head takes the nuclear stress; it is signalled, intonationally, as being of maximal prominence:

(47)   "I còuldn't# "literally còuldn't# "stay to the ènd# (S.2.5.277/8/9)

The strength of the association leaves no doubt as to the status of the adverb. The intonational aspect of modal–adverb combinations is examined in 4.6.

We shall return to a more detailed examination of individual items and their characteristic behaviour in modal environments after consideration of their syntactic features.

4.3.2.1 *Syntactic features*

Emphasizers invariably occur at medial (*M*) or a variant of *M*. They may be placed after the modal auxiliary (*M*) but for special emphasis precede it (*iM*):

(48)   The result easily could be a big minus, indicating that you're spending or planning to spend more than your projected income. (J 1975: 188)

(49)   Regardless of what field you prefer, applying for employment is something you undoubtedly will do several times in finding a suitable place in the world of work. (J 1975: 242)

(50)   I "really mŭst be getting 'home in a 'moment# (S.2.2.831)

(51)   "oh well 'that sounds like something I 'actually 'might be 'able to sày 'something a'bout# (S.9.1.1007)

This position is more common in spoken than in written English, although the norm is *M*, regardless of medium:

(52)   He invents an occasion on which the glasses may very easily have been lost or stolen. (SB/78)

(53)   I "certainly did nòt think 'this mèant# that it "must in'evitably 'mean wèlcóming# the "lowering of 'academic stàndards# (S.11.2.935/6/7)

With the negated modals, emphasizers regularly occur at *iM* and co-occur with clausal negation; HONESTLY, JUST and SIMPLY show a marked tendency to do so:

(54)   "I 'honestly can't re'member where it wàs# (S.2.10.1079)

(55)   "wèll# one "just mûstn't mind# (S.2.5.756/7)

(56)   it "really còuldn't be done# "yòu know# (S.3.2.388/9)

(57)   my "father cèrtainly couldn't speak 'German# (S.213.470)

(58)   "I còuldn't# "literally còuldn't# "stay to the ènd# (S.2.5.277/8/9)

(59)   They certainly wouldn't be on the watch for as small a bulge as that. (CG/284)

(60)   No I bloody well won't come and be your valet. (CG/250)

Semantically, this position is associated with particularly strong emphasis and the effect is to clearly focalize the negated modal.

ACTUALLY, DEFINITELY, and REALLY may fall within the scope of clausal negation:

(61)   I can't actually/definitely/really confirm the precise details.

but this creates considerable ambivalence as to which part(s) are being emphasized.[10]

Emphasizers do not co-occur with modals in questions, although other categories of subjunct do (see 4.3.3); they do not usually co-occur within the same clause, although in spoken language they may combine to produce an exaggerated effect:

(62)   the "one that 'you 'obviously 'absolutely mùst watch# (S.9.1.799)

and, with the exception of DEFINITELY, which is sometimes preceded by QUITE or VERY, they are rarely modified.[11]

4.3.2.2 Emphasis or intensification?

In many works on adverbials (for example, Greenbaum 1970; Bolinger 1972a) emphasis is treated in terms of intensification and a distinction made between standard intensifers (emphasizers) and degree intensifiers (intensifiers). While both semantic processes entail a heightening effect on the force of the modal, it is primarily with emphasis that there is interaction with modal meanings. This is due to the difference between the two types of intensification: 'In adding to the force (as distinct from the degree) of a constituent, emphasizers do not require that the constituent concerned should be gradable. When, however, the constituent emphasized is indeed gradable, the adverbial takes on the force of an intensifier' (CGEL: 583). The difference can be illustrated with reference to REALLY in the following:

(63)   He *really* must have performed well.

(64)   He must *really* have performed well.

(65)   He must have *really* performed well.

In (63) and (64), with REALLY at *iM* and *M*, the adverb focalizes the modal and operates as a pure emphasizer. But with (65), where the adverb occurs at *eM*, it is now the lexical verb which is primarily modified: the implication is of a high level of performance as well as affirmation of certainty. Adverbial scope and focus is a complex matter; the question of ambivalence and indeterminacy is discussed further, in 4.5.1. Modal-(degree) intensifier co-occurrence is considered in 4.3.3.

4.3.2.3 *Emphasizers and truth*

Bolinger (1972: 93) records that most emphasizers 'are terms that originally expressed some relationship between what is said and the declarativeness of saying it, or the certainty or emphasis or truth attached to it'. Disjuncts which are used to refer to the truth–value of a sentence are the most productive but not the only external source.[12]

Bolinger differs from the CGEL in his notional groupings. REALLY, HONESTLY, ACTUALLY, INDEED are described as adverbs which 'comment on truth versus non-truth', and CERTAINLY, SURELY, DEFINITELY, FRANKLY as adverbs which involve the 'affirmation of truth'. In practice, the distinction is a fine one, because emphasis involves only adding to the force of what is modified; the heightening or lowering effects associated with intensification (see 4.3.3) are, in principle, absent. And yet it is possible to identify differences in their asseverative value which may determine their appropriacy in certain contexts. We discuss the main adverbs individually, making comparisons where appropriate.

REALLY is by far the most versatile emphasizer and freely combines with all modals: as a disjunct it makes explicit the speaker's view that what he is saying is in fact true, and so Greenbaum (1969: 144) concludes that: 'It is often difficult to distinguish between the disjunct and the intensifying [emphasizing] functions of this item.' However, his own tests into native speaker sensibility over the issue demonstrate that most speakers make a sharp distinction between the two functions. It regularly co-occurs with nonepistemic MUST, and clausal negation:

(66)   We really must get down to business.

(67)   She really couldn't see any alternative.

Although far less frequent, ACTUALLY operates in a similar way, except that it additionally implies that the speaker is surprised:

(68)   They actually must have survived long enough to complete their report.

HONESTLY is not fully divested of its disjunct status, as it is restricted to contexts where the speaker appears to be making an admission:

(69)   I don't know how you cope – I did a part time teaching thing for a bit but honestly could not carry on. (W.7.3.44)

(70)   ?/*They honestly may have forgotten.

REALLY or ACTUALLY are more natural in the second example.

INDEED again retains something of its lexical meaning, 'in fact it can be added that . . .':

(71)   You could – indeed should – be more expansive in your commentary.

When postposed, however, it functions as an intensifier:

(72)   He can indeed produce good work if he wants to.

Like REALLY, CERTAINLY collocates with all modals, although restrictions apply in the case of combinations with the epistemic modals of possibility, unless the adverb is used concessively:

(73)   *He certainly might/may be there.

It also shows a general tendency to co-occur with clause negation:

(74)   He certainly can't remember.

In contrast to REALLY, it seems to convey straightforward affirmation of truth without there being the implication that an assertion is being made in opposition to the contradictory notion of non-truth. Thus:

(75)   I really can't remember, if truth be told.

sounds more natural in comparison with:

(76)   ?/*I certainly can't remember, if truth be told.

DEFINITELY functions in a similar way and is also subject to collocational restrictions. It remains too lexically loaded to occur in the environment of epistemic MUST, where CERTAINLY may be a more natural choice:

(77)   His behaviour must certainly/?definitely bring him to grief sooner or later.

It is probably more emphatic in nonepistemic contexts:

(78)   I definitely won't do it and let that be an end to the discussion!

There were no instances found in the data of FRANKLY emphasizing a modal. Greenbaum (1969: 114) draws attention to the fact that there are restrictions on the types of auxiliary with which emphasizer FRANKLY can collocate. It clearly focuses DO in:

(79)   I frankly don't know the answer to that question.

But in a modal environment, the direction of modification is less clear:

(80)   ? I frankly can't understand what he wanted.

HONESTLY would seem the more natural choice. To some extent, it depends on the nature of the lexical verb in the verb phrase. In:

(81)   I frankly can't say what he wanted.

the lexical affinity between adverb and main verb is collocationally too strong; the disjunct status of the adverb becomes apparent if an emphasizer is interpolated in the sentence:

(82)   I frankly just can't say what he wanted.

SURELY differs from all other emphasizers in two respects: when it immediately follows the modal, it openly invites agreement from the person(s) addressed in order to confirm the speaker's assessment of the truth of what he says, and in doing so lacks the forcefulness of other members in this category:

(83)   they must "surely ap'ply this to pèacetime condítions#
        mústn't they# (S.2.3.1103/4)

In pre-auxiliary position, however, SURELY functions in a similar
way to other emphasizers and could be replaced by CERTAINLY
without there being any major shift in meaning:

(84)   At the same time she set a terrible trap for him out in the
        swamp that surely would have killed him if he had got
        caught. (J 1975: 362)

In his seminal work on English adverbial usage, Greenbaum
(1969: 127f) reports the findings of his research into the discrim-
inations native speakers make between modal adverbs operating as
disjuncts and their homonymous forms functioning as emphasizers.
The results of his tests show that those adverbs which have clear
modal connotations, CERTAINLY, INDEED, SURELY, are felt to exhibit
greater affinity in meaning in their two functions than ACTUALLY
or REALLY, which are modally less marked. The former have a more
diffuse semantic role, especially in the environment of the modals.
Although it is this feature which has promoted the view that modal
adverbs are necessarily sentential in scope, the results of Greenbaum's experiments indicate that native speakers do discriminate
adverbial function on the basis of their position, associated
intonation (or punctuation), and immediate context. The greater
distinction made between the two functions of REALLY (and to a
lesser extent ACTUALLY) indicates that it has attained full status as an
emphasizer with no remnant of the sentence adverb, hence its
freedom to co-occur with all modal forms.

4.3.2.4 *Emphasizers in restricted environments: ALWAYS, WELL, EASILY, READILY, LITERALLY*

These are a small group of items which are common uniquely in
certain modal environments. Both epistemic and nonepistemic
senses of the modals may be emphasized.

ALWAYS only functions as an emphasizer in the environments of
CAN or COULD in a positive declarative clause:

(85)   I "mean if I don't líke it# I can "always 'send it bàck"#
        "càn't I# (S.1.4.561/2/3)

(86)   if there was "something 'nice coming ŭp# you could
        "always 'ring us ŭp you know# (S.2.5.1188/9)

The temporal meaning of ALWAYS can be ruled out by adding an
adverbial with specific time reference: TONIGHT, SOME TIME NEXT
WEEK. If the modal is negated, however, ALWAYS reverts to its
temporal meaning and loses its subjunct status:

(87)   I can't always send it back.

WELL uniquely combines with MIGHT, MAY or COULD in positive
declarative clauses to produce idiomatic modal expressions of
epistemic probability:

(88)   I "might wèll# be "having some mòre 'tickets 'given to
        me# (S.7.1.1038/9)

(89)   I know a dinner and a cocktail party may well be on the
        programme of our four days there. (W.16.4.260)

(90)   I a"gree with him that it could 'well hăppen# I "don't see
        that it 'necessarily něed 'happen# (S.2.8.510/11)

For greater emphasis, the adverb may precede MIGHT or MAY, but
not COULD:

(91)   [he's] "looking 'very happy on 'this dày# as "well he
        m̀ight# with "such a lovely dàughter# (S.10.6.230/1/2)

(92)   This is not to say that the movement of each tiny particle
        is not governed completely by the laws of classical
        mechanics. It well may be. (J 1975: 206)

If unmodified, MIGHT, MAY, and COULD simply express epistemic
possibility. WELL is the only emphasizer to transform rather than
heighten or reinforce the meaning of the epistemic modals with
which it combines. The strength of the collocational attraction can
be demonstrated by examining the behaviour of WELL in the
environment of CAN; now it is not the auxiliary but the adjacent
lexical verb which is focused:

(93)   She would be greatly missed, both socially and academi-
        cally, if she left but I can well understand that after ten
        years she feels the need for a new environment.
        (W.7.6.284)[13]

The defective relationship between the two forms further points to the marginal epistemic status of CAN when compared with MAY or MIGHT (see 3.4.1).

When intensified by VERY, however, WELL is no longer restricted to positive declarative clauses and may also combine with CAN:

(94)   They can't very well drop the project at this stage.
         [They can't very easily . . .]

But here VERY WELL purely emphasizes the negated dynamic modal, it does not transform the meaning as in the previous examples.

In spoken discourse, WELL frequently combines with the slang intensifiers, BLEEDING, BLOODY, DAMN and an assortment of other taboo expletives:

(95)   and "he lost 'four pints of blòod# and he "bloody well 'shouldn't have púlled through# (S.2.12.186/7)

These intensifier–emphasizer phrases co-occur with all the modals:

(96)   He bloody well might/may/can/could/will/would/ shall/should/ought to/must do it!

The effect is one of simple reinforcement.

Occasionally, fronting of WELL occurs with MAY and MIGHT, but again, the semantic effect is simply to emphasize, although it is conveyed with greater force:

(97)   [he's] "looking 'very happy on 'this dày# as "well he mìght# with such a lovely dàughter# (S.10.6.230/1/2)

This is particularly noticeable in the following example, due to Jacobson:

(98)   Does the fact that we cannot localize magnetic poles . . . undermine your first enthusiastic acceptance? It well might do so. (J 1975: 57)

EASILY and READILY tend to co-occur with MIGHT, MAY, CAN, and COULD, focusing the idea of possibility.[14] The adverb invariably occurs at M:

(99)   Take two words which might easily affect the same

important modern argument, barbarism and colonialism. (W.9.3.49)

(100)   Now it may easily happen that the activation energy is large compared with the transition temperature. (W.9.9.153)

(101)   oh "dèar# "but 'it can eàsily be 'rubbed 'out# (S.8.3.765/6)

(102)   . . . a large proportion of motor horns . . . were dented and badly polished but could easily have been made merchantable at a trifling cost. (W.14.2.64)

EASILY is the more frequent of the two and together with MIGHT and MAY is similar in effect to their combination with WELL, if not quite as idiomatic. Jacobson (1964: 213) records that EASILY more frequently occurs at M than in any other position and that 'the reason is probably that its force of manner is often mixed with some force of mood'. His illustrations all involve combinations with MIGHT, and it could be that there is a stronger attraction between these two forms than between EASILY and MAY. Jacobson (1975: 58) also suggests that EASILY 'has a somewhat weaker emphatic character than WELL . . . , and still weaker is that of READILY'.

LITERALLY, although not widely represented in the data, sometimes functions as an emphasizer in the spoken language and mostly with negated modals:

(103)   "I còuldn't# "literally còuldn't# "stay to the ènd# (S.2.5.277/8/9)

Bolinger (1972a: 107) remarks that this is a hypostatic use of language because 'the speaker in effect comments on the appropriateness of the word': the impossibility expressed by COULDN'T is focalized as being maximally impossible; the effect is to emphasize. SIMPLY and JUST are used in a similar way:

(104)   I "just 'couldn't bêar it# "in the ĕnd# (S.2.7.772/3)

They are far more common because there are objections to the use of LITERALLY in this sense. The CGEL (619) notes that 'in careless and informal speech, and even indeed in writing, the adverb comes to be used in ways that are "literally" absurd'. They condemn such usages as:

(105)   She literally flew out of the room.

However, in modal environments, where there is greater lexical reduction, there are no such objections. Jacobson records a use of LITERALLY in the environment of WILL, where he suggests there is a mixture of degree and modality, with degree as the dominant sense (which he captures with the paraphrase 'indeed, in the full sense of the word'):

(106)   A person whose whole view of himself includes the cultural meanings inherent in a magical society will literally die if that culture indicates that he should.
(J 1975: 63)

Although the lexical verb is the main item focused, the modal also clearly receives emphasis.

4.3.2.5 *The emphasis of* MUST: *APPARENTLY, CLEARLY, EVIDENTLY, INEVITABLY, OBVIOUSLY, NECESSARILY*

There is a marked tendency for epistemic MUST to attract adverb satellites where the combinations endorse the inference–confidence distinction we discussed in 3.3 and 3.4.3. The range of adverbs involved – APPARENTLY, CLEARLY, EVIDENTLY, INEVITABLY, OBVIOUSLY – otherwise function as content disjuncts (see 4.4.2) which are generally used to express the speaker's conviction by making an appeal to available evidence. In the immediate environment of MUST (usually at *M*), they retain something of their superordinate status but at the same time they focalize the unique inferential quality of the modal. In combination with these adverbs, which can be notionally categorized as evidentials, MUST constitutes an epistemic subsystem which is at once judgemental and evidential. The latter component is made explicit by the adverb, which additionally reinforces the speaker's confidence in the truth of what he is saying. These emphasizers convey the notion that such is the evidence available to the speaker that no other conclusion can possibly be drawn:

(107)   I "certainly did nòt think 'this mèant# that it "must in'evitably 'mean wèlcóming# the "lowering of 'academic stàndards# (S.11.2.935/6/7)

(108)   In these circumstances, the Government must clearly rely on a full turnout . . . of the payroll vote. (W.12.3.19)

(109)   Moreover, its extent must obviously increase with the reactivity of the aromatic substrate . . . (W.9.10.136)

Of course, these adverbs also co-occur with other modals, such as WOULD and WILL (see 3.4.5), but to a lesser degree; neither modal is as central to the epistemic system as MUST, and neither is as marked for its inferential quality.

NECESSARILY uniquely functions as an emphasizer in combination with both epistemic and deontic MUST:

(110)   Any history of art written for the consumption of twentieth-century Europeans must necessarily regard the Giotto-Cézanne period as the most important section of art history. (J 1964: 298)

(111)   The judgement in these matters must necessarily be a harsh one. (J 1978: 63)

4.3.3 Subjunct intensifiers

In contrast to emphasizers, subjunct intensifiers (or intensifiers for short) express the semantic category of degree and have either a heightening or a lowering effect on what they modify. In denoting degree, or degrees of intensity, intensifiers may either scale upwards from an assumed norm:

(112)   I must absolutely insist that there be complete silence.

or scale downwards:

(113)   She could hardly keep a straight face.

The CGEL (589f) distinguishes two main categories of intensifier: 'amplifiers', which scale upwards (ABSOLUTELY), and 'downtoners', which scale downwards (HARDLY). This scaling implies that the constituent under focus by the intensifier is gradable.

In principle, the modals are not gradable and, with certain exceptions (see 4.3.3.4), are only susceptible to intensification indirectly. But they do occur in the environment of lexical verbs which can be assessed as a gradable constituent, as with INSIST in

(112). Although the effect of ABSOLUTELY is primarily to focalize the main verb, it also heightens the force of the modal: the implication is of a high degree of insistence as well as affirmation of the speaker's authority. This again illustrates the ambivalence of adverbial function in modal environments (see also the discussion in 4.3.2.2). In (113) COULD is more clearly susceptible to intensification, where HARDLY appears to diminish the force of the modal: 'In fact she did not keep a straight face.' Downtoning, or diminution, does involve direct intensification of the modals but is mostly restricted to the co-occurrence of HARDLY, SCARCELY and AT ALL with CAN and COULD. Otherwise, intensification applies only indirectly to the modal and occurs when an emphasizer or content disjunct is present:

(114)   They will almost certainly be here next week.

Very few intensifiers are involved:

Type A   *Amplifiers (which scale upwards from an assumed norm)*
          MOST, VERY

Type B   *Downtoners (which scale downwards from an assumed norm)*
          ONLY; SIMPLY, JUST; HARDLY, SCARCELY, AT ALL; ALMOST,
          QUITE

4.3.3.1 *Syntactic features*

In general, intensifiers favour *M* but there can be quite considerable variation (including *E*) according to which constitutent is being modified. For instance, amplifiers co-occur only with gradable verbs which they tend to precede at *eM*:

(115)   He may well have completely misunderstood what you said.

Here COMPLETELY focalizes the main verb and not the modal. Where the modal is modified, the intensifier is almost always at *M* as, for example, when the downtoner HARDLY modifies COULD:

(116)   The extent that profits were hit by an abnormally low level of output is difficult to assess but it could hardly have been less than £750,000. (W.12.6.183)

A few, like AT ALL, are restricted to *E*:

(117)   I "cannot 'see them pro'ducing it at àll# (S.5.5.479)

(118)   They couldn't sing a/one bit.

The data revealed one instance of SCARCELY occurring at *iM* in the environment of COULD:

(119)   The elopement was not successful; the abbot shortly returning home so humbled and amended that he scarcely could be said to have erred. (W.11.3.45)

Due to the association of *iM* with particularly strong emphasis, the status of SCARCELY is ambivalent; it could be replaced by the emphasizer REALLY: '. . . that he really couldn't be said to have erred'.

In the restricted environments of negated CAN and COULD, intensifiers may co-occur with clausal negation and clause interrogation (see 4.3.3.4).

The CGEL establishes further subcategories of amplifiers and downtoners and explores their syntactic behaviour in some detail, but the focus is primarily on the intensification of attitudinal verbs. Furthermore, it is apparently the authors' intention that the notional subclassification of both types of intensifier be treated with circumspection. Thus they note in relation to amplifiers: 'the distinction between maximizers and boosters [the two subdivisions] is not a hard and fast one' (591); and that 'the assignment of individual downtoners to particular groups [approximators, compromisers, diminishers, minimizers] would vary from speaker to speaker', (CGEL: 597).

4.3.3.2 *Amplification:* MOST, QUITE, VERY[15]

Amplifiers intensify the modals indirectly by modifying their emphasizer or content disjunct satellites:

(120)   I shall most probably [certainly/definitely] be gone by then. (W.7.2.11)

(121)   If we were satisfied with the spirit of a performance, but wanted to excise a fluffed note here, a pedal bang there, we could quite easily do so. (MD/157)

(122)   It would be more sensible if you would send her an

appointment as she may quite well need weekly visits for gold injections. (W.7.12.114)

(123)   Houston ... thought that she very easily could if she put her mind to it ... (W.16.7.322)

(124)   in "higher educàtion# it may "very 'well bè that# "they will sáy# (S.11.2.273/4/5)

Ultimately, the effect in each case is to enhance the modality so that the overall semantic process is best described in terms of emphasis. This can be illustrated with reference to the type of multiple co-occurrence exemplified in (127) below. Consider:

(125)   It may be that they were wrong.
          [It is possible that they were wrong.]

(126)   It may well be that they were wrong.
          [It is probable that they were wrong.]

(127)   It may very well be that they were wrong.
          [It is highly probable/likely that they were wrong.]

Pre-modification of the emphasizer WELL leads naturally to modification of the modal itself and the effect is of course to both reinforce the truth-value expressed in the sentence and additionally reflect the strength of the speaker's conviction. Multiple co-occurrence of this kind is largely restricted to the spoken language.

4.3.3.3 Diminution (downtoners): ONLY, SIMPLY, JUST; HARDLY, SCARCELY, AT ALL; ALMOST, QUITE

The three sets of intensifier identified for discussion here are the most regular items to occur in modal environments.

ONLY, SIMPLY, AND JUST are described by the CGEL (598) as 'attitude diminishers' which 'seek to imply that the force of the item concerned is limited'. This can be demonstrated through the co-occurrence of JUST with 'LL(WILL):

(128)   well there's "only a 'month till 'Christmas 'now# I'll just go and 'work in 'one of the stòres# (S.2.12.118/19)

By contrast, when JUST functions as a focusing subjunct and precedes the item focused (in our example a lexical verb), it is usually associated with a nuclear stress (see 4.6) on the item concerned:

(129)   "three hĭgher 'notes# and we'll just lĭsten to them# "first of àll# (S.10.8.948/49/50)

(The same is true of ONLY and SIMPLY.) Both functions can be distinguished from JUST operating as a subjunct emphasizer, especially to reinforce a negated modal:

(130)   but I just "couldn't imàgine# "what I was 'going to dò# (S.5.9.670/1)

JUST also regularly operates as an intensifier in the environments of MAY, MIGHT, CAN and COULD, delimiting the force of the modal in each case:

(131)   now "may I 'just 'talk to 'Mr Dánby for a moment# (S.5.6.486)

And it may also combine with a disjunct when doing so:

(132)   I should just perhaps add that I am at the moment engaged on research for a possible book on a very difficult subject . . . (W.7.8.202)

SIMPLY functions in a similar way, although the expression of intensification is not always so readily distinguished from focus where the written language is concerned:

(133)   He must simply have burned with hatred not to send some sort of conciliatory signal to me. (MD/268/9)

Emphasis is more easily discriminated:

(134)   I simply cannot believe that your discovery of my multiple dalliance alone could lead you to state that I was 'depraved'. (MD/31)

In modal environments, there can be ambivalence as to the precise status of these adverbs and it may be impossible to make a sharp distinction between their different roles, especially without intonation as a guide, as in the written language (see 4.5). For example, in:

(135)   And if this is so, then some of the more outdated practices

at Camphill can only be working against the needs of the very people the village is trying to help. (W.11.4.43)

native speakers may well be undecided as to what precisely ONLY modifies. The example recalls (26) in Chapter 3, where it is argued that the CAN ONLY combination is almost on a par with MUST; we repeat it here for ease of reference:

(136)   Rubbish! You can only be about fifty. (S.10.568)

It seems that CAN ONLY may be expressing epistemic modality and its equivalence to MUST can be captured in an example such as the following:

(137)   It can only be the case that someone was informing (no other conclusion is possible).

(138)   It must be the case that someone was informing (everything points to that conclusion).

HARDLY, SCARCELY, AT ALL are negative intensifiers ('minimizers'), so called because, although not negative in form, they are negative in meaning. They tend to co-occur with CAN and COULD directly modifying the modal:

(139)   "they   can   hàrdly   'snub#   five   vice-présbyters#
        (S.1.2.442/3)
        ['In fact they did snub five vice-presbyters']

(140)   I could hardly keep a straight face when one old girl brought Robert Service from which to read in the discussion on modern poetry. (W.7.5.66)
        ['In fact I did not keep a straight face ...'.]

The CGEL (599) argues that this group of intensifiers provides 'a modification towards a version that is more strictly true than a denial of the truth-value of what has been said'. In (139) and (140) the added clauses in parentheses demonstrate the point by turning the partial denial in the illustrations into a full denial. POSSIBLY and CONCEIVABLY, when they operate on CAN and COULD in non-assertive clauses function in a similar way (see 4.3.3.4).

AT ALL may focus the negated modal alone or intensify the entire clause depending on intonation and its position in the clause:

(141)   the "face 'jumps oùt of the pàinting# but I "can't at àll 'tell you what I dó# (S.1.8.839/40)

(142)   I "cannot 'see them pro'ducing it at àll# (S.5.5.479)

Both examples illustrate the resemblance between intensifiers and emphasizers in their semantic effect: AT ALL denies the truth-value in each utterance by emphasizing the negative pole of the statement.

Neither ALMOST nor QUITE operate directly on the modal but, by modifying other adverbials (CERTAINLY and DEFINITELY in our examples) that do, they ultimately affect the intensity of the force of the verb:

(143)   In 1967 ... the capital employed in Group companies averaged £23,000 per employee ... and this is a figure which will almost certainly continue to rise steadily in the years ahead. (W.13.2.78)

(144)   There's only one thing – if you come next week, on the 26th, she will probably almost definitely be here, so I leave it to you. (W.7.1.259)

Without the modification of DEFINITELY by ALMOST in (144), co-occurrence with WILL PROBABLY would be anomalous. The example clearly shows how dramatic the intensifying (lowering) effect of the modifier can be on the modified:

(145)   *She will probably definitely be here.

Downtoner QUITE usually combines with negated CAN or COULD and has to be distinguished from its function as an amplifier, as in (121) and (122) above:

(146)   A: "sórry#
         B: "I 'couldn't quite cătch 'that# "sòrry#
             (S.8.4.867/8/9)

4.3.3.4 *Intensifiers in restricted environments: POSSIBLY, CONCEIVABLY; NEVER EVER*

In addition to those items listed in 4.3.3, these adverbs function as intensifiers in restricted environments. The most idiomatic are the combinations represented by the collocation of POSSIBLY and

CONCEIVABLY with CAN and COULD in non-assertive (negative and interrogative) contexts:

(147)   I "cannot 'possibly stày# in a "hospital in Mŏscow# (S.6.6.240/1)

(148)   "no it couldn't pòssibly 'happen twice# (S.9.1.1125)

(149)   What could possibly have troubled her so much that she'd needed to talk to him? (AA/102)

(150)   But what could Galloway conceivably know? (AA/302)

The intensifying function of these adverbs contrasts with their use as disjuncts; the difference in meaning and effect can be demonstrated by reference to potential variant positions of the disjunct POSSIBLY:

(151)   Possibly, I cannot stay in a hospital in Moscow.
I possibly cannot stay in a hospital in Moscow.
I can possibly not stay in a hospital in Moscow.
I cannot stay in a hospital in Moscow, possibly.

Perkins (1983: 92) records the objections of some linguists to the occurrence of modal adverbs in interrogative contexts; they 'do not feel comfortable' (Jackendoff 1972: 84), or they quite simply 'do not occur' (Bellert 1977: 344).[16] In fact, in epistemic contexts, both intensifiers, POSSIBLY and CONCEIVABLY, co-occur with CAN, COULD and MIGHT (but not MAY) in deliberative questions:

(152)   Can/Could this possibly be love at first sight?

(153)   Might they just possibly have overlooked some procedure?

The effect is rhetorical: the speaker assumes the role of both speaker and addressee so that the truth-value of the proposition is determined by his worldview and not that of the person addressed (if, indeed, an interlocutor is present at all!). The rhetorical nature of these questions can be caught by tagging on the modal lexical verb WONDER:

(154)   Can this possibly be love at first sight, I wonder?

Similar examples arise with the emphasizer REALLY, as with example (30) in 3.4.1:

(155)   Could Madeleine really have retired in her prime,
         become a country woman on her own, her days plotted
         by the seasons, evenings alone with books and wireless, or
         writing letters to her children; a friend occasionally for
         weekends perhaps. (W.16.1.16)

As Lyons remarks (1977: 756): 'Wondering, like entertaining a
proposition, is first and foremost a mental act.'
    NEVER (a negative amplifier) frequently behaves as an intensifier
in a modal environment; this use parallels that of ALWAYS in
conjunction with CAN or COULD (see 4.3.2.3). The following are
typical:

(156)   The burden of his remarks is that Britain will never
         change the status of the colony against the population's
         wishes. (W.12.4.121)

(157)   "you must nèver say thàt Ralph# (S.5.11.565)

As with ALWAYS, the temporal meaning of NEVER can be ruled out
by interpolating an adverbial with specific future time reference:

(158)   They'll never catch the ferry this evening.
         [They will not under any circumstances catch the ferry
         this evening.]

As an intensifier, NEVER is always stressed and may be additionally
intensified through asyndetic repetition:

(159)   but "we shall 'never 'never im'prove our ac'commodà-
         tion# un'til we have 'central tìmetabling# (S.3.4.535/6)

A similar effect is produced when it co-occurs with EVER:

(160)   You must never ever say that again.

    In non-assertive clauses, EVER replaces NEVER, although a hint of
temporal suggestion remains:

(161)   But so far, there had been no signs that it would ever be
         realized. (W.16.4.330)

4.3.4 Focusing subjuncts

The role of focusing subjuncts (FS) is to draw attention to a part of a sentence which may be as broad as the predication (everything in the sentence bar the subject and the auxiliary) or as narrow as a single constituent, such as the modal verb. The CGEL (604) distinguishes two main categories: 'restrictives' (which indicate that 'the utterance concerned is true in respect of the part focused') and 'additives' (which indicate that 'the utterance concerned is *additionally* true in respect of the part focused'). The following examples illustrate the two types of focus involved and each modal is placed in angle brackets to indicate that it is the part focused:

(162)   It's just that he <mày> have gone (I don't know whether he has).

(163)   John càn and also <will> learn that I'm the one in charge here.

Restrictives include such adverbs as JUST, ONLY, SIMPLY which may also function as emphasizers or intensifiers. Additives include AGAIN, ALSO, EVEN, FURTHER, SIMILARLY.

Normally the item selected for being the focus is what is called 'new' information – that is, information that is new to the receiver and has not already been supplied or 'given' by the context. The point of a message is the new as opposed to the given information it contains. In speech this is identified by intonational stress while, in careful writing, it is usually marked by the proximity of the adverb to the item focused (see also the discussion in 4.6.3):

(164)   You còuld – and simply shòuld – be more expansive in writing an introductory survey.

The correlative construction highlights the contrast between COULD, and SHOULD focused by SIMPLY. Semantically, the contrast is based in different modal values, COULD denoting dynamic possibility (see 3.4.1) and SHOULD denoting obligation (see 3.4.4).

FS usually precede the item they focus, and occur at *iM* when this is an auxiliary. It will be remembered that this position is also associated with particularly strong emphasis. Of course, by focusing attention on the modal, the effect is to reinforce it and for this reason it can be argued that restriction in modal environments is a special case of emphasis:

(165)   "well I 'just mìght be 'there# "round about 'sort of 'seven to 'half păst# (S.7.3.223/4)

4.4 CO-OCCURRENCE WITH DISJUNCTS

Disjuncts contrast with subjuncts in that they have a superior role compared with other sentence elements. Their relative peripherality to sentence structure gives them superordinate status and thus their scope seems to extend over the sentence as a whole. Their grammatical status makes them ideal for identifying speaker presence and authority, and for reinforcing the subjective quality of the sentences in which they occur.

It is rare that an utterance is made which could be considered wholly objective; there is usually some implication of our attitude. The unqualified assertion:

(166)   The drugs they give have a detrimental effect on the powers of concentration.

involves assumptions about the 'authority' on which the statement is based which the interpolation of disjuncts can make more or less explicit. For instance, if the speaker in (166) were unable himself to confirm the veracity of the claim, he could say:

(167)   The drugs they give could apparently have a detrimental effect on the powers of concentration. (W.7.3.98)

Or, if the available evidence were substantial, he might comment:

(168)   The drugs they give will undoubtedly have a detrimental effect on the powers of concentration.

Alternatively, the speaker could be more direct in both the style and the content of his utterance:

(169)   Frankly, the drugs they give have a detrimental effect on the powers of concentration.

The adverbs APPARENTLY (167), UNDOUBTEDLY (168) and FRANKLY (169) all make the speaker's authority explicit, although

they differ in the way they function. APPARENTLY and UNDOUBT-
EDLY belong to a subcategory of disjuncts known as 'content' or
'attitudinal' disjuncts, which are by far the most important category
in relation to co-occurrence; FRANKLY belongs to the other,
smaller, category, known as 'style' disjuncts. We examine each in
turn, beginning with style disjuncts.

4.4.1 Style disjuncts

Style disjuncts convey the speaker's comment on the style and form
of what is being said, and in some way define under what
conditions the speaker acts as 'authority' for the utterance. They
differ from content disjuncts in that they are not directly concerned
with its truth-value and therefore co-occur with the modals
without any notable restrictions coming into play.

In general, style disjuncts correspond to a clause in which a verb
of speaking is present. Thus the relationship of FRANKLY to its
sentence in:

(170)   Frankly I would like to see the overdraft completely
         repaid as soon as possible. (W.7.9.37)

can be demonstrated by several different correspondences:

(171)   I am speaking frankly when I say that . . .
         I say frankly that . . .
         If I may speak frankly . . .
         If I may put it frankly . . .
         In all frankness . . .

Style disjuncts therefore not only draw attention to what is being
said, but how it is being said, thereby incorporating metalinguistic
comment into the sentences in which they occur.

Style disjuncts have a wide variety of realization types, such as
clauses and prepositional phrases similar to those exemplified in
(171), but they also commonly occur as single word items. They are
typically associated with *I*. The CGEL (615f) distinguishes two
subtypes; we only list and comment on the most common items.

Type A   *Style disjuncts expressing the semantic categories of modality and*
            manner: FRANKLY, HONESTLY, SERIOUSLY, TRULY; BRIEFLY,
            GENERALLY, SIMPLY

Type A is a miscellaneous assortment, although two semantic categories in this particular grouping quite clearly emerge. The modal credentials of the first four items render them similar to content disjuncts like CERTAINLY or DEFINITELY in that they all express conviction. However, while content disjuncts assert the truth of what is said, these style disjuncts merely assert that the speaker is saying something sincerely. They do not impinge on modal meanings since their role is essentially metacommunicative:

(172)   Frankly, there's no-one else here who very well could do the job.

(173)   Honestly, he must be joking! He can't be serious!

(174)   Truly, they will undoubtedly run into problems before long.

(175)   Seriously, you can't really be thinking she's the murderer, surely?!

Greenbaum (1969: 93) suggests that this category of disjunct is very often used when in fact the speaker is not being sincere, although this is more an issue for psychology than linguistics.

The remaining items in this subcategory indicate that the speaker is making a rough generalization and are unexceptional in modal environments.

Type B   Style disjuncts expressing the semantic category of respect:
LITERALLY, PERSONALLY, STRICTLY

Respect is an abstract semantic notion but, in broad terms, adverbs in this category provide some point of reference in respect of which a sentence derives its truth-value. Again, a verb of speaking is understood and may, of course, be made explicit:

(176)   Personally (speaking), I think they may well/must be raving mad.

(177)   Strictly (speaking), they should have asked for permission.

There can be an element of modal concord between the style disjunct and an auxiliary, even though the relation lacks the synergy which typifies co-occurrence with subjunct emphasizers. In (176), PERSONALLY emphasizes that it is the speaker alone who is the authority and explicitly the point of reference for the modal judgement. However, content disjuncts are of much greater significance in modal environments, and these we examine in greater detail below.

4.4.2 Content disjuncts

More frequent and almost as central to modal–adverb co-occurrence as subjunct emphasizers, content (or attitudinal) disjuncts express direct observations about the truth-value of the sentence in which they occur or express an evaluation or attitude towards what is said. The CGEL (620f) therefore identifies two subtypes of content disjunct: those concerned with degree of truth (relating to notions of certainty/uncertainty) and those concerned with value judgement (relating to evaluation). The first category is by far the more important of the two, although the latter also merits attention.

Semantically, disjuncts expressing value judgement characteristically presuppose the positive truth-value of the sentence in which they occur; they therefore contrast markedly with disjuncts expressing degrees of truth:

(178)   Hopefully, the scheme would remove a substantial amount of traffic from Great John Street and Thurnham Street, allowing introduction of an environmental improvement scheme. (W.12.7.283)

(179)   Take poetry as literal description, and you'll probably find yourself very wide of the mark. (W.15.2.89)

The distinction is all the more poignant where there is no modal in the accompanying predication:

(180)   Fortunately, cannibalism is dying out.

(181)   Probably, cannibalism is dying out.

In (180), the clause is implicitly considered true; this is manifestly not the case with (181). However, the evaluation of an event or state of affairs as a fact does not necessarily mean that it actually is a fact. Assumptions can be made irrespective of the degree of likelihood of what is said actually being or becoming true. For example, a speaker can make an assessment about the likelihood of a state of affairs being true and mark the lack of conclusive evidence by interpolating an appropriate modal adverb:

(182)   Hopefully, the tax office may well have overlooked the additional income.

(183)   Rightly, they will probably have to take the exam again.

Value judgement disjuncts comprise a variety of seemingly quite disparate items which can be notionally grouped according to the type of evaluation they denote. For instance, they may express the judgement that what is being said is fortunate or unfortunate (FORTUNATELY, HAPPILY, LUCKILY; UNFORTUNATELY, UNHAPPILY, SADLY, TRAGICALLY); is a cause for satisfaction or the reverse (PLEASINGLY, REFRESHINGLY; ANNOYINGLY, REGRETTABLY); is surprising or unexpected (AMAZINGLY, CURIOUSLY, FUNNILY, ODDLY, STRANGELY); is appropriate or expected (INEVITABLY, NATURALLY, UNDERSTANDABLY); is right or wrong (CORRECTLY, RIGHTLY, WRONGLY); is deemed wise or artful (CLEVERLY, SENSIBLY, WISELY; FOOLISHY, UNWISELY). There are no obvious restrictions in their occurrence with sentences containing a modal verb or a modal–adverb combination. The significance of value judgement disjuncts is that they enable the speaker to qualify or characterize his attitude towards the truth-value of an utterance without this in any way interfering with his assessment of the likelihood of what he is saying being or becoming true.

Content disjuncts expressing degree of truth are in turn subdivided according to whether they categorically endorse the truth-value of what is said, make appeal to the observation or perception of some state of affairs, express shades of doubt, or assert the truth or falsity of what is said:

(184)   No doubt similar schemes will in due course be submitted by other Schools of the University. (W.13.1.29)

(185)   The drugs they give could apparently have a detrimental effect on the powers of concentration. (W.7.3.98)

(186)   Perhaps your friend – the fat one – might give some useful leads if subtly approached. (W.7.32.228)

(187)   Actually, as you are aware, there ought to be no overdraft at all.(W.7.9.44)

The content disjuncts concerned with truth-value and which most regularly occur with the modals fall into three categories:

Type A   *Content disjuncts expressing conviction:* ADMITTEDLY, CERTAINLY, DEFINITELY, INDEED, SURELY, UNDOUBTEDLY, CLEARLY, EVIDENTLY, OBVIOUSLY, OF COURSE, PLAINLY

With the exception of the underlined forms, these items also operate as emphasizers in modal environments (see 4.3.2).

Type B   *Content disjuncts expressing doubt:* ARGUABLY, APPARENTLY, CONCEIVABLY, DOUBTLESS, (QUITE/VERY) LIKELY (informal), MAYBE (informal), PERHAPS,[17] POSSIBLY, PRESUMABLY, PROBABLY[18]

The underlined forms also function as intensifiers in non-assertive (negative and interrogative) contexts.

Type C   *Content disjuncts expressing assertion in reality:* ACTUALLY, REALLY, IN FACT

By conveying the speaker's conviction and asserting the reality of what is said, this group is doubly emphatic; there is a clear contrast with group B adverbs where there is reference to a lack of reality. Contrast:

(188)   In fact, the consignment may well be delivered next week.

(189)   Apparently, the consignment may be delivered next week.

4.4.2.1   Syntactic features

Whilst disjuncts have considerable freedom in positional terms and may appear at several places in clause structure, they most usually occur in initial position at *I*:

(190)   "obviously you 'can't 'break 'up a pa'rticular còmpany# into its con'stituent pǎrts# (S.11.5.36/7)

(191)   per"haps we 'could maintaìn her# (S.2.6.690)

(192)   "prŏbably#   I   "would   im'agine   she   ĭs   in   'fact#
         (S.2.14.719)

As these examples demonstrate, peripherality is not simply a matter of syntax and position; there are different nuances suggested by prosody in speech. The adverb PROBABLY in (192), which occupies its own tone unit, is more peripheral than either OBVIOUSLY or PERHAPS in (190) and (191). Semantically, I can be associated with the thematic role of disjuncts (see 4.4.2.2): their scope is sentential making them ideal 'scene-setters' for what is to follow.

Content disjuncts can be interpolated within clause structure at M, or a variant of M, depending on the complexity of the verb phrase in which they appear (see 4.1.2):

(193)   Had he been a contemporary of Velasquez he would probably never have been heard of. (J 1964: 321)

(194)   If he'd wanted tea, he could presumably have asked for it. (CG/151)

(195)   A: Is there something else you've thought of?
         B: Yes there quite possibly may be. (CG/107)

This position is associated with the semantic process of approximation (see 4.4.2.3) where the adverb has a lesser scope than when at I.

Content disjuncts may also occur at E, even though this position is not readily associated with the expression of modality. The central modal adverbs POSSIBLY, PROBABLY, CERTAINLY do not usually occur in final position and, when they do, there is often the implication that they are tagged on as an afterthought, thereby increasing or weakening the effect of what has just been said:

(196)   He could get back to Dijon, possibly, though even that did not seem very certain. (J 1964: 318)

The most common items to occur at E are type C content disjuncts expressing assertion in reality, but this is more a feature of spoken than written discourse:

(197)   it "must be a 'very pe'culiar coĭnage 'actually# (S.2.5.564)

(198)   "prŏbably#   I   "would   im'agine   she   ĭs   in   'fact#
         (S.2.14.719)

(199)   "yès I thìnk you mùst 'do rèally# (S.5.9.550)

On account of their tendency to occur at *I*, content disjuncts frequently lie outside the scope of clause negation:

(200)   Maybe we cannot care enough unless the information is presented to us in a certain way. (W.7.17.127)

(201)   "obviously you càn't 'break 'up a partìcular còmpany# into its con'stituent pǎrts# (S.11.5.36/7)

(202)   it "probably 'wouldn't suit Nìce# (S.5.4.1154)

Similarly, if they occur at *E*, they are too peripheral to fall within its scope:

(203)   He may well not be coming next week, in fact.

When content disjuncts co-occur with clausal negation and are placed at *iM* in a modal environment, the overwhelming tendency is for them to take on the role of a subjunct emphasizer (see 4.3.2.1), especially when the modal verb is focused prosodically:

(204)   it "really còuldn't be done# "you knòw# (S.3.2.388/9)

Content disjuncts do not normally have the freedom to appear in any position in a direct or indirect question and in this respect contrast with style disjuncts, which may occur even initially:

(205) ?/*Certainly, must he really have access to all the details?

(206)   *She asked whether, certainly, he really must have access to all the details.

(207)   Frankly, must he really have access to all the details?

(208)   They asked, frankly, whether he really must have access to all the details.

However, type B content disjuncts, which involve the expression of doubt, represent some important exceptions, although they still do not appear initially:

(209)   Can you possibly/perhaps see the patient now?
        [Is there a possibility of your seeing the patient now?]

(210)   She asked him whether he could possibly see the patient now.

(211)   Could there conceivably have been an error?
         [Is it possible that an error was made?]

(212)   He asked if there could conceivably have been an error.

Examples such as these also contradict the view that modal adverbs do not occur in questions (see the discussion in 4.3.3.4). Their status here as disjuncts also contrasts with their use as intensifiers in interrogative contexts, where the questions in which they appear are deliberative or rhetorical in nature, and more the countersign of introspection than a genuine appeal for outside comment:

(213)   Can this possibly be the last time we'll meet?
         [Is it at all possible that this is the last time we'll meet?]

Content disjuncts are subject to modification by intensifiers such as ALMOST, VERY or QUITE and they may also co-occur in informal speech and writing:

(214)   There's only one thing – if you come next week, on the 26th, she will probably almost definitely be here, so I leave it to you. (W.7.1.259)

(215)   "possibly next Mŏnday perhaps might be best# (S.7.1.1145)

4.4.2.2 Content disjuncts and thematization

The constraining factors which affect adverbial placement are not just a matter of syntax and prosody: their distribution is also a matter of pragmatics and discourse or information structure and the contexts in which they are actually used. Placing a content disjunct such as OBVIOUSLY in initial position provides the speaker with the means to characterize his attitude towards what he is saying, where the effect is to focus the entire propositional content. It is normally the case that a speaker expects the addressee to believe what he asserts; the fronting or topicalization of modal values facilitated by placing a disjunct at I, is both a means of establishing the speaker as the source of authority and signalling his underlying attitude to the content of his utterance.

All subcategories of content disjunct can be associated with thematization; different modal values are topicalized according to the semantic status of the adverb and the modal in the adjoining clause. Disjuncts are not usually the key information point of the sentence to which they are related, but they focalize the modal elements present and thereby underpin the speaker's attitude to the content and the salient information point(s) he wishes to convey. (To some extent, this accounts for their placement in positions other than initial.) In:

(216)   Obviously one of the two must have been a better candidate than the other. (J 1964: 306)

OBVIOUSLY implies that the writer is basing his assertion on seemingly irrefutable evidence; this endorses the use of inferential MUST to make the strongest of all possible judgements about the likelihood of the proposition being true. The cumulative effect of the two modal elements is to endorse the strength of the speaker's conviction and to imply that the judgement is based in the mental perception of available evidence, rather than in mere caprice.

Occasionally, content disjuncts may be the major information point in the clause (see 4.6), especially when used as responses to questions or as a comment on a previous utterance :

(217)   A: They will surely have left for Bucharest by now?
        B: "Wèll# Pǒssibly#

(218)   A: He could have problems
        B: He "còuld# And he "will#

In addition, a few style disjuncts (see 4.4.1), such as HONESTLY or SERIOUSLY, are used as verbless questions but these imply all the other items stated in the previous utterance:

(219)   A: He's running for the Presidency.
        B: "Hǒnestly# / "Sěriously#
            [Were you speaking honestly/seriously when you just said what you did?]

The content disjunct REALLY is commonly used in this way:

(220)   A: She's resigned, at last!
        B: "Rěally#

Where thematization involves disjuncts concerned with the expression or assertion of truth-value, as in example (216), the semantic attraction between the adverb and the modal verb is much stronger than in cases where the disjunct conveys the speaker's value judgement. Where the speaker's evaluation is involved, there is no overlap in modal values, because evaluating and thus thematizing an utterance in terms of its propositional content being fortunate or unfortunate, satisfactory or the reverse, strange or unexpected, expected or appropriate, right or unjust in no way impinges on the degree to which it may be considered true or false. The speaker's evaluation operates independently of considerations of truth-value. This reflects the characteristic difference between what might be regarded as central modal adverbs and evaluative adverbs: 'while an evaluative adverb presupposes the positive truth-value of the ... predication with which it is in construction and offers an evaluation (value-judgement) of it, a modal adverb assigns a degree of likelihood (a probably truth-value) to the associated predication' (Schreiber 1971: 88). For this reason, evaluatives or value judgement adverbs show no particular tendency to combine with modal verbs, although the combinations illustrated in the following frame are perfectly plausible:

(221)   Fortunately/Luckily/Unfortunately/Sadly/Regrettably/
Amazingly/Curiously/Oddly/Understandably/Sensibly/
Wisely/Foolishly, they could/might (well)/may (well)/
should/would/will/must have decided not to press char-
ges and I think they should/shouldn't.

No noteworthy trends were uncovered in the data. Furthermore, Jacobson's dictionary of adverb placement (1964), the source of several of our examples illustrating modal–adverb concord, records no instances of co-occurrence between evaluatives and a modal verb. One significant exception is NATURALLY, which could plausibly be reclassified as a type A content disjunct expressing the speaker's conviction, on the grounds that, in modal environments, it is virtually synonymous with OF COURSE. Under Jacobson's entry for NATURALLY (1964: 297), all but one of his five illustrations involve co-occurrence with a modal form. Although less common, INEVITABLY behaves in a similar way; the selection of either adverb lends the accompanying proposition an air of factuality:

(222)   Naturally Palaeolithic man's interest in bison cannot have
been purely aesthetic. (J 1964: 217)

(223)   Inevitably, there will be those who see only the earthen
        vessels. (W.9.2.281)

Accordingly, we focus on thematization in relation to adverbs
expressing truth-value and where the contexts of co-occurrence
are almost always epistemic.

The modal values which are thematized depend primarily on
the type of disjunct involved: whether it simply asserts the truth-
value of what is said (ADMITTEDLY, CERTAINLY, DEFINITELY, OF
COURSE, SURELY, UNDOUBTEDLY), relates to the perception of
evidence (APPARENTLY, CLEARLY, EVIDENTLY, OBVIOUSLY), implies
a measure of doubt (CONCEIVABLY, MAYBE, PERHAPS, POSSIBLY,
PROBABLY), affirms what is said as a matter of fact (ACTUALLY,
REALLY), or is suppositious (PRESUMABLY, SUPPOSEDLY). We shall
examine thematization in relation to these notional groupings.
They represent a refinement of the categories established in 4.4.2
in that now, for instance, distinctions are made between adverbs
such as CERTAINLY, by which the speaker makes a direct claim to
'knowledge' and those like EVIDENTLY, which involve an appeal to
general perception. These subdivisions of modal adverbs do not
have clear-cut membership criteria but they do represent plausible
notional categorizations.

ADMITTEDLY, CERTAINLY (the most common item in the group),
DEFINITELY, OF COURSE, SURELY, UNDOUBTEDLY are all high
probability adverbs which convey the speaker's strength of conviction in the truth of the adjoining proposition; by topicalizing the
firmness of the speaker's belief the effect is, of course, to emphasize
it. At the same time, the adverb interacts with the modal verb by
focalizing or objectifying (see the discussion of objectification in
2.5) the modality expressed by the modal: possibility in the first two
examples, and prediction in the latter.

(224)   Certainly if the artist could speak at all, his command of
        spoken language must have been more primitive than his
        command of graphic language. (J 1964: 240)

(225)   Of course, when the subject-matter concerns very recent
        events it may not be easy to use this technique, and if the
        matter is trivial it may not be worthwhile. (W.9.3.9)

(226)   of "course he'll be working with overseas stùdents#
        (S.1.2.656)

(227)   Undoubtedly some of this extra production was uneco-
         nomic and would never have been countenanced in
         peacetime. (J 1964: 356)

Regardless of its syntactic position, SURELY functions to seek
agreement in anticipation of some opposition and is not purely
used for the reinforcement of truth-value (see also 4.3.2.3); it also
tends to precede a question:

(228)   Surely they couldn't have expected you to complete the
         project so soon (could they)?

(229)   Surely the run must be nearly over now. (W.11.2.203)

Formally, OF COURSE is an adverb phrase and not an adverb but
it is included here on the grounds that it functions as a single item.
Sinclair (1991: 110) notes that 'the word space, which is structurally
bogus, may disappear in time, as we see in *maybe*, *anyway*, and
another'.

Despite their syntactic peripherality, disjuncts in this group
remain subject to the constraints of modal harmony when
adjoining clauses contain MIGHT, MAY or MUST:

(230)   *Possibly, she must be at home.

(231)   *Definitely, she might/may be at home.

ADMITTEDLY, CERTAINLY and OF COURSE also function concessively
and imply that the speaker is reluctant to accept the truth of what
is being said. In these cases, the normal collocational rules of modal
harmony do not necessarily apply:

(232)   Of course, Heathrow [London airport] could keep
         expanding. Much of Hounslow could be bulldozed to
         make way for it ... but the government might find a
         sensible pricing regime politically easier to implement.
         (Ec/26.08.95/32)

(233)   This I can believe, but I hardly feel that she will be the
         sweeter for it – but of course I could be wrong.
         (W.7.31.99)

(234)   Certainly, she might be there, but somehow I don't think
         so.

In the case of ADMITTEDLY, there is the additional suggestion that the speaker is reluctant to mention the acceptance (see Greenbaum 1969: 203):

(235)   Admittedly his picture will be a set of references to actual appearances, but its raison d'être will not be to impart information about appearances. (J 1964: 216)

The evidentials APPARENTLY, CLEARLY, EVIDENTLY, OBVIOUSLY all refer to the observation or perception of a state of affairs and express either the speaker's conviction or his measure of doubt, according to the strength of evidence they convey. They therefore represent a mix of high and low probability adverbs. CLEARLY and OBVIOUSLY express a higher degree of conviction than either EVIDENTLY or APPARENTLY:

(236)   Clearly, a mutation in a regulatory gene could bring about a substantial change in the appearance of an organism at one blow. (W.11.7.251)

(237)   "obviously you 'can't 'break 'up a par'ticular còmpany# into its con'stituent pårts# (S.11.5.36/7)

(238)   Obviously, elements as subtle as attitudes could never be attributed to one generation or one decade. (W.11.1.123)

(239)   Evidently there must still be other receptors, able to respond to changes of light intensity in the wall of the diencephalon. (W.9.7.252)

APPARENTLY denotes doubt and distances the speaker from the source of evidence to the extent that it may be used 'to show that the speaker is aware of false evidence' (Swan 1981: 432):

(240)   Apparently, there might have been a mistake but the situation is unclear.

APPARENTLY and EVIDENTLY signal in an explicit way that the source of information is not the speaker and that the evidence on which his assessment is based is therefore second-hand. There is doubt as to the veracity of the adjoining proposition because what is said can only be understood as the speaker's interpretation rather than as a personal assessment of a particular state of affairs. As Blakemore (1992: 105) remarks: 'A speaker who intends his utterance to be understood as an interpretation cannot be creating expectations of truthfulness, since his utterance does not purport to be a description of a state of affairs.' The nature of the proposition in these contexts corresponds to the second type of proposition recognized by Givón (1982: 24) and which he describes as follows: 'Propositions that are asserted with relative confidence, are open to challenge by the hearer and thus require – or admit – evidentiary justification.'[19]

CLEARLY and OBVIOUSLY are among those adverbs which Corum (1975: 134) observes are 'sprinkled throughout the speech (and literature) of some speakers, but the content of the adjoining proposition is not always *obvious* at all'. Their use may be 'devious' because they occur 'in precisely those areas where speakers have something to gain or lose by their addressee's acceptance or rejection of what they are saying' (see 4.5.4).

These adverbs constitute the epistemic evidential subsystem in English and correspond to the formal 'hearsay particles' found in other languages. Palmer's conclusion (1986: 54) that the epistemic system of English 'has only judgements' is perhaps misleading because it does not take into account the type of disjunct–modal co-occurrences discussed above, nor the tendency for evidential collocations with MUST (see 3.4.3.2; 4.3.2.5). Although these adverbs denote evidential values which only indirectly impinge on the expression of degrees of likelihood, restrictions apply with respect to the modal values they can thematize in epistemic contexts. While APPARENTLY and EVIDENTLY freely co-occur with clauses containing any of the central epistemic modals, CLEARLY and OBVIOUSLY are mostly restricted to those with WILL, WOULD or MUST:

(241)   Apparently/Evidently they might/may/will/would/must have already arrived.

(242)   Clearly/Obviously they will/must have already arrived.

(243) ?/*Clearly/Obviously they might/may have already arrived.

None of the evidentials in this group seems harmonious in the environment of COULD, whose less central epistemic status sets it apart from the other epistemic modals:

(244)?/* Apparently/Evidently/Clearly/Obviously   they   could have already arrived.

Conversely, where epistemic readings are plausible, these restrictions on co-occurrence with evidentials do not apply:

(245)   If I were out in the world, I could consult the books that had been written on the subject, but here in the convent, obviously, there could be no access to atheistic literature. (H 1969: 221)

When the modal expresses dynamic rather than epistemic modality, as in example (228) above, or in the following paradigm, combinations are more plausible:

(246)   Apparently/Evidently/Clearly/Obviously they can/could finish the project on schedule, if they want(ed) to.
[There is evidence to support the view that it is possible for them to finish the project on schedule.]

Measured in terms of likelihood, PRESUMABLY, SUPPOSEDLY and PROBABLY allow for some doubt but imply the speaker's reasonable certainty that the propositional content of what he is saying is in fact true. Both items convey what might be described as medium probability. PROBABLY is the more common item and the strength of likelihood it conveys is best understood if it is contrasted with the much weaker adverbs CONCEIVABLY and POSSIBLY:

(247)   *Probably/Presumably they'll be at the reception this evening, on the other hand, probably/presumably they won't.

(248)   Possibly/Conceivably they'll be at the reception this evening, on the other hand, possibly/conceivably they won't.

The tendency for PROBABLY and PRESUMABLY to combine with WILL and WOULD has been noted elsewhere (see 3.4.5). PRESUMABLY is the more loaded item and functions in stark contrast to the evidentials, because now the truth of the proposition is assumed or taken for granted until the contrary is proved. It neither seeks nor anticipates dissent from another party and its use may therefore seem rather arrogant or imperious in certain contexts:

(249)   Presumably your mother will have your addresss and will forward it. (W.7.4.5)

(250)   The legend that Milton was an unpopular poet has lived
         so long that probably it will never be destroyed.
         (J 1964: 321)

SUPPOSEDLY, like PRESUMABLY, conveys the speaker's presumption
of truth but is uncommon and rarely occurs in initial position as the
latter form is preferred.

CONCEIVABLY, MAYBE, PERHAPS, POSSIBLY denote low probability
values, and are all clearly epistemic. They imply that the speaker
'does not accept responsibility for, or particularly believe in the
propositional content' of what he is saying (Swan 1987: 445):

(251)   Maybe we cannot care enough unless the information is
         presented to us in a certain way. (W.7.17.127)

(252)   Perhaps I ought to be miserable because you are not with
         me. (W.7.4.18)

(253)   Possibly you may have considered . . . that the proceeds of
         sale of the car . . . would supplement the proceeds of sales
         of securities already received . . . (W.7.9.87)

Only with MUST do restrictions come into play:

(254)   *Conceivably/(?)Maybe/(?)Perhaps/Possibly there must
         have been a mistake.

However, combinations with MAYBE and PERHAPS are not entirely
implausible:

(255)   A: You think maybe there must have been maybe a
             mistake somewhere?
         B: I consider it extremely probable, Mr Aaronson.
             (DM/217)

The thematization of modal values is more typical of epistemic
rather than nonepistemic contexts, although it also occurs with the
latter, as in examples (236) to (238). In epistemic environments,
however, both the adverb and the modal simultaneously convey the
speaker's opinion on the truth-value of what is being said, whether
this is expressed in terms of his relative doubt or certainty, or is
related to his observation or perception of a state of affairs. In
nonepistemic (deontic) environments, formulaic combinations of
PERHAPS and POSSIBLY with CAN, COULD, WILL, WOULD and

SHOULD commonly mark the sentences in which they occur with
the illocutionary force of a request:

(256)   Perhaps/Possibly you can/could/will/would/should meet
them at the airport, as I shall be busy.

In this usage, these adverbs have the unique function of not so
much thematizing the modality expressed as mitigating its impositive force. Hence they may combine with such courtesy subjuncts
as PLEASE or KINDLY (see 4.3.1) which function as pragmatic
markers of politeness or mitigation:

(257)   Perhaps you would kindly call at my offices when this is
convenient.

(258)   Could you possibly get the pending file for me, please.

4.4.2.3   Content disjuncts and interpolation

Interpolation involves the same items as thematization except that
now the disjunct is inserted parenthetically within clause structure
at M, or a variant of M, depending on the complexity of the verb
phrase in which it appears (see 4.1.2). Like sentence-initial/-final
disjuncts, these items are similar in effect in their role of interpreting the text to the addressee in order to encourage a particular
attitude. Evaluative adverbs may be involved, subject to the
observations made in the previous section. Interpolation, like
thematization, is mostly restricted to epistemic contexts:

(259)   I "probably 'could have gìven it# (S.5.9.6)

(260)   Among other things, there is a limit in the supply of food
and the materials which conceivably could be turned into
food. (J 1975: 245)

(261)   Mr. Lindsay, meanwhile, repeated his view, calling the
clash 'an unfortunate incident that possibly could have
been averted'. (J 1975: 242)

(262)   The drugs they give ... could apparently have a detrimental effect on the powers of concentration. (W.7.3.98)

(263)   Manner of speaking; the use of urban dialects, accents,

and intonations, could probably indicate even more. (W.11.1.94)

(264)   It's now the end and might conceivably be masquerading under the title of phylogenetic change. (W.7.2.45)

(265)   How pervasive this historical background is may perhaps be best realized through the way it affects the meaning, and colour, of words in common use. (W.9.3.48)

(266)   This vessel is decorated with masks, projecting spiked triangles, and reticulated rectangles which might possibly represent fishing nets. (W.11.6.152)

(267)   That food is in some way limiting for nestling robins can scarcely be doubted – otherwise the average size of the brood would presumably be increased by natural selection until the food limit was reached. (J 1964: 320)

Modal environments tend to favour the interpolation of adverbs which express dubitative meanings, conveying the speaker's relative degree of uncertainty. The CGEL (627f) also records that content disjuncts like PROBABLY and POSSIBLY normally occur at M, or a variant of M. Such adverbs occupy the middle ground between modal reinforcement (involving emphasizers and intensifiers which have a strengthening effect) and modal diminution (involving intensifiers which have a weakening effect).

Indubitative adverbs, on the other hand, which convey the speaker's conviction, regularly shed their status as disjuncts to function as emphasizers. Unless marked off intonationally, or by punctuation, their proximity to the modal verb head undermines their independent status and they become more readily associated with emphasis rather than interpolation:

(268)   You will undoubtedly have a very strong field for this appointment. (W.7.6.90)

(269)   The statutory implied conditions would certainly seem to be material parts of a contract so that any breach of them, however slight, would seem to entitle the buyer to reject the goods, treat the contract as repudiated, and recover the price. (W.14.2.109)

(270)   for the "second force àirline# "well I would 'cèrtainly#
        re"grèt it# (S.11.4.181/2/3)

This is also true of adverbs expressing semantic roles other than
modality and degree (see 4.1.2). However, indubitatives may be
interpolated at M, where their more peripheral status is invariably
signalled by a pause in speech, or commas or parenthesis in
writing:

(271)' Plato, certainly, would have none of it. (J 1964: 241)

(272)   This would, clearly, be a fault. (J 1964: 242)

(273)   Everyone in the household, obviously, can't keep per-
        fectly still just because some one member is playing the
        piano. (J 1975: 306)

(274)   Other people using the same supply can, of course, apply
        for shares in the same way as other members of the public
        who are not British Gas customers. (W.15.5.326)

Where the adverb is not marked off intonationally or by
punctuation, it may have a more restricted scope for some native
speakers and to have as its focus the modal constituent rather than
the sentence as a whole. In these cases, there may be indeterminacy
between interpolation and emphasis and it is not always clear
whether a significant distinction can be made. In (270), either
interpretation seems plausible, although the true emphasizer status
of the adverb is revealed when it occurs in pre-auxiliary position:

(275)   That certainly would be very convenient, wouldn't it?
        (J 1975: 165)

Corum (1975: 137), circumvents the problem of indeterminacy by
referring to what we have called approximation (the main category
of disjunct-type modification) as niching (after Ross 1973) and by
describing the processes involved simply in terms of focus: 'A
speaker may employ NICHING to emphasize a particular constituent
or the whole proposition'. For similar reasons, it could be argued
that CONCEIVABLY and POSSIBLY (see 4.3.3.4) function as intensifiers (downtoners) in the environments of MIGHT and MAY, where
they are virtually equivalent to JUST:

(276)   This vessel is decorated with masks, projecting spiked

triangles, and reticulated rectangles which might possibly [just] represent fishing nets. (W.11.6.152)

Indeterminacy is inevitable when such closely related semantic roles are contrasted with one another, but there are also relatively clear-cut cases of modal–adverb interaction which justify the present approach.

4.4.2.4 Content disjuncts and tagging

In addition to the type C adverbs ACTUALLY, REALLY, IN FACT (see 4.4.2), other content disjuncts may occur in final position. Their effect is to emphasize the propositional content of the utterance to which they are attached and to endorse the speaker's authority:

(277)   I "don't know what I'd 'do if she lĕft# she "will of 'course# (S.1.8.295/6)

(278)   "we shall be 'giving it 'very 'very 'careful 'thought indèed# (S.11.4.295)

(279)   they're "all very Kèntish# they "may be in Sùssex áctually# (S.7.3.587/8)

(280)   'That's not exactly the kind of picture of her that I had gathered from Mr. Pettigrew', said Mallett, 'but you may be right, of course.' (HB/134)

(281)   'What I was wondering was whether it would be better to have her under Mrs. Clarke – that would be a bit too obvious, perhaps. (HB/28)

(282)   And Rose will be a mother certainly, and Sheila – she may be a mother too. (J 1964: 240)

As Corum remarks (1975: 137): 'Putting a strong [adverb] at the end of a proposition is a way of reminding the hearer that his acceptance of the content of the proposition is the desired effect.' From a pragmatic point of view, it is easy to understand how such artifice could be used for rhetorical purposes.

4.5   SUBJUNCTS AND DISJUNCTS IN CONSPECTUS

4.5.1   Adverbial scope and ambivalence

Modal adverbs have been partly defined in terms of their scope: subjuncts typically focus on a constituent or group of constituents in clause structure, while disjuncts modify the entire clause. The one is syntactically and semantically subordinate, the other superordinate. In reality, however, adverbial scope is often an ill-defined and elusive concept which cannot, by itself, account for differences in modal–adverb behaviour or use. To some extent this is due to the practical difficulties involved in making hard-and-fast distinctions between sentence and word or word-group modifers. Hence Jacobson (1964: 29) remarks that 'Though grammarians are fully agreed that a division of adverbials into sentence-modifiers and word or word-group modifers can be made, they usually show a great deal of hesitation about how to distinguish between these two categories in practice.' Examples (13) and (14) with POSSIBLY, discussed in 4.1.1 above, demonstrate that the distinction can be made and to striking effect. But often there is ambivalence, and theoretical niceties can become blurred in actual usage. For instance, it is not obvious that in terms of scope there is a substantial difference between the way SURELY behaves in (283) and (284) where, as a subjunct emphasizer, it focalizes the co-occurring modal, and its more peripheral role in examples (285) to (288), where its scope seems to extend over the sentence or clause as a whole:

(283)   Some England fans might save up to make such a trip, but they would surely be extremely thin on the ground. (W.12.8.7)

(284)   Although previous police investigations have turned up no significant National Front influence in soccer violence these shameful events must surely lead to a call for further enquiries. (W.12.8.23)

(285)   Surely the run must be nearly over now. (W.11.2.203)

(286)   There is no hell of course but surely there ought to be one for such a woman ... (H 1969: 146)

(287)   But they must have already delivered the parcel, surely?

(288)   What if the old man complained ... to the Provost himself? It would mean, surely, Bruno's being chucked out of the college on his ear. (H 1969: 232)

Emphasizer SURELY, in (283) and (284), clearly focalizes and reinforces the auxiliaries it adjoins, but it would be tenuous to claim that emphasis is restricted to these constituents without in any way affecting other parts of the clause, or perhaps the clause as a whole, even if the locus of reinforcement is primarily the modal verb. At the same time, while disjunct SURELY in (285) to (288) is highly mobile, occurring in initial, medial and final positions, it clearly interacts with the modal present in the accompanying clause, regardless of the effects on scope brought about by its superordinate status. Such freedom of movement is bound to create ambivalence over what is focused, especially in the written langure, but in everyday speech, even at its most relaxed and informal, prosodic information normally provides most of the necessary clues as to what is focused and carries most information value (see 4.6).

Bolinger (1972b: 34) argues that there is no sharp distinction between sentence and word(-group) modifers, but if one were to be drawn, adverbials which occupy initial position, or gravitate towards it, would tend to be sentential in scope. According to his principle of 'linear modification' a preposed adverb (which has the status of a disjunct) will modify, or have within its scope, everything which it precedes. Initial position can be most readily associated with this principle of 'inclusiveness'. The adverb establishes the modal theme of the utterance and gives it prominence through an extensive association with the modal auxiliary:

(289)   At the same time, the novel as we know it to-day is a late growth ... Certainly it cannot, in England, be traced back earlier than the sixteenth century. (J 1964: 240)

(290)   The legend that Milton was an unpopular poet has lived so long that probably it will never be destroyed. (J 1964: 321)

(291)   She's bent, I think, on growing a different kind of sensory equipment. Maybe she will, and it will save her. (J 1964: 293)

Yet, even where the adverb is tagged on (287) or interpolated (288), its scope may also be inclusive, especially when the adverb and the verbal constituent it modifies share the expression of similar modal values. In the case of approximation (thematization, interpolation and tagging) there is a natural tendency for the diverse modal elements to combine and interact intrasententially because the adverb modifiers involved, disjuncts, are only loosely tied to their modal verb heads.

Despite their greater degree of integration, subjuncts may also be ambivalent with regard to scope. In principle, a distinction could be drawn between the primary locus of modification (the modal verb head) and the secondary locus of modification (the verb phrase as a whole and/or the rest of the clause) but this would sometimes be difficult to uphold in practice, especially when native speaker perceptions differ as they do (see Greenbaum 1969: 127f). The CGEL (583F) warns of this pitfall in the section on subjunct emphasizers: 'When ... emphasizers are positioned next to a part of the communication, without being separated intonationally or by punctuation, their effect is often to emphasize that part alone, though there may be ambivalence as to whether the emphasis is on the part or on the whole.'

Another factor influencing scope is the concept of speaker-orientation. This is more clearly associated with disjuncts than subjuncts on account of the former's greater mobility and autonomy in relation to clause structure. Overt marking of the speaker's intrusion and his authority to comment on the relevance of what he is saying are given a prominence which tends to override purely syntactic considerations of scope. Hence Halliday (1985: 51) remarks that modal disjuncts 'tend to be given thematic status, and so typically occur in first position. But this is not obligatory; they can come elsewhere in the clause, and they may be added as an afterthought at the end.' Their freedom of movement is therefore significant for discourse structure. The concept of speaker-orientation alone would imply that the scope of adverbial modification is generally more extensive than in the case of modal subjuncts, which simply assert speaker-presence through reinforcement of the co-occurring modal verb. Clearly, a valid distinction on the grounds of scope can be drawn between the two types of adverbial, but in some contexts indeterminacy is inevitable.

4.5.2 Adverbial homonymy and polysemy[20]

The ambivalence associated with adverbial scope is also related to the fact that many modal adverbs are multifunctional, combining two or more different functions. As a rule these can be easily distinguished; there is unlikely to be confusion between the use of CLEARLY to express the notion 'in a clear manner' (where it functions as a manner adjunct); its use to add reinforcement to a part of an utterance (where it functions as a subjunct emphasizer); or its use to convey the speaker's attitude towards the content of his utterance (where it functions as a content disjunct):

(292)   I think he'd be good – he can expound things clearly, and he is a really nice humane person. (W.17.2.271)

(293)   She is more at home in Name than in Name and would clearly have no problems about settling down in Name if appointed. (W.17.1.59)

(294)   Clearly, a mutation in a regulatory gene could bring about a substantial change in the appearance of an organism at one blow. (W.11.7.251)

The use of one adverbial form, in this case CLEARLY, to fulfil a number of different functions appears to be a feature of English which is unparalleled in other Germanic languages (see Swan 1987: 523). No doubt, the predominance of -LY adverbs in English has itself facilitated adverbial shifts between the different functions because, as Swan (1987: 523) points out, 'adverbs need not change morphologically, but can by degrees change from one function to another'.

The mechanism of adverbial shifts, and the direction of shift (from sentence modifier to word(-group) modifier, or vice versa) are complex issues and the situation varies according to the item concerned. Swan (1987: 519) concludes that 'SA [sentence adverb] shifts can be seen as including the presence of word-modifiers ... and a speaker comment concept. These blend in the adverbial form which becomes SA or rather, the SA usually becomes polysemous and functions both as SA and non-SA.' Adverbs associated with the expression of modality or degree are often at different stages in their progression from one function to another, and this sometimes results in a certain blending or mixing of their different roles. In:

(295)   They truly cannot stop talking about the very pleasant
         times they had and the kind hospitality of the Swedish
         people. (J 1975: 158)

the modal force of TRULY is tinged with some force of manner but
is more nearly an emphasizer than HONESTLY, which still clearly
retains something of the sentence adverb, as it is restricted to
contexts where the speaker is making an admission:

(296)   "I 'honestly can't remember where it wàs# (S.2.10.1079)

In other cases the adverb has maximally lost semantic content and
become increasingly grammaticalized, as in the case of REALLY in
the environment of MUST, or when it focalizes the negated modals:

(297)   and "time's 'running òut# we "really mŭst get it con-
         'clùded# mùstn't we# (S.5.11.239/40)

(298)   "yòu know# it "really còuldn't be dòne# (S.3.2.387/8)

However, in other modal environments, REALLY has just a hint of
its sentential function ('it would be true to say that'):

(299)   We have already asserted that the initial paradox is not
         resolved, as it really would be in a poem which hymned
         the joys of nature as opposed to art. (J 1975: 270)

In contrast to REALLY, ACTUALLY is less advanced in the shift cycle
and in current usage never seems to fully divest itself of its sentential
status ('in actual fact'):

(300)   If there was a controlling power outside the universe, it
         could not show itself to us as one of the facts inside the
         universe – no more than the architect of a house could
         actually be a wall or staircase or fireplace in that house.
         (J 1964: 218)

This is arguably still true even in the environment of MUST:

(301)   Here the words 'whip of cords' ... represent a sort of
         minimal toning down of what actually must have been a
         massive undertaking. (J 1975: 361)

These examples demonstrate that there are perceptible differences
in the truth-emphasizer status of the modal adverbs. It is intuitively
obvious that such differences correlate with the greater frequency

of use of those items where the shift is complete. In time, the same adverbial form develops different uses or functions which semantically are often quite closely related.

Sameness of form and its relationship to meaning is usually discussed in terms of homonymy (two or more lexical items which have the same spoken and written form but differ in meaning) and polysemy (a single lexical item which has a range of different yet related meanings). MUST (denoting an essential and necessary thing), MUST (denoting the newly pressed fruit of grapes) and MUST (denoting a state of frenzied sexual excitement in a male elephant) are considered homonyms because the various meanings are unrelated. Conversely, MOUTH (of a human), MOUTH (of a river) and MOUTH (as in the jaws of a vice) share a metaphorical connection and may be considered a single polysemous lexical item with multiple meaning. Unrelatedness versus relatedness of meaning is probably the most relevant criterion for distinguishing between homonymy and polysemy, but it is an elusive yardstick since relatedness of meaning is a matter of degree and clear-cut distinctions between the two concepts are not always easy to make. This is no less true when the principles of homonymy and polysemy are applied to the function of adverbs.

The classification of modal adverbs presented in this chapter has been based on both syntactic and semantic criteria. More than any other adverb group, modal adverbs are particularly difficult to assign to discrete classes because there is often a continuum from class to class, rather than clear-cut demarcations between them. As we have already seen, many modal adverbs contain features belonging to more than one class with the result that there can be blending or mixing of semantic roles. To this extent the system of classification proposed in the CGEL can appear somewhat arbitrary: the semantic effects of subjunct emphasizers, subjunct intensifiers and focusing subjuncts in modal environments frequently represent cases of mixture or overlap, and the subjunct function of modal adverbs, at least in terms of adverbial scope, is not always readily distinguished from their function as disjuncts. Modal adverbs are therefore truly multifunctional: individual items regularly have two or more different syntactic functions in which their spoken and written forms are identical and where there is often a degree of semantic affinity between their different roles. Greenbaum (1969: 4) refers to these items as 'syntactic homonyms'.

Many style disjuncts, especially those expressing the semantic categories of modality and manner (see 4.4.1) and some content disjuncts expressing conviction (see 4.4.2) also function as manner adjuncts (CGEL: 557f) and can generally be paraphrased by 'in a . . . way, or manner', with an appropriate adjective base such as HONEST, SERIOUS, FRANK, CLEAR, EVIDENT, OBVIOUS inserted in the frame. There may be as many as four separate uses of the same item and this, of course, raises the vexed issue of adverbial homonymy and polysemy outlined above. To illustrate the relevance of these concepts to the account of modal adverbs, we examine the behaviour of SIMPLY in its range of syntactic and semantic roles, and conclude the section with some examples of modal adverb homonyms in context.

Dictionary definitions of SIMPLY assign the entry up to four separate meanings: in a separate manner; merely, only; absolutely, altogether, undoubtedly, really; frankly, candidly. In the CGEL classification, these meanings correspond to four identifiable functions of the adverb, which we illustrate as follows:

(302)   [Manner adjunct: SIMPLY (A)]
        He must just do the right thing simply, even surrepti-
        tiously, and let what would follow follow mechanically.
        (H 1968: 228)

(303)   [Focusing subjunct: SIMPLY (B)]
        He must simply have <burned with hatred> not to send
        some sort of conciliatory signal to me. (MD/268/9)

(304)   [Subjunct emphasizer: SIMPLY (C)]
        He's worried . . . but he simply will not face anything.
        (J 1975: 334)

(305)   [Style disjunct: SIMPLY (D)]
        So I will conclude my preamble by remarking, simply,
        that I am proud to be present. (H 1968: 228)

Each of these sentences represents a more or less distinct use of SIMPLY where, in order to retain its function, the adverb is restricted to a particular syntactic position. The questions now arise: Is SIMPLY operating homonymously and expressing four separate meanings? Or is SIMPLY operating polysemously as one lexical item and expressing a range of different meanings?

To some extent these questions can be answered by examining the different uses of SIMPLY to see if they share any relatedness of meaning. SIMPLY (A) can be roughly paraphrased as 'in a manner or way that is straightforward and uncomplicated'. By indicating that the sentence is true in respect to the part focused (indicated by angle brackets), SIMPLY (B) signals that the propositional content is easy or straightforward to understand; it also serves to reinforce the modal verb. SIMPLY (C) and SIMPLY (D) have their modal force tinged with some force of manner so that there is an indication that the speaker chooses to express himself in as simple a way as possible. SIMPLY (C) is less marked in this respect because of its proximity to the modal and its primary semantic role of reinforcement. SIMPLY (D), which has been interpolated in our example, makes overt reference to the form and content of what the speaker is saying: 'to express what I feel as simply as possible . . .'.

Relatedness of meaning is a matter of degree and so it is to be expected that some instances of the adverb are closer in meaning than others; (B), (C), and (D) share a greater semantic affinity, perhaps, than any of these in contrast with (A). But there is clearly some connection between the senses of the four instances of SIMPLY and so SIMPLY could therefore be regarded as polysemous, a single lexical item which has a range of different meanings. Indeed, this is the view put forward by Swan (1987: 519). But, if SIMPLY is a case of polysemy, how can we account for the differences in its syntactic function in each of the above examples? Even allowing for the degree of neutralization between its different subjunct roles, each instance of SIMPLY represents an identifiable and separate syntactic function. It would be misleading to assign the four manifestations of SIMPLY to membership of the same syntactic class as this would obfuscate any description which sought to account for differences in its behaviour. Assigning the different functions to different classes of items helps us to make sense of what would otherwise be 'diffuse transitions from class to class' (Jacobson 1975: 49). Greenbaum's use of the notion 'syntactic homonymy' helps to circumvent the problem of drawing a sharp distinction between homonymy and polysemy because it also includes cases which might otherwise be ascribed to polysemy.

The following instances of modal adverb homonymy illustrate the syntactic function of each item according to its status, which is indicated in parentheses: HONESTLY (manner adjunct/subjunct emphasizer), INEVITABLY (content disjunct/subjunct emphasizer), OF COURSE (content disjunct/subjunct emphasizer) and POSSIBLY (content disjunct/subjunct intensifier) as syntactic homonyms, in their respective roles as disjuncts and subjuncts:

(306)   Not infrequently in controversy we encounter definitions which cannot honestly be regarded as corresponding to ordinary usage. (J 1975: 454)

(307)   I honestly would not have minded, because I know apprentices are exploited. (J 1975: 141)

(308)   Inevitably, there will be those who see only the earthen vessels. (W.9.2.281)

(309)   As prices go on rising and the value of money declines (as, it seems to me, must inevitably happen) . . . (W.11.2.147)

(310)   Of course, if anyone knows of any vacant office space where we could also house our growing collection of paraphernalia at a very low cost or free, then that news would be welcome too. (W.6.5.16)

(311)   there "must of course be a 'post'script to all this# (S.12.1.531)

(312)   Possibly you might try the effect of the slow release preparation of Indomethacin . . . (W.7.13.86)

(313)   "no it couldn't pòssibly 'happen twíce# (S.9.1.1125)

4.5.3 Modal adverbs or modal particles?

The familiarity of the term 'adverb' belies its reputation as the most problematical of all word classes to define; the properties of invariability of form, scope of modification, optionality versus peripherality, and transmobility are all valid criterial notions but none is a necessary or sufficient condition for membership of the category of adverb. Adverbs are invariable and have a fixed form of realization (allowing for such derivational variation as the formation of the comparative) but so do adjectives. Their scope is determined by a host of variables (context of utterance, stylistic choice, information structure, and so on) and certainly not just restricted to the modification of the verb, as the term 'adverb' misleadingly implies. Not all adverbs are optional; some may be obligatory (such as the locative adverb in 'Ann is here'). Whilst English generally favours the 'middle field' for adverb placement, adverbs have considerable freedom of movement in relation to clause structure. Despite such heterogeneity, there has been widespread consensus about when a word is an adverb, even when there are differences over terminology and approaches to classification, because of the default status accorded this category.

Recently, however, a number of linguists have proposed that certain categories of adverb, primarily those adverbs with only faint shades of meaning, be treated as 'particles'. In English, the term 'particle' is used in grammatical description to refer to words like UP, OUT, OVER (see the CGEL: 1151f) which combine with a verb to form a separate lexical item, such as TO LOOK OVER, but which in themselves are rather abstract in meaning and usually context-dependent for their interpretation. Languages such as Classical Greek, Russian and German have a much wider range of particles than English. Particles are distinguished from other uninflecting word classes, such as adverbs, primarily on the grounds that they are a closed class, have multiple membership of several word classes, are restricted to the so-called 'middle field' in clause structure and, unlike adverbs, prepositions, and conjunctions, behave as function words, that is words whose role is largely or wholly grammatical. In practice, the delimitation of particles from other invariables is highly controversial: definitions of 'particle' vary, and even then the extent of their lexical redundancy defies semantic description. But, particles can be identified: modern descriptions of German regularly identify over twenty modal particles. The concept of 'modal particle' is relevant to the classification of modal adverbs in English because, as we have seen, according to the degree of their integration in clause structure and the nature of their association with the modal verb head, they display various degrees of lexical redundancy and grammaticalization.

The distinction between particle and adverb broadly matches the division between subjunct and disjunct. Subjuncts have maximally lost semantic content and become increasingly grammaticalized, whereas disjuncts more clearly express lexical meanings in their characterization of the speaker's orientation, comment-wise or content-wise, towards his utterance. The meaning subjuncts convey, if they can be said to convey meaning at all, is to be found not so much in their semantic make-up as in their use: they focalize and thereby reinforce the modal verb in a way that has a perceptible effect on the sentence as a whole. CERTAINLY, JUST, REALLY and SIMPLY, the most lexically reduced items of the subjunct emphasizer set, come close to the notion of modal particle in English, especially in the environment of negated modals, where they are maximally redundant as regards independence of meaning (see note 3 to this chapter, and also 4.3.2.1):

(314)   While greater resources is not the only solution, it certainly must be regarded as a principal one.
(J 1975: 295)

(315)   You just can't convict a man on evidence like that – you can't. (J 1975: 272)

(316)   She really could not remember the words, but she supposed that the scene was true and that he actually remembered. (J 1975: 306)

(317)   Finally, mail order simply cannot generate enough buying power to keep a business going. (J 1975: 282)

When adverbs combine with modals to form idiomatic expressions, as in MIGHT/MIGHT WELL (emphasizer) or COULDN'T/ CAN'T POSSIBLY (intensifier), the process of delexicalization, integration and grammaticalization has moved a step further. In the restricted environment of MIGHT or MAY, WELL signifies a transformation in the epistemic value of the auxiliary, which now denotes probability rather than possibility, and thus alters the status of the speaker's attitude and commitment towards the 'known facts':

(318)   We are told that Ezekiel 38 and 39 may well be describing Russia and the mighty power of Communism.
(J 1975: 347)

Restricted in this role to non-assertive contexts, the function of POSSIBLY in the environment of the modals COULD and CAN is to intensify; no essential shift in meaning takes place, but whereas POSSIBLY otherwise denotes uncertainty, here it signifies the reverse:

(319)   No man who rises to command of a United States naval ship can possibly be a coward. (J 1975: 57)

(320)   They cannot possibly repair their losses. (J 1964: 318)

(321)   What could he possibly tell him which would pass for valuable information. (J 1964: 318)

CLEARLY, EVIDENTLY, INEVITABLY, and OBVIOUSLY behave in a similar way in the environment of MUST (see 4.3.2.5): they assign the epistemic system an evidential dimension (see 3.4.3) and are consequently more loaded for meaning than other modal subjuncts, although they still retain their function as emphasizers:

(322)   In these circumstances, the Government must clearly rely on a full turnout . . . of the payroll vote. (W.12.3.19)

(323)   They must evidently be related.

(324)   Color customs in America (and elsewhere) inevitably will yield to the larger realities of today and tomorrow. (J 1975: 175)

(325)   In addition to these primary functions, each State obviously must maintain a legal department, a department of finance and taxation, and certain record offices. (J 1975: 296)

(326)   Nevertheless, metaphysics has to begin with something, and since it obviously cannot begin with things that are proved, it must begin with things that are believed. (J 1975: 364)

Of course, none of the items discussed here is fully grammaticalized with, say, the equivalent status of a verbal inflection: inflectional mood as represented, for instance, by the subjunctive, is a clear example of a grammatical category. But as Palmer (1986: 5) suggests, 'grammaticalization is a matter of degree, of more or less rather than yes or no'. As we have seen, there are syntactic restrictions which determine the status and function of subjuncts and which define them as a limited and not an open-ended class of items. The extent to which they have become delexicalized is a measure of the extent to which they have become grammatically and semantically dependent on their modal verb heads. The nature of that dependency can be demonstrated by contrasting subjuncts with their homonymous forms as disjuncts, or adjuncts, as in examples (306) to (313) above.

It would not be implausible to redefine subjuncts expressing modality as 'modal particles', subdivided into the following categories: evidential particles (CLEARLY, OBVIOUSLY); hearsay particles (APPARENTLY); reinforcement or emphasizing particles (CERTAINLY, SURELY, WELL); and focus particles (ONLY, SIMPLY). The grounds for doing so involve both syntactic and semantic criteria. Syntactically, modal particles are integrated with their modal verb head and are thus restricted to medial position and the verb phrase; they are a limited rather than an open class range of items; and they are polyfunctional in that most may additionally function as sentence adverbs (adjuncts or disjuncts) according to their position in the sentence and the general context. Semantically, modal particles express abstract sense relations rather than literal meanings. This accounts for the collocational versatility of such prototypical emphasizers as REALLY and SIMPLY. Ultimately, it may be more appropriate to consider modal particles as a special subset of modal adverbs rather than as an entirely separate word class and to define them according to their use rather than in terms of any meanings they might possibly convey. What is clear is that there are grounds for distinguishing the subjunct class of items from other, more lexically loaded types of adverb, and for recognizing their unique characteristics in the environment of their modal verb heads.

4.5.4 The pragmatic dimension of modal adverbs

The occurrence and placement of adverbs cannot be accounted for by reference to syntactic and semantic explanations alone: their distribution and function are also determined by pragmatic or discourse considerations and are thus influenced by a range of contextual factors such as the relationship between the speaker and addressee, their respective attitudes, beliefs and individual motivation, the topic under discussion, the setting where the linguistic interaction takes place, and so forth. These constraining factors have often been overlooked and the placement of sentence-modifiers seen as a random process, principally on account of their optional syntactic status in clause structure. As a general rule, sentence adverbs (disjuncts) have the characteristic functions of indicating the speaker's degree of affinity or commitment to the proposition being conveyed, or interpreting what is said (or written) to the addressee (the hearer or reader) by encouraging a particular reaction. Initial, medial and final positions can all be associated with these functions and the overt marking of speaker presence and subjectivity.

Indication of the speaker's attitude is most pronounced and its scope least ambivalent when the adverb is placed initially; it immediately establishes the speaker's authority and the stance he wishes to adopt towards what he is about to say. He may well have a vested interest in securing the addressee's acceptance of his point of view: the manipulative use of adverbs (and adverbials in general) is commonly encountered in situations 'where speakers have something to gain or lose by their addressee's acceptance or rejection of what they are saying' (Corum 1975: 134).[21] Assertions which involve the use of adverbs like OBVIOUSLY, CLEARLY, NATURALLY may be uttered rhetorically in an attempt to persuade, influence or please. The content of the adjoining proposition may be anything but obvious, clear, or a matter of course from the addressee's point of view:

(327)   Obviously one of the two must have been a better candidate. (J 1964: 306)

(328)   Clearly they should exercise ordinary civil and criminal jurisdiction. (J 1964: 241)

(329)   Naturally, if you're thinking about the country we shall have to go back and run through this whole matter over again. (J 1964: 297)

When in initial position, factive adverbs – that is, adverbs which express the speaker's value judgement (see 4.4.2.2) and presuppose the truth of the adjoining proposition – render the speaker's assertion all the more forceful and, like modal adverbs in general, can be used in a manipulative sense 'to seduce the addressee into believing the content of the proposition' (Corum: op. cit.).

When tagged on in end position, sentential adverbs again signal speaker presence. The tagging of modal adverbs is unusual because end position is mainly reserved for other types of adverbial, such as those conveying the notions of time, place or manner; they are more lexically weighted and more suited to their role as carriers of new information. Tagging often gives the modal adverb a contextual prominence it would otherwise lack and may have the fundamental purpose of signalling to the addressee that his acquiescence with respect to the content of the proposition is openly being sought:

(330)   No, Nox, you are here for more than learning. You will absorb knowledge, certainly. At least I hope you will. (H 1969: 191)

(331)   We must write it down a failure, definitely. (H 1969: 196)

(332)   I am afraid she will be upset, though I shall make a point of explaining things to her after lunch, naturally. (H 1969: 218)

The interpolation of a modal adverb in mid-sentence often has the effect of focalizing the modal verb head, which is then highlighted, or even emphasized if indubitative adverbs are involved. An interpolated adverb may appear to function as if it were an incidental component, used only to give information in passing and having no significant bearing on the basic message being conveyed. This may of course be the case: modal adverbs are more or less incidental or essential components of sentences, according to the contexts in which they are used. However, the apparent casualness with which adverbs can be interpolated, possibly to add emotional overtones or to make the propositional content sound more acceptable, may be deceptive and the speaker's strategy nothing less than a subtle manoeuvre to obtain a given response from the addressee:

(333)   Dear me! That means, conceivably, they might fail to send you a card. But I'll see to it. (H 1969: 139)

(334)   Why hadn't they told her who the other nominees were? There was no particular reason why they should, perhaps, but it somehow looked odd when they didn't. (H 1969: 147)

(335)   Editors choose the Quarto reading, arguing, presumably, that Shakespeare would have chosen the common, proverbial phrase 'last but not least'. (H 1969: 148)

On other occasions, the speaker may wish to at least appear to dissociate himself from his source: this could simply be the recognition that the available evidence is second-hand and insufficient to warrant more than a tentative assessment, or it may be that there is genuine doubt as to the veracity of what is being reported. Evidential adverbs are frequently used in this way (see 4.4.2.2). In his discussion of the connection between adverb placement, medium, text category and stylistic province, Jacobson (1975: 164) refers to the role of adverbs in the discourse of newspaper reports. He suggests that the most plausible reason for the greater frequency in medial position of adverbs like APPARENTLY and PROBABLY in this text category, as opposed to other types of discourse, 'is that newspaper editors and journalists in their discussion of current events often find it necessary to emphasize that they have not had sufficient time for thorough penetration of a subject and therefore have to tell their readers only what appears to be the truth'. The use of these adverbs relegates the adjoining proposition to the realm of hearsay by clearly dissociating the speaker from the source of his information and attributing it to others. Fairclough (1995: 131) argues that even relatively extensive modalization of media texts does not diminish their authoritativeness because it evokes 'the cautious (and authoritative) discourse of science and other academic disciplines in their careful specification of probabilities'. Carefully formulated expressions of the speaker's relative doubt lend the discourse official status and may even reflect official influence upon the formulation of media reports.

The functional significance of medial position is developed by Jacobson in a later study (1978) in which modal adverbs are associated with the following categories of use: to mark a conclusion, signal confirmation or correction, indicate sincerity, make an evaluation, and signal illocutionary force:

(336)   Christine will probably/undoubtedly be coming.

(337)   Although they were found guilty, it now seems that they must actually have been innocent.

(338)   The company frankly couldn't condone that sort of behaviour, so he was dismissed.

(339)   She, fortunately, will probably be released tomorrow.

(340)   Could you please close the window?

Reference is also made to their roles as intensifiers, emphasizers, and markers of courtesy. Contexts of use are specified in only the broadest of terms. In connection with the epistemic function of marking of a conclusion, for instance, Jacobson suggests that 'if the evidence is clear, the force of the conclusion is usually not marked in any special way' (1978: 22). Thus:

(341)   Christine will arrive before long.

is based on the speaker's assumption and involves no explicit reference to the evidence by which such a conclusion has been reached. Where he suspects the addressee may doubt the content of the proposition, he may be motivated to thematize, interpolate or tag an appropriate adverb to strengthen his assertion:

(342)   Christine will undoubtedly arrive before long.

Conversely, if the nature of the evidence leaves room for doubt, a dubitative adverb can be used:

(343)   Christine will probably arrive before long.

While pertinent, the categories described are based on highly conventionalized instances of potential language use and the different contextual factors influencing speaker motivation and addressee interpretation are left largely unexplored. However, Jacobson does refer to the use of modal adverbs for manipulative purposes, recalling Corum's observation that: 'The TV news commentator, the columnist, and the politician all exploit [the manipulative] use of sentential adverbs . . . to lend strength to their assertions' (1975: 134). The pragmatic function of these adverbs may therefore be at variance with their inherent content: the more indiscriminately they are used, the more 'diluted' their literal meanings become.

Where the modal auxiliary functions as a pragmatic particle (see 3.5.1), the modal adverb interacts synergetically, serving to reinforce, focus, highlight or soften impositive force at the semantic level, in the service of the speaker's design and intentions at the pragmatic level. Jacobson's exploration of the association between position, effect and use convincingly demonstrates the interdependency of syntactic and semantic factors and the pragmatic behaviour of modal adverbs in modal environments.

4.6 INTONATION AND MODALITY

Intonation signals the division of undifferentiated speech into tone units or intonation phrases which are usually co-extensive with grammatical structures, be these realized as a single item, a clause or an entire sentence. The pitch patterns associated with intonation give prominence to a syllable within the tone unit, thereby highlighting the relative communicative value of the item(s) involved. The shape of the tunes or 'melodies' produced by variations in pitch convey a range of attitudinal meanings which interact with those expressed lexically in the utterance. The most important pitch movements are associated with different types of nuclear tone and each type conveys a range of meanings which vary, to a greater or lesser extent, according to the context.

The meanings of nuclear tones which convey modal values are either attitudinal and indicate the speaker's doubt or certainty, or semantic and co-occur with lexical meanings which have a reinforcing or limiting effect, such as those expressed by content disjuncts and subjuncts. The attitudinal aspect of intonation is probably the most difficult of all to characterize. Firstly, there is no agreed list of descriptive labels applicable to different attitudes and, secondly and more importantly, the same intonation pattern may have different meanings or signal different attitudes in different contexts. The point is taken up by Cruttenden (1994: 243):

> ... it should be remembered that the attitudinal meaning of an utterance must always be interpreted within a context, both of the situation and also of the speaker's personality. It may well happen that an intonation which is neutral in one set of circumstances might, for instance, be offensive or patronizing when used by another person or in other circumstances.

The 'local' meanings of nuclear tones in English – that is, meanings associated with isolated utterances – were outlined in Chapter 1, section 1.3.1 and these are now examined in relation to modal contexts. For the convenience of the reader, the key to the prosodic notation used is repeated below:

Onset stress	:	"
Normal stress	:	'
Tone unit boundary	:	#

Nuclear stress
Fall   : `
Rise   : ´
Fall–rise   : ˇ
Rise–fall   : ^
Fall + rise : `+´
Rise + fall : ´+`

4.6.1 Intonation and the modals

Coates (1983: 6) records the fact that, despite the recognition in theoretical linguistics of the primacy of speech, surprisingly little attention has been paid to the expression of modality in spoken English. Palmer (1979) was the first account to use spoken examples but both in this and his later edition of the work (1990), he deliberately excludes prosodic and paralinguistic information chiefly on the grounds that 'it is, a little surprisingly, almost completely irrelevant to a study of the modals' (Palmer 1990: 26). The results of Coates' study, and our own investigations in this area, refute Palmer's findings, although in his typological survey on modality (1986) he does acknowledge that 'intonation and other prosodic features . . . can clearly be regarded as modality in a purely semantic sense. Indeed, doubt and lack of commitment are often expressed by intonation in English.'

At the root of Palmer's disquiet is the fact that, while there are statistical correlations between stress patterns and the different types of modality expressed, stress, including nuclear stress, is not a formal indexation of modal contrasts in any grammatical sense, because there is no one-to-one correspondence between a particular intonation and the formal realization of a modal value. As Cruttenden (1986: 96) remarks, 'it is not difficult to find examples, at least in English, of almost any nuclear tone combined with any syntactic type'. However, the expression of modality by modals and adverbs, individually or in combination, does interact with the linguistic category of intonation, and patterns do emerge, even if these merely indicate probabilistic tendencies within the range of intonational choices available.

The most striking correlation between intonational pattern and modal expression occurs in the case of epistemic modality.[22] This can be regularly associated with the fall–rise or fall–plus–rise intonations used in what the CGEL (1600) refers to as 'contingency' environments, even though the lexical carriers of modality do not necessarily attract stress themselves:

(344)   I "think it's unlĭkely actually# but he "might 'do it todăy# (S.8.1a.18)

(345)   I "may be wrŏng# (S.1.2.38)

(346)   well you "ought to 'have some 'thing to kèep réally# for your "twenty-first# (S.7.2.1247/8)

(347)   he "used to 'come in 'regularly and collĕct them# but we "think he must nŏw have 'gone 'back# to Ni"gèria# (S.8.3.1086/7/8)

(348)   B: "Gŏd#
        A: they 'can't there "must be a 'lot more 'to it than thăt# I'm "sùre it 'wasn't just thát# (S.2.14.860/1/2)

This is not to say, of course, that modal expressions are unstressed or even that they may not take the nuclear stress:

(349)   B: there's an A. C. on Mònday ísn't there#
        A: "think there mùst be mústn't there#
        B: "or was it làst Monday# (S.7.2.L.9) (cited in Coates 1983: 49)

(350)   "wéll# I "think it shòuld be quite 'good 'actually# I mean 'it's a ter'rific thĭng# (S.7.3.712/3/4)

(351)   I "don't know what I'd 'do if she lĕft# she "wĭll of 'course# (S.1.8.295)

The CGEL (1372) records that the fall–rise nucleus on epistemic modals 'often signals a contrast between the supposed real state of affairs, and a state of affairs thought desirable or likely':

(352)   The op"inion 'polls măy be 'right# ['but I suspect they're not']

This is also a matter of focus which we discuss further below. The contrastive potential applies primarily to unmodified modals, so that a similar inference is implausible in:

(353)   The o"pinion 'polls mǎy 'well be 'right# ['but I suspect they're not']

Example (348) illustrates the difficulty in attaching a meaningful or at least all-embracing attitudinal label to the fall–rise (or any other tone); the context reveals not only A's sense of reservation, but additionally there appear to be extralinguistic conditioning factors creating a sense of urgency or dismay; from a pragmatic point of view, these latter emotions may carry more significance than the expression of the speaker's reserve. No one abstract basic meaning has the explanatory power to characterize the use of the fall–rise in this dialogue.

Coates' (1983: *passim*) compilation of data on the patterns of stress associated with individual modal forms suggests that the modals which regularly express epistemic meanings, COULD, MIGHT, MAY and MUST, normally receive some kind of stress and that they can be regularly associated with fall–rise or fall–plus–rise intonation, as a number of the preceding illustrations have shown. By contrast, the percentage of stressed modals expressing non-epistemic meanings is considerably lower:

(354)   well ap"parently I càn# because "Hàrold said what 'I was in a po'sition to 'do# (S.1.5.961/2)

(355)   "well a vèry little# because I "really mǔst be getting 'home in a móment# (S.2.2.830/1)

Obviously, Coates' findings must be treated with circumspection because statistical trends are at best probabilistic and not wholly reliable given the finite extent of the corpus data consulted. But they do provide further empirical evidence to support the recognition of epistemic modality as a distinct semantic category. Non-epistemic modality, as we have seen, is far less homogeneous and covers a wider semantic range; the interaction with intonation is too varied for any ready conclusions to be drawn.

4.6.2 Intonation and modal adverbs

In spoken English, the prominence of an adverbial in a clause is signalled not primarily by its syntactic and lexical statuses but rather by its stress and intonation. These linguistic features operate synergetically to mark the relative communicative significance of the adverbial in its clausal context, and as a result they index its degree of peripherality or integration in grammatical structure.

Modal adverbs which have a reinforcing role, subjunct emphasizers and some intensifiers (see 4.3.2), regularly receive emphatic intonation (corresponding to the writer's use of italics in written English), commonly in the form of a fall:

(356)   and "this is what you 'know I 'think we rèally 'ought to#
        to "qùestion 'very 'very stròngly# (S5.7.870/1)

(357)   "wèll# it "cèrtainly would re'strìct it# I mean you
        "couldn't de'velop on the èast side of 'Sete very 'well#
        (S.2.13.895/6/7)

(358)   A: be "very 'kìnd#
        B: "of 'còurse I will# (S.8.4.505/6)

(359)   and we "used to thìnk# "oh that 'couldn't 'pòssibly 'be#
        our "soldiers are 'thère# (S.6.6.453/4/5)

In (356) and (357) the adverb is given additional prominence by its placement in pre-auxiliary position at *iM*. Alternatively, the adverb may be given less prominence and attract only normal or onset stress:

(360)   "they would 'rănge# from "people who 'really 'wŏuld
        say# the "thing to do with 'strikers is to shòot them#
        (S.2.11.573/4/5)

(361)   and "time's 'running òut# we "really 'mŭst get it con-
        'clùded# "mùstn't we# (S.5.11.339/40)

The item focused by focusing subjuncts is also clearly discriminated by intonation, where in writing there can be uncertainty (see CGEL: 605):

(362)   I "merely said he 'còuld go# not that he "shòuld#

While tone units tend to correlate with quite large syntactic constituents, realized as an independent clause or the main clause in complex sentences, they may also correspond with smaller units, such as sentence-modifying adverbs like content (attitudinal) disjuncts. In general use, adverbs which express dubitative meanings (see 4.4.2, type B) and which have their own separate tone unit can be associated with the fall–rise regardless of whether they occur initially, medially, or finally:

(363)   "prŏbably# I "would im'agine she ĭs in 'fact# (S.2.14.719)

By contrast, adverbs of an indubitative or assertive character (4.4.2, types A and C) more often take a falling intonation:

(364)   oh "maps 'must have exĭsted# cèrtainly# (S.2.3.72/3)

There were relatively few examples of modal adverbs occupying their own intonation group actually attested in the spoken data of the Survey. In the environment of modal verb heads, it is more common for sentential modal adverbs to occur within the same tone unit. The general tendency for dubitatives to receive a fall–rise and indubitatives a fall still applies, although other stress patterns do occur, which correspond with clausal meaning, speaker intent and speaker–listener relations (see 4.6.3):

(365)   if "Carol thìnks that we 'ought to 'look at him# per"hǎps we should 'look at him# (S.2.6.1130/1)

(366)   it would "prŏbably be# a "little more mòney# (S.8.1.494/5)

(367)   "and I as'sure the 'honourable géntleman# "we shall be 'giving it 'very 'very 'careful 'thought indèed# (S.11.4.294/5)

(368)   and "this is what you 'know I 'think we 'rèally 'ought to# to "quèstion 'very 'very stròngly# (S.5.7.870/1)

(369)   "that could indĕed 'lead to 'strangulàtion# (S.11.4280)

(370)   "I 'think most of the women in this àudience# would prôbably agree# with "mé# (S.5.4.579/80/81)

In all of these examples, the adverb is marked for maximal prominence because it carries the nuclear tone; otherwise, it may simply receive normal or onset stress. In the majority of cases, the adverb is stressed in some way, as a sign of its relative communicative importance:

(371)   well I "think 'Geoffrey perfectly rêalized 'this# I mean âctually I tóld him 'that quite 'possibly it didn't I mean

there's 'no reason why it 'should 'maybe# come "over in
this prŏgramme# (S.2.14.562/3/4)

4.6.3 Intonation and co-occurrence

Modal–adverb combinations generate a variety of intonation
patterns and, again, the most marked correspondence is the
association of these forms with the fall–rise or fall–plus–rise
intonations in epistemic contexts. Both subjuncts and disjuncts
(regardless of position) are regularly involved:

(372)   and we'd been "talking to 'hèr# it may "well have bĕen#
        that "we'd have been 'able to 'help 'hèr to sée#
        (S.6.5.526/7/8)

(373)   it "may wèll bé# that "there were faults# (S.12.4.1120/1)

(374)   they must "surely ap'ply this to pèacetime cónditions#
        (S.2.3.1103)

(375)   oh "maps 'must have exìsted# cèrtainly# (S.2.3.72/3)

(376)   because I "think they 'wìll# and "must strìke in fãct# at
        the "ròots# (S.11.2.910/11/12)

(377)   "and of'course it 'may ălso pro'vide you# with "topics for
        the philòlogy 'paper 'then# (S.6.2.132/3)

(378)   I "think it 'shòuld be quite 'good áctually# I mean 'it's a
        ter'rific thìng# (S.7.3.713/14)

(379)   you'd prŏbably 'have some 'other 'reason# "I don't
        knòw# (S.2.14.788/9)

(380)   I "don't know what I'd 'do if she 'lĕft# she "wìll of
        'course# (S.1.8.294/5)

There is also a noticeable correspondence between the falling
tone, fall–plus–rise, onset and normal stress and the emphasis or
intensification of negated modals, whether epistemic or nonepistemic (see 4.3.2.1):

(381)   it "cèrtainly would re'strict it# (S.2.13.896)

(382)   B: "wèll# one "just mustn't mînd#

A: I "don't mind 'being re'corded 'surreptĭtiously#
(S.2.5.756/7/8)

(387) and "he lost 'four pints of blòod# and he "bloody well
shouldn't have púlled through# (S.2.12.186/7)

(384) then you "shouldn't go 'in for it at àll# (S.5.10.306)

(385) but al"ready 'I was beginning to thĭnk# I "cannot pòssibly
'stay# in a "hospital in Mŏscow# (S.6.6.239/40/41)

(386) "no it couldn't pòssibly 'happen twíce# (S9.1.1125)

The correlation between a falling tone and the intensification of
the negated modals in the above examples could be regarded as an
intonational idiom, to the extent that the lexical sequence of
negated modal and intensifier are yoked to a particular pitch
pattern.

The reinforcing effect of the fall is marked in contexts where
several nuclei follow in rapid succession to emphasize the speaker's
sense of urgency:

(387) "I còuldn't# "literally còuldn't# "stay to the ènd#
(S.2.5.277/8/9)

Gimson (1980: 279f) explains that:

> Such a series of nuclear syllables, often occurring rhythmically at
> equal intervals of time, may produce an effect of a categoric,
> downright, hectoring, insistent, self-assertive way of speaking.
> Nevertheless, such multi-nuclear patterns are extremely com-
> mon in ordinary conversation and often serve no other purpose
> than to produce a lively, animated effect . . . .

The communicative value of modal–adverb combinations in
spoken language is conveyed not only by their lexical and
grammatical status but also by their associated intonational patterns.
Except for the general correspondences outlined in this and
previous sections, the patterns used by a speaker vary, often having
significant implications for meaning; such conditioning factors as
speaker–listener relationships, the role of the preceding utterances,
and the physical circumstances of communication are all contextually influential but their relative importance has not yet been
fully described. Cruttenden (1986: 112f) observes that: 'the

question of what actually brings about ... slight or considerable variation in meaning ... is a very ill-understood area of intonational and pragmatic study'. This is not to deny the validity of the correspondences in meaning outlined here, such as the association between the fall–rise and the expression of doubt or conviction in epistemic contexts, but they are not hard-and-fast and other tonetic meanings may additionally become intertwined.

The placement of a simple or complex nuclear tone on the modal or the adverb, or a compound tone spanning both, is the intonational means of focusing the item(s) in question. In English, it is the principal means of doing so; lexical and grammatical means are less pervasive (see Cruttenden 1986: 80f). The item(s) highlighted by the nucleus corresponds to a piece of information, and the tone unit in which it occurs is co-extensive with an information unit. The word 'information' is used in a very broad sense to cover referential and abstract meanings, events, states of affairs and adverbial frames. However, the correspondence is less direct between intonational prominence and information value because, as the CGEL (1357) points out:

> Prominence by stress or intonation is realized on a *syllable*, a unit that has no necessary correlation with meaning, let alone information value ... The effect of prosodic prominence is to draw attention to the semantic unit within which the prominent syllable occurs ... and hence to give that unit information prominence.

In the second tone unit in the following example (the first is supplied to give it some context):

(388)   does he "want me to cŏme for the 'day# I probably "will 'anyway áctually# (S.8.3.505/6)

the effect of the nuclear tone and other less prominent forms of stress is to highlight the modality of the utterance and in this example to convey the relative strength of the speaker's declared intention. Altering the intonation – for example, focusing the personal pronoun 'I' rather than the modal expressions in the above example – would change the information focus of the tone unit and hence the general meaning conveyed.

Generally, what is focused is 'new' information and what is left unfocused is 'given' information. Given information is basically what a sentence is about: it constitutes what the speaker assumes the listener is already aware of and is usually a combination of linguistically given information (basically what has been said before), known as the 'theme', and contextually given information (extralinguistic clues provided by the physical situation in which the communication actually takes place). Given information normally provides enough context for the new information to be readily and unambiguously understood: new information is the actual point of the communication (or 'message') to which the listener is expected to pay special attention and is · focused by intonation accordingly.

The informational value of modal–adverb expressions resides in their potential to characterize the speaker's attitude or disposition towards states-of-affairs or events (see Chaper 2, section 2.4.2). Prominence is ascribed to the attitudinal dimension of an utterance where attitude rather than propositional content or the realization of an event is the focus of the message:

(389)   it "may wèll bé# that "there were faults# (S.12.4.1120/1)

(390)   "I còuldn't# "literally còuldn't# "stay to the ènd# (S.2.5.277/8/9)

Even where modal–adverb combinations are not marked by a nuclear tone for maximal prominence, their association with particular types of tone still gives them informational value. In modal environments, therefore, nucleus placement alone does not necessarily indicate the scope of focus.

The identification and description of the intonational patterns which regularly co-occur with the modals and their adverb satellites, individually and in combination, demonstrates the importance of including spoken analysis in a linguistic account of modality. In general, modal-adverb expressions which are used epistemically often attract some type of stress and, even if neither element receives the nucleus, either or both can usually be associated with it, and in particular the fall–rise and its compound equivalent.

The interaction of intonation with grammatical and lexical carriers of modality allows for subtle variations in the way modal contrasts are expressed, and further enables the speaker to tinge his utterance with the desired overtones or to inject it with an appropriate measure of innuendo. Modality is an elusive phenomenon and by its nature ambivalent: however, it is this very ambivalence which speakers can actively exploit in pursuit of their desired communicative goals.

NOTES

1 Bache and Davidsen-Nielsen (1995: 59) point out that: 'Traditionally, the adverbial is regarded as the *default* sentence function in the sense that it characterizes any function at sentence level that is *not* a subject, predicator [the verb phrase], object or complement.'

2 The different types of adverbial realization are distributed with widely different frequencies in the SEU: closed class items, account for about 40 per cent of all occurrences in both speech and writing. See the CGEL (501).

3 In traditional grammatical classifications, a distinction is drawn between closed class and open class items – that is, between sets of items which have a finite membership (prepositions, pronouns, determiners, conjunctions, modals and primary verbs) and those where membership is in principle unlimited and indefinitely extendable (nouns, objectives, full verbs and adverbs). The distinction between open and closed word classes, however, must be treated with caution. Adverbs *typically* belong to the open class category but not exclusively so: several items constitute a closed subsystem. The latter consists primarily of the common monosyllabic adverbs such as JUST, NOW, THEN, WELL, and frozen prepositional phrases like OF COURSE (cf. MAYBE), which function as single units. The meaning of closed class items is closely linked with that of the construction of which they form a part: for instance, the meaning of the constituent WELL in the modal idiom MAY WELL ('They may well have forgotten') is entirely dependent on its combination with the modal verb head. The reduction in its independent lexical status suggests that it could be treated as a particle. See the CGEL (71f) for further discussion of the two word class categories and section 4.5.3 in this book for an examination of the modal adverb/particle question.

4 Adverbials express a wide range of semantic roles; see the CGEL (479f).

5 The adverbial category is extremely heterogeneous in terms of semantic role, grammatical function, formal realization and linear position. Adverbials vary considerably in their relative centrality/peripherality. Most are highly mobile and optional, and can be

omitted or moved to another position without this affecting the grammatical integrity of the clause in which they occur: '(*Sometimes,*) They (?*sometimes*) would (*sometimes*) take (*sometimes) a walk (?*sometimes*) along (?*sometimes*) the (*sometimes) seashore (*sometimes*).' Some adverbials however, are less mobile and others still are obligatory and essential to the specification of the verb: '*(*Downstairs*) They (*downstairs) might (*downstairs) be (*downstairs*); 'They'll be playing *down by the lake*'. See the CGEL (51f).

6   It is noted in the CGEL (478n) that the adverbial element is the next most frequent after subject and verb, and that there are approximately 15 adverbials every 100 running words in the spoken and written material of the Survey of English Usage corpus. In his comments on frequency, Crystal (1980: 153f) demonstrates that for a sentence in English not to include an adverbial is the exception not the rule; 59 per cent of clauses in his spoken language material contain at least one adverbial. The statistic points to the general significance of adverbials in discourse and their relatively high frequency in speech as opposed to writing. Certainly, modal–adverb co-occurrence is more common in speech, although overall frequencies vary according to the source of the data, the communicative aims and stylistic preferences of the speaker/writer, the subject, and genre. For example, in the supplementary data, drawn primarily from recent novels, frequencies of modal–adverb co-occurrence range from 3 to 26 co-occurrences per 80,000 words in our chosen sample. In English, the adverbial has a particularly heavy workload, possibly to match the range of its realization types.

In what can be understood as support for a corpus-based approach to the treatment of adverbials and in recognition of their relatively high frequency of occurrence, Crystal also observes that when contrived data are cited in sentence grammar, adverbials are usually omitted from clause structure unless they are being specifically discussed.

7   From a personal communication quoted by Perkins (1983: 104).

8   The CGEL (485) uses 'approximation' in a different sense to refer to the middle ground between emphasis on the positive or negative poles of a statement:

(a)   They must certainly have been happy with their pay award.
(b)   They may well have been happy with their pay award.
(c)   They could hardly have been happy with their pay award.
(d)   They can't have been happy with their pay award at all.

9   Generally, courtesy subjuncts do not carry nuclear stress or occupy a

separate tone unit unless the speaker has reason for insisting (which might suggest irritability, for instance); see 4.6.

10   Where REALLY falls within the scope of clause negation as in : 'It couldn't really be done, you know', the effect is to slightly reduce the force of the negation.

11   Bache (private communication) has suggested the following as a working definition of the subjunct category of adverbial: 'A subjunct may be defined as any one-word realization of the adverbial element which occurs non-parenthetically at M (or a variant of M) and which cannot be focalized by means of a cleft sentence.'

12   See Swan (1987: 513f) for a detailed treatment of adverbial shifts and the influence this has on the syntactic and semantic status of adverbs.

13   See Chapter 3, note 15.

14   In the environment of CAN, EASILY and READILY are ambivalent; when the modal co-occurs with verbs of saying or thinking, the latter may exert a stronger pull than the modal. Contrast:

(a)   I may well accept that excuse.
      [It is possible that I will accept it]

(b)   I can readily [well] accept that excuse.
      [It is possible for me to fully accept it]

See Bolinger (1972a: 40f).

15   These items occur as dependents within adverb phrase structure, where the adverb functions as head. They are omissible but the head is obligatory: 'They WILL (MOST) PROBABLY be there this evening', *'They will MOST be there this evening'.

16   See Palmer (1990: *passim*; 1986: 30f) and Perkins (1983: 111f) for treatment of the interrelationship between interrogatives and modality.

17   Bellert (1977: 344) argues that adverbs such as PERHAPS 'are not purely modal' because they 'have an additional meaning component'. In the case of PERHAPS, there is 'an implication that gives a suggestion as to a possible answer':

(a)   Has John PERHAPS been here before?

(b)   Have you PERHAPS misunderstood the question?

Yet there are plenty of examples where there is no such implication, as in the following epistemic context:

(c)   They may perhaps stimulate him to a higher pitch of sensitiveness than I am capable of myself. (J 1964: 316)

In support of her claim, Bellert adduces that purely modal adverbs do not occur in questions: PERHAPS, which is not purely modal, does. But what is a purely modal adverb? Consider:

(d)   COULD he POSSIBLY do it later?

(e)   WILL they CERTAINLY be there?

See the discussion in 4.3.3.4.

18   See Schreiber (1971: 94f) and Bellert (1977: 343) for distinctions between their definition of modal adverbs (content disjuncts expressing conviction or doubt) and evaluatives (content disjuncts expressing value judgement). They note, for instance, that adverbs of likelihood have no corresponding negative forms (*IMPROBABLY), while evaluatives do (UNFORTUNATELY), although they may combine with ENOUGH: IMPROBABLY ENOUGH. UNDOUBTEDLY contains a negative morpheme but is not negative in meaning.

19   See Chapter 3, note 19.

20   See Lyons (1977: 550f) for further discussion of homonymy and polysemy.

21   Corum (1975: 134) suggests that the language of courtroom advocacy is a paradigm example of the manipulative use of sentential adverbs; the way counsel uses language to plead his case has a significant effect on the jury.

22   Coates (1983: 246) suggests prosodic contrasts, such as the fall–rise, may serve as a diagnostic for disambiguating between epistemic and deontic readings.

Five

Modal–adverb collocations in English with reference to Spanish

5.1 GENERAL INTRODUCTION

In the previous chapters, to which the present is by way of an addendum, we presented a detailed analysis of modal–adverb combinations in terms of their syntax, semantics and pragmatics. The aim here is to assess how the association between the two forms can best be evaluated, particularly with such applications in mind as the teaching of English modal expressions.

In 5.2, we begin by examining the notions of collocation, idiom and lexical phrase and discuss the implications of using these as a basis for describing modal–adverb expressions. In the following section (5.3), the strength of attraction between selected combinations is tested through recourse to native and non-native speakers of English and a comparison of the results obtained informs the pedagogical proposals presented in section 5.4. These are by no means exhaustive and are merely intended to provide an outline exercise typology. For ease of reference, the major trends in modal–adverb co-occurrence are summarized in the form of a data profile which can be found at the end of the chapter (5.5).

5.2 COLLOCATION, IDIOM OR LEXICAL PHRASE

In the course of the description so far, modal–adverb combinations have been loosely referred to as modal–adverb collocations or modal–adverb idioms. In this section, we take a detailed look at the notions of collocation, idiom and lexical phrase in order to assess their relevance for the evaluation of modal–adverb phrases as prefabricated units of modal expression.

5.2.1 Collocation and idiom

The term 'collocation' is normally used to refer to the regular or repeated co-occurrence of two or more lexical items and it is in this sense that the word has been used in this book. The frequency with which each item occurs in the environment of the other can be measured using the concordancing techniques of corpus linguistics. Statistical evidence demonstrates, for instance, that there is a greater-than-chance likelihood of MAY and WELL co-occurring in a text as a recurring pattern of lexical co-occurrence: the syntagmatic affinity between WELL and MAY accounts for nearly three in four emphasizer combinations with MAY in the SEU (Survey of English Usage) spoken and written data! The strength of this association, and of other modal–adverb combinations examined in this study, might suggest that the items with the strongest lexical affinity have the highest probability of occurring together. This would be a misguided assumption: the semantic link between COULD and POSSIBLY is very strong but this does not mean that the modal verb will usually or even often be associated with this particular adverb modifier or any other modal adverb modifier. An important distinction needs to be made between syntagmatic relations as repeated actual occurrences of two or more items and as an associative phenomenon marking the potential for two or more items to combine.

Actual co-occurrence, which may include frequent co-occurrence, is a surface- or text-related phenomenon referred to in linguistics as collocation. In the collocation REALLY MUST, MUST is the 'node', in effect the item whose lexical behaviour is under scrutiny, and the word located to its left, REALLY, is called a collocate. The linear relationship between REALLY and MUST is a syntagmatic relation. There is a paradigmatic class of words that enters into the syntagmatic relation: other adverbs which function as reinforcement particles, such as JUST and SIMPLY, or modal adverbs designating a high degree of likelihood, such as CERTAINLY, DEFINITELY, SURELY or UNDOUBTEDLY. These adverbs constitute the 'collocational range' of MUST. In the SEU, there were no attested cases of MUST co-occurring with DEFINITELY or UNDOUBT-EDLY, although other collocates exhibiting similar grammatical and semantic characteristics were found to co-occur, to wit CERTAINLY and SURELY. A textual analysis of the Survey would thus permit the observation that MUST collocated only with such and such an item but that, by a process of analogy, it is 'collocable' with other, specifiable forms, according to a permissible sequence of co-occurrence. In contrast to collocation, the notion of collocability is therefore not tied to the frequency with which a group of items may co-occur in the language. It indicates what is conceptually admissible. Both concepts, however, are concerned with the syntagmatic combinability of items which has as much to do with meaning as with grammar.

The syntagmatic affinity between collocated items is marked lexically and grammatically. Any alteration to the pattern affects its structure, its meaning and ultimately its use; the invariability of these relations can be shown in relation to the collocation MAY WELL. If WELL is positioned syntactically in pre-auxiliary position, to produce the syntagm WELL MAY, the collocational tie is of a different order; whereas MAY WELL has a unity of meaning and signifies probability, WELL MAY more clearly carries the independent meanings of its constituent items and denotes 'indeed possible'. CAN'T POSSIBLY behaves in a similar way and, again, the invariability of the syntagm brooks no disruption. POSSIBLY is collocable with CAN'T as in POSSIBLY CAN'T, but this sequence expresses a quite different meaning. MAY WELL and CAN'T POSSIBLY are also more predicatable as likely collocations than where the order of the items is reversed; predictability is related to the concept of idiomaticity.

The collocations represented by modal–adverb combinations are tendencies of association rather than the frozen stretches of syntactic patterns which distinguish collocations from idioms, or the longer stretches of prefabricated speech known as clichés. In this book, the collocations of WELL with MIGHT, MAY and, to a lesser extent, COULD (see 4.3.2.4) or CONCEIVABLY or POSSIBLY with

CAN'T and COULDN'T (see 4.3.3.4) have been referred to as idiomatic modal expressions. It has been implied that these combinations exhibit a greater degree of idiomaticity than, say, the co-occurrence of REALLY or SIMPLY with MUST, or any of the other collocates from its collocational range, mentioned above. We have seen that MAY WELL is invariable and resistant to any form of modification; paradigmatic substitution of other adverbs, while possible, disrupts the integrity of the meaning this particular collocation conveys. In the environment of MUST, however, there is greater flexibility of association between the adverb collocates and the node with little if any impact for meaning when these are interchanged. Modal–adverb collocations exhibit idiomaticity in different measure: what constitutes an idiomatic rather than a collocational pattern is relative and a matter of degree rather than kind. But to what extent can any of the modal–adverb combinations discussed here be considered as true idioms on a par with, say, 'step on the gas' or 'kick the bucket'?

Idioms consist of a group of two or more words which combine to produce a specific meaning or effect. They are semantically and syntactically restricted and tend to function as a single unit. The meaning of the idiomatic expression as a whole cannot usually be derived from the meanings of the individual words, and these brook little or none of the grammatical variation they display in other contexts. 'He kicked the bucket' does not (normally) permit variations such as ?/*'He may kick the bucket', *'He will kick a bucket', or *'He kicked the pail' because the idiom as it stands intact uniquely produces the required meaning. Idioms and collocations obviously overlap because both involve the selection of two or more words, and the line between them is not easily established. However, in standard definitions, co-occurrences are treated as idioms if they can be interpreted as giving a single unit of meaning, and as collocations if the constituents retain some meaning of their own (Sinclair 1991: 172).

Let us take the example of MAY WELL. In common with idioms, as we have defined them, this combination represents a unity of meaning which amounts to more than the sum of its individual parts. WELL not only functions as a semantic marker of reinforcement, it operates uniquely as an agent of transformation in the restricted environment of MAY. (The unmodifed modal conveys possibility, whereas the combination designates probability.) The adverb displays a high degree of lexical redundancy and grammaticalization, and to all intents and purposes can be treated as a modal particle (see 4.5.3).

Now, it is a feature of idioms and clichés that, as they are fixed patterns, allowing for little if any syntagmatic and paradigmatic variation, the presence of one constituent predicts the occurrence of the other(s). In the case of a two–word pattern, co–occurrence becomes a matter of 'mutual expectancy' (Nattinger and DeCarrico 1992: 36). As collocations become more fixed, their predictability increases and lexical content diminishes. To return to our example MAY WELL, the combination produces a single unit of meaning which cannot readily be derived from the meanings of the individual constituents, if WELL as an emphasizer and not a manner adjunct can be considered to have any meaning at all. If WELL is removed, the special meaning of probability disappears. WELL has a variety of current uses, for instance, as a manner adjunct in 'She sang well' or as an intensifier in 'I knew him well', but such meanings, while related to its status as an emphasizer, are semantically distinct. It must be remembered that WELL is an emphasizer uniquely in the restricted environments of MIGHT, MAY and COULD.[2] Furthermore, given an appropriate context, the presence of one word, the modal MAY, to some extent predicts the occurrence of the other, the adverb WELL. Admittedly, the degree of expectancy is not as high as it would be in the case of EKE combining with OUT, KITH with KIN, or SPICK with SPAN, where the association can be predicted with nigh on 100 per cent certainty, but the strength of the association is nonetheless strong. On the basis of these arguments, MAY WELL appears to be a modal idiom, on a par with other verbal constructions like HAD BETTER or WOULD RATHER which are widely accorded the status (see CGEL: 141f).

Measured in terms of a continuum ranging from complete frozenness or idiomaticity at one extreme to unlimited freedom of combination at the other, the distribution of modal–adverb combinations differs considerably. The phenomenon of idiomatization implies that idioms have a specialized meaning which can be inferred partly or not at all from their constituents. MAY WELL matches this criterion more closely than any other modal–adverb collocation. In their turn, the restricted combinations of CAN'T and COULDN'T with CONCEIVABLY or POSSIBLY are more unitary, and hence idiomatic than, for example, WILL with its wider and more disparate range of collocates, such as POSSIBLY, PRESUMABLY and CERTAINLY: 'as collocations become less fixed ... predictability lessens and meaning increases' (Nattinger and DeCarrico 1992: 20).

As a general principle, collocations (and more elaborate structures to which we shall turn below) with little syntagmatic or paradigmatic variation are more easy to predict than those with a lot. The concepts of idiom, collocation and lexical patterns generally depend for their relevance on the extent to which they can be predicted and processed with the minimum of effort: 'the degree to which words constrain those around them, and the assurance we have that certain words are going to follow certain others, are the facts we use to make sense of language and to create all sorts of subtle variations and surprises' (Nattinger and DeCarrico 1992: 34). The more idiomatic or frozen the expression, the less amenable it is to variation, although variation is still possible if a particular effect is desired, as in the foregrounding of the adverb-modal sequence in this headline taken from a British newspaper: 'Yes Mr Mitterrand we absolutely, categorically, possibly, maybe, could be going into Europe.' The concatenation of modally non-harmonious collocates represents a deviation from the expected; the string is possibly unique and its novelty a psychological fillip.

It was remarked at the beginning of this section that a preliminary, although potentially misleading, definition of collocation relates co-occurrence to frequency and that the combination of two or more items could be established with reference to a sample corpus of the language. The deficiencies of this approach are especially noticeable when examination is restricted to a particular text. Some of the illustrative material in this study derives from the written works of well-known authors and, if frequency of co-occurrence had been used as a collocational yardstick, it is doubtful whether the present study could have been written at all. The frequency of modal-adverb co-occurrence and the variety of collocations involved varies enormously, ranging from 3 to 25 recorded instances in different works, each consisting of about 80,000 words of running text! In none of the sample material cited was any reference made to EKE OUT or SPICK AND SPAN, but as native speakers we know these expressions form part of our idiomatic and hence linguistic repertoire. Idioms and collocations have a psychological reality which also mirrors how language is stored and processed; in Greenbaum's (1988: 116) words:

> ... collocation is more than a statistical matter: it has a psychological correlate. We know that items are collocated just as we know that one sequence of items is part of our language and another is not. And just as we recognize degrees of acceptability (some sequences seem more obviously all right than others), so we can recognize degrees of collocation (some co-occurrences seem more frequent than others).

The extent to which native and non-native speakers recognize modal-adverb collocations as prefabricated units is examined in section 5.3.

5.2.2 Lexical phrases

Idioms and collocations do not account for all the regular and pervasive co-occurrence relationships found in language. The computational analysis of extensive spoken and written texts, often comprising corpora running into several millions of words, indicates that linguistic patterning is more extensive and more significant than was once thought: it is one of the principal factors of organization underlying the functional connectedness and coherence of spoken and written discourse. While idioms and collocations lend themselves relatively easily to isolation from their context, it is more difficult to circumscribe larger stretches of language, although the existence of intricate patterns of language which knit discourse together is not in doubt. Text-based studies (see, for instance, Sinclair 1991; Nattinger and DeCarrico 1992) identify a large number of partial or holistic preconstructed phrases, known as 'lexical phrases'. These are distinguished from clichés, idioms and collocations in that they are ascribed functional value, as their definition by Nattinger and DeCarrico (1992: 1) clearly suggests: '[lexical phrases are] multi-word lexical phenomena that exist somewhere between the traditional poles of lexicon and syntax, conventionalized form/function composites that occur more frequently and have more idiomatically determined meaning than language that is put together each time.' They resemble lexicon in being treated as units of meaning, yet most are multi-word constructions, susceptible to derivation by the same syntactic rules as govern the generation of grammatical structures in the language as a whole.[3]

Lexical phrases differ in complexity and the extent to which they allow for variation, but their lexical and grammatical structure is always a function of the uses they are required to serve. Modal–adverb collocations are associated with the types of lexical phrase referred to as 'sentence builders'. In the expression of epistemic modality, two closely related types of syntactic frame are involved, pronoun + modal + adverb + VP or adverb + pronoun + modal + VP:

(1)   He + may + well + be late;

(2)   Obviously + she + must + have forgotten

Nonepistemic modality involves just the one basic frame, (adverb) + modal + you + (adverb) + VP + (adverb):

(3)   Perhaps + you + could + fill the car up.

(4)   Will + you + close the door + please.

(5)   Could + you + possibly + close the door.

There are further permutations which would generate sentences like: 'Perhaps you would like some more coffee' or 'You really must have some more cake'. The basic frames are syntagmatically simple, allow for paradigmatic substitution, and are flexible enough to cover a wide range of functions, such as making an assessment (epistemic), a request or an offer (nonepistemic). The combined flexibility, simplicity and relatively high frequency of these lexical phrases and the reduced processing effort they entail, since they come ready-made and involve little encoding or decoding work, may well account for why they have become the conventionalized form/function composites in their respective domains.

The strength of the form/function association suggests that these modal sentence builders are as psychologically real as clichés, idioms or collocations. The close relationship between their particular, conventionalized forms and associated functions has prompted some linguists to invoke the notion of 'pragmatic competence', the pragmatic correlative of general linguistic competence or the speaker's abstract knowledge of the language system and its rules of use: 'Although grammatical competence encompasses the knowledge of the lexical forms and their internal syntax, pragmatic competence accounts for the speaker's ability to continue to access these forms as pre-assembled chunks, ready for a given functional use in an appropriate context' (Nattinger and DeCarrico 1992: 13).[4] Any implication that there are 'rules of use', on a par with grammatical rules, and that these are amenable to a comparable degree of formalization and exposition is misleading. Many conditioning factors of a non-linguistic kind can affect the dynamics of a given communicative situation, so that a lexical phrase normally associated with one set of functions may come to be used in ways not readily ascribed it by convention (see the discussion in 3.5). However, a lot of language used every day is routine and predictable: modals and adverbs occur in frames where the form/function association simply reflects regular, conventionalized instances of language use.

5.2.3 The classification of modal–adverb collocations

The association of modal–adverb collocations with epistemic and nonepistemic categories of modality has been examined at all levels of language description, in terms of: phonology, grammar, semantics and pragmatics. As the descriptions in Chapters 3 and 4 have demonstrated, the category of epistemic modality is more homogeneous and easier to define than those related to nonepistemic domains, which cover a much wider semantic range: the association between modals and modal adverbs is correspondingly more transparent and amenable to categorization. In this section, we now outline a descriptive framework for the classification of these synthetic expressions within an epistemic framework, where modal–adverb synergy is most clearly marked.

The two notions central to epistemic modality – possibility and necessity – are obvious co-ordinates in a scale of likelihood, ranging from 'doubt' through various intermediate stages to 'certainty'. There have been various proposals for such scales: Halliday (1970); Horn (1972); Lakoff (1973, 1974; cited in Bîrâ 1979); Close (1975); Matthews (1991) and Hoye and Zdrenghea (1995). They all represent hierarchies of epistemic senses and have been variously referred to as scales of tentativeness, indirectness or formality. Close

Table 5.1 Epistemic modal classification

A Possibility	B Probability	C Certainty
MIGHT	SHOULD	MUST
MAY	OUGHT TO	CAN'T
COULD	WOULD	
CAN[†]	WILL	

† Only in rhetorical questions: 'Can this be love at first sight?'

(1975) typifies the general approach and arranges the (unmodified) modals in terms of a scale of tentativeness, ranging from tentative to non-tentative: MIGHT, MAY, COULD, CAN, SHOULD, OUGHT TO, WOULD, WILL, MUST. An alternative classification is plausibly suggested in Table 5.1 by the epistemic trichotomy of certainty, probability and possibility. The adverbs which collocate with the epistemic modals can be classified in a similar way, as shown in Table 5.2.

Neither classification claims to be definitive but, taken together, they provide a workable framework for assessing and predicting trends in modal–adverb collocation in the epistemic domain. It is immediately apparent that, in terms of the extremes of the scales, represented by the modals MIGHT and MUST and the adverbs

Table 5.2 Epistemic modal–adverb classification

A Possibility	B Probability	C Certainty
POSSIBLY	PROBABLY	CERTAINLY
CONCEIVABLY	QUITE LIKELY	DEFINITELY
PERHAPS	MOST LIKELY	INDEED
MAYBE	WELL[†]	PRESUMABLY
		SURELY
		FOR CERTAIN
		OF COURSE
		UNDOUBTEDLY
		NECESSARILY

† Only after COULD, MAY and MIGHT.

POSSIBLY and CERTAINLY, collocational restrictions apply, demonstrating the incompatability of:

(6)   *He might/may certainly be at home.

(7)   *He must possibly be there.

Lyons (1977: 807f) discusses these collocational restrictions in terms of 'modally harmonic' and 'modally non-harmonic' combinations: 'POSSIBLY and MAY, if each is being used epistemically, are harmonic, in that they both express the same degree of modality, whereas CERTAINLY and MAY are, in this sense, modally non-harmonic' (see also 1.4). In modally harmonic combinations, the epistemic sense of each modal is captured by the adverb collocate so that there exists a concord of modality running through each sentence. In cases such as:

(8)   Certainly he may be there.

where there is an implied objectivity, 'it is certainly the case that he may be there', the adverb acts independently of the modal, since they are non-harmonic, and signals concession rather than certainty, allowing for the following types of interpretation:

(9)   Certainly, he may be there and we have to investigate that possibility.

(10)   Certainly, he mày be there – there's always a possibility – but somehow I doubt it.

It is obviously easier to predict the restrictions on co-occurrence, and to identify trends in collocability, when the extremes of the scale are involved. The stages in between are less determinate and allow for greater latitude. Thus, while MIGHT cannot normally combine with adverbs from categories B and C, or MUST with those from category A, all other modals are, in principle, free to combine with adverbs listed in all three categories. However, the description of modal–adverb co-occurrence presented in this book suggests that there is a marked tendency for the modals to combine with adverbs of an equivalent epistemic status, for category A modals to combine with A adverbs, and so forth. There are predictable trends and patterns in co-occurrence, at least in terms of the combination of items from the three main categories. The more idiomatic or regular the expression the more confidently it can be predicted.

The predictability of trends in association between modals and adverbs is assessed by testing native and non-native speaker performance in the modal–adverb domain (see 5.2).

An obvious omission from the adverb classification is the small group of evidential adverbs whose role is not simply to reinforce the modality but to provide an evidential submodification of an epistemic system which is essentially judgement-based. The items concerned are: APPARENTLY, CLEARLY, EVIDENTLY, OBVIOUSLY and MANIFESTLY. On account of their inferential nature, the epistemic modals combine freely with these items. The evidential quality of MUST (see 3.4.3.2) accounts for the regularity and significance of their association with this modal. Otherwise, the only likely restriction is one of a stylistic kind:

(11)   ?/*Manifestly, there might/may have been an error.

REALLY and ACTUALLY have also been omitted because they are collocable with all modals.

The nature of the attraction between modals and adverbs of equivalent epistemic status can be illustrated in terms of a paradigm of speaker assessments, where each collocation correlates with the relative strength or weakness of the speaker's epistemic knowledge. Again, three broad categories of speaker assessment can be distinguished, in terms of possibility, probability and certainty:

A   *Possibility*
      could conceivably, could possibly, could maybe, could perhaps, might conceivably, might possibly, might perhaps may conceivably, may possibly, may perhaps

      . . . .

B   *Probability*
      might well, might easily, could well, could easily, may well, may easily would probably, would presumably, should probably, should presumably, will probably, will presumably

      . . . .

C   *Certainty*
      would certainly, would undoubtedly, should certainly, ought to certainly, will certainly, will undoubtedly, must

certainly, must surely, must evidently, must obviously, must necessarily

. . . .

A   *Negative possibility*
mightn't (rare) necessarily, may not necessarily

. . . .

B   *Negative probability (unlikely)*
probably wouldn't, probably won't

. . . .

C   *Negative certainty (impossibility)*
couldn't possibly, couldn't conceivably, can't possibly

The dotted lines represent the boundaries of transition from one type of likelihood to another; the hierarchical listing is to some extent arbitrary and native speakers might well differ as to the precise ordering of certain collocations: MAY WELL might be considered by some as indicating a stronger likelihood than WILL PROBABLY on account of perceived differences in the semantic effects of reinforcement in the one and of approximation in the other.

The list does not reflect syntactic variation. CONCEIVABLY, POSSIBLY, PROBABLY, PRESUMABLY, CERTAINLY, SURELY and UNDOUBTEDLY are happy in either pre- or post-auxiliary position, the former position being reserved for emphatic reinforcement. In combination with OUGHT TO, however, they are mostly restricted to pre-auxiliary position. EASILY is restricted to post-auxiliary position, and CONCEIVABLY, POSSIBLY and NECESSARILY to post-negated auxiliary position. In general, the pre-positioning of adverbs, where this is syntactically permissible, tends to objectify the modality; this is especially noticeable with CERTAINLY and CONCEIVABLY:

(12)   They conceivably might consider their available options now.

(13)   She certainly will be attending the meeting.

Significantly, the collocations involving the positive forms of the modals demonstrate that MAY and MIGHT are linked to the notion of possibility (but not probability, other than in combination with WELL), while WILL, WOULD and SHOULD are connected both with notions of probability and certainty, but not necessity, which uniquely involves MUST. The principle observed is that the adverb harmonizes with the modality expressed by the auxiliary. Collocations with the negative forms show the tendency to formulate negation in terms of possibility or non-possibility where, again, the adverbs reflect the modality of the auxiliary. They do not, however, where the proposition rather than the modality is negated, as in the combinations of MIGHT NOT and MAY NOT with NECESSARILY (see 2.4.3). The affinity of MUST for the evidentials and, in fact, for SURELY is due to its inferential nature.[5]

5.3 NATIVE SPEAKER AND NON-NATIVE (SPANISH) SPEAKER PERFORMANCE IN THE MODAL–ADVERB DOMAIN

The description and evaluation of modal–adverb co-occurrence has been based on an analysis of primarily the spoken and written data of the SEU. To provide a more secure basis for evaluating the strength of particular modal–adverb collocations, native speaker performance in the modal–adverb domain was assessed by means of a simple completion test. A similar test, and a translation exercise (see 5.3.3), were administered to educated, non-native speakers of English to help determine the nature and extent of their linguistic sensitivity to the use of modal–adverb collocations. In general, modality is a notoriously difficult area for learners of English.

The test used for this study was narrower in scope and simpler in design than the kind involved in the preparation of the CGEL. There elicitation experiments were used to obtain data not only on native speaker performance but on native speaker attitudes towards the acceptability of given instances of language usage.[6] The present study is not primarily concerned with issues of language variation and acceptability, important though these are in the wider context of language description.[7]

The performance test used here is a type of completion test loosely based on the forced-choice selection model proposed by Greenbaum and Quirk (1970: 3f). The sentences it contained were based on attested examples of language use drawn from the corpus but, for the purposes of the test, the adverb satellite was omitted and the modal verb left unmodified. The alterations in no way affected the acceptability of the sentences. When informants performed the required task ('Please complete the following sentences by inserting a word or phrase in the space provided'), they had to choose a word, or a phrase, they considered appropriate in the context. The sentences represented a limited set of environments and there was no restriction (other than the contextual) on the potential range of items from which they could make their selection. The usual procedure with completion tests is to provide informants with a limited set of items from which to select, but in this instance it was felt that the absence of any such constraint would be less inhibiting on performance and encourage a more natural set of responses, consistent with the informants' own intuitions about language use.

There are problems with this approach, of course. It could be argued that, by requiring informants to complete the sentences, they felt obliged to make a selection and insert an item in the sentence frame, even in contexts where they might otherwise have been happier to leave the modal unmodified. However, there were cases where informants did not comply either because they failed to select an item or felt so compelled by the test instruction that they actually produced deviant structures. This naturally occurred more frequently in the case of the non-native informants.

More seriously, it could be argued that, however elaborate test procedures are, they are contrived and the nature of the evidence they generate is inevitably compromised by the subject's awareness that he is performing under test conditions. This is a view put forward very forcefully by Sinclair (1991: 39): 'The problem about all kinds of introspection is that it does not give evidence about usage. The informant will not be able to distinguish among various kinds of language patterning – psychological associations, semantic groupings, and so on. Actual usage plays a very minor role in one's consciousness of language and one would be recording largely ideas about language rather than facts of it.'[8] Quirk (1995: 129) also warns that informants may become accustomed to what is required of them and this could well compromise the validity of their responses: 'Elicitation testing runs into greatest difficulty where a single problem or a narrow range of problems is being investigated. The unwanted habituation factor is adequately offset, however, if the goal is to seek data on a number of disparate issues.' Some of the more ingenious elicitation techniques devised by Quirk and others (see, especially, Quirk and Svartvik 1966, and Quirk 1995: 145f) in order to counteract habituation involve aural presentation of the test material, and require subjects to produce oral responses within a set time limit (between 3 to 5 seconds) depending on the complexity of the linguistic operation concerned. This technique reduces 'deliberation time', thus inhibiting any tendency towards conscious prevarication, and it also helps avoid ambivalent types of response, especially relevant in the case of acceptability experiments.[9]

Ideally, the tests used for this brief account would have focused on a range of linguistic issues (and not just those concerning modality) and the elicitation techniques would have reflected the complexity of the undertaking and entailed the administration of a whole series of test batteries, both in aural/oral and written formats. Such an approach would have been insatiable in the context of this study. However, the results we obtained largely corroborate and supplement the evidence on collocational trends provided by the corpus data and are useful, if not unassailable, indicators of native and non-native speaker performance in the modal–adverb domain. But, clearly, unless more sophisticated elicitation techniques are deployed, a properly cautious use should be made of the results.[10,11]

5.3.1 Background to the completion test: procedure, format, informants

The experiment was conducted in the form of a completion test which consisted of 15 sentences requiring completion by the insertion of an appropriate word or phrase in a blank space. Each contained a modal form whose original adverb collocate had been omitted, as in this example:

(14)   He _____ ought to have arrived in Paris by now.

The sentences all derive from either the spoken or written part of the SEU, although some have been slightly modified to accord with the design of the test. Informants were not acquainted with the aim of the test and the instructions for its completion were accordingly non-specific: 'Please complete the following sentences by inserting a word or phrase in the space provided.' In most cases, the contexts allowed for the selection of an item only from the adverb class, but there were no restrictions on the choice of type. Five of the 15 sentences making up the test were included as distracters to help reduce the risk of habituation.[12] For the assessment of results, the selection of non-adverbial forms, phrases, miscellaneous structures or the failure to complete a sentence invalidated the response, even where the grammatical integrity of the sentence was preserved.

Two groups of informants participated in the test: 20 educated native speakers employed in the overseas diplomatic service, and 20 educated non-native Chilean speakers of English with Spanish as their mother tongue, who were either undergraduate students or teachers of English.

The aim of the test as administered to the native speaker subjects was to evaluate the descriptive framework proposed in 5.2.3. We hypothesized that native speaker performance would endorse the patterns of association predicted by that classification and corroborate the general principle that modals and adverbs of equivalent epistemic value show a marked tendency to combine, especially in relation to the possibility and necessity poles of the epistemic continuum. The consistency with which informants selected either the original collocate, or an item belonging to the same category, and thus respected the collocational associations described in Chapters 3 and 4, would at least give some indication as to the reliability of the classification and its usefulness as a tool for predicting different types of epistemic modal–adverb collocation.

The same test was also administered to non-native informants to help identify how their responses deviated from the original versions of the test sentences and, of course, from the responses of their native speaker counterparts. Analysis of their performance in this test and the subsequent translation exercise highlights points of contrast and similarity between English and Spanish and provides valuable insights into how the two languages formulate idiomatic modal expressions. This information offers a useful basis for developing appropriate language learning materials.

The combinations included in the test were chosen to reflect the strength of different collocational links, and hence varying degrees of idiomaticity and predictability. Except for (15)(a) and (15)(f), which is ambiguous between a deontic and epistemic reading, the sentences express epistemic modality, where trends in co-occurrence are most amenable to investigation. The letters *A*, *B* and *C* after the selected items refer to the classification presented in 5.2.3. The five sentences which figured as distracters attract no commentary in the discussion of the test results.

(15)　　(a)　REALLY *A B C* + MUST *C*
　　　　　　I kept thinking when I was doing my revision that I really must look up rickets, but I never did.

　　　(b)　SHALL *B* + PROBABLY *B*
　　　　　　I shall probably be there by then.

　　　(c)　MIGHT *A* + WELL *B* (modal idiom)
　　　　　　They might well be pushed off their territories.

　　　(d)　PERHAPS *A* + MIGHT *A*
　　　　　　Perhaps your friend – the fat one – might give some useful leads if subtly approached.

　　　(e)　WOULD *B* + CLEARLY *C*
　　　　　　She is much more at home in the town than in the country and would clearly have no problems about settling down in Scunthorpe if appointed.

　　　(f)　MUST *C* + CLEARLY *C*
　　　　　　In these circumstances, the Government must clearly rely on a full turnout of the payroll vote.

　　　(g)　SURELY *C* + OUGHT TO *B*
　　　　　　He surely ought to have arrived in Paris by now.

　　　(h)　WILL *B* + PROBABLY *B*
　　　　　　What they are thinking of and what they will probably come up with at the end of the day need not concern what we propose here.

　　　(i)　WOULD *B* + PROBABLY *B*
　　　　　　I am sure that with weight reduction his risk of gout would be much reduced and he would probably not have to take Allopurinol at all.

　　　(j)　CAN'T *C* + POSSIBLY *A* (modal idiom)
　　　　　　Rubbish! You can only be about 50 – you can't possibly have aged that much!

5.3.2   The test results

In the ensuing discussion, the above sentences and their associated modal–adverb collocations are referred to as (a), (b), and so on. We set out the results of the completion test in Table 5.3, followed by brief commentary. Ns and Ss stand for native speakers and non-native Chilean (Spanish) speakers, respectively. There were 20 participants in each informant group and their responses were measured as percentages: those in italics are the results of the Ns group, and those in normal typeface the results of the Ss group. Four types of response were categorized:

1. Percentage of informants who selected the original collocate.
2. Percentage of informants who selected a collocate within the same category as the original.
3. Percentage of informants who selected a collocable item from a category other than the original.
4. Percentage of informants whose responses were invalid (failure to fill in blank; selection of an inappropriate adverb or structure; grammatical deviance).

The relatively high percentages for Ns recorded in column 1 in connection with (c), (d) and (j) indicate that the collocational attraction between modals and adverbs at the extremes of the

Table 5.3 Completion test: summary of results (percentages)

	1		2		3		4	
Collocations	*Ns*	Ss	*Ns*	Ss	*Ns*	Ss	*Ns*	Ss
(a) REALLY + MUST	*All*	10	–	20	–	–	–	70
(b) SHALL + PROBABLY	*12*	5	–	–	*66*	25	*22*	70
(c) MIGHT + WELL	*60*	–	–	–	*20*	20	*20*	80
(d) PERHAPS + MIGHT	*65*	–	–	5	*10*	5	*25*	90
(e) WOULD + CLEARLY	–	5	*85*	35	*10*	10	*5*	50
(f) MUST + CLEARLY	–	–	*50*	30	–	–	*50*	70
(g) SURELY + OUGHT TO	*15*	–	*80*	40	–	5	*5*	55
(h) WILL + PROBABLY	*15*	5	*20*	–	–	20	*65*	75
(i) WOULD + PROBABLY	*15*	10	*10*	–	–	30	*75*	60
(j) CAN'T + POSSIBLY	*65*	30	–	–	*25*	–	*10*	70

epistemic scale of likelihood is stronger than with intermediate values. This is what one would expect from our description of the trends in co-occurrence attested in the Survey. The status of the idiomatic combination of MIGHT with WELL (c) is widely recognized, as is its association with possibility (d). Again, the results for (j) indicate the idiomaticity of the association. The 100 per cent result in relation to the nonepistemic combination in (a) is surprisingly consistènt but it does confirm the association between REALLY and this modal when the latter is used with the sense of 'self-admonishment' (see 3.4.3.3). Half the Ns informants associate epistemic MUST in (f) with category C collocates, all of them adverbs expressing high epistemic values. Both results point to the singular status of MUST as the co-ordinate of necessity in epistemic and deontic contexts.

The results among Ns in column 2 broadly correspond with what could be predicted from the modal and adverb categorizations listed in 5.2.3. Although the link between WOULD and CLEARLY (e) is not accorded idiomatic status, the high proportion of informants selecting other evidential adverbs indicates the strength of the attraction in contexts of use which evidently involve the speaker's inference rather than mere prediction of a future state-of-affairs (see 3.4.5). The selection of a category C emphasizer by 95 per cent of Ns in connection with (g) points to the affinity between pre-auxiliary position and especial emphasis. A number of informants opted for REALLY, the item most commonly associated with this position and function.

The relatively low percentages recorded for Ns in columns 3 and 4 correlate with their recognition of the collocational ties predicted by the system of classification used in 5.2.3. There are four notable exceptions. In column 3, in connexion with (b), 66 per cent of Ns selected items from category C rather than category B, suggesting a collocational attraction inclining towards epistemic necessity, although the epistemic status of the modal is debatable (see 3.4.6). More significant are the invalid responses in column 4 with reference to (h), (i) and (j) where informants either failed to complete or selected adverbs belonging to other classes (EVENTUALLY and THEN were chosen by a number of informants). There was a marginal tendency for WILL and WOULD to be associated with category B adverbs, otherwise informants failed to record any noteworthy collocational ties. It may be that since these modals permit a much wider range of adverb collocate than any other epistemic modal, the semantic attraction towards modal adverbs from any particular category is correspondingly weaker and quite random (see also 3.4.5.2).

In comparison with Ns, and perhaps not surprisingly, Ss consistently neglected the potential for modals and adverbs to combine, that is, their collocability with certain types of adverbial. This was most noticeable in the case of the idiomatic collocations MIGHT WELL (c) and CAN'T POSSIBLY (j); broadly similar results were produced by Romanian informants when they were administered a similar test in an earlier research exercise.[13] The failure of Ss to recognize modal–adverb collocations and the lack of conformity in their responses with either the original sentences or those produced by the native speaker informants are no doubt due in part to their level of competence in the foreign language. In terms of an error analytical approach, Ss performance errors could be described as mistakes in language use, brought about mainly as the result of interlingual lexical error and the selection of inappropriate forms. On the other hand, the propensity for Ss to select an inappropriate (non-modal) adverb or to omit selection of an adverb altogether might be accounted for in terms of 'avoidance', or what has been referred to as 'linguistic (syntactic or idiomatic) disbelief' (van Els *et al.* 1984: 63). In this view, learners may over-value or underrate the use of certain structures or elements in the target language (L2), according to how they perceive the similarities or differences between this and their native tongue (L1). There are, in other words, points of contrast and equivalence between the L1 and the L2 which may lead to 'negative transfer' or interference and actively impede the learner's level of performance in the L2. While interference from the L1 may not be the sole source of 'error' or insensitivity to the L2 norms of performance, it is not implausible to suggest that differences in the way English and Spanish express modal contrasts, and the extent to which they deploy modal–adverb combinations, have an important influence on the learner's ability to operate competently within the L2 modal system. The salient differences between the two systems and the translatability of modal meanings, especially those conveyed by modal–adverb collocations, are outlined and discussed in the next two sections.

5.3.3 Modal–adverb expressions and their Spanish equivalents: background to the translation exercise

The translation exercise was not intended as the basis for a systematic appraisal of the Spanish modal system but as a framework for examining points of contrast and equivalence between the L1 and the L2 in the modal–adverb domain.[14] It was not expected that there should be a one-to-one correspondence between either form or function: it is unlikely that languages as different as English and Spanish would conceive of modality or express and apply modal contrasts in the same way, although both languages recognize the grammatical category of mood and express a similar range of modal meanings. In his typological survey of modality, Palmer (1986: 7) observes that 'it is probable that there are very few languages that do not have some kind of grammatical system of modality', although they may differ as to which parts of the semantic system they grammaticalize, how they organize the semantic field, and which grammatical devices are involved.

While Spanish and English share similar modal concepts, they differ considerably in the way these are expressed linguistically. The main points of contrast are as follows. The Spanish equivalents of the English modals are fully conjugated in the same categories as main verbs and are therefore inflected for tense and mood. In contrast, the English modals are defective: they do not normally combine; they are uninflected for person, and they are severely limited with respect to tense (see 3.1). Their morphologically past tense forms are not necessarily related semantically to the past ('Next week, he could/might/should go to the dentist's'). Since in English, the modals do not usually combine, the expression of 'posteriority' (future and conditional) is less distinct than in Spanish, where tense distinctions are conveyed purely through inflection, and do not involve the support of other verbal forms. Thus, the Spanish for 'he should have tried it' is expressed simply by 'debió intentarlo'.

WILL, SHALL and WOULD, SHOULD, as markers of futurity and conditionality, are matched by the future and conditional tenses in Spanish. But the uses of WILL and WOULD to convey willingness are conveyed by another verb in Spanish, QUERER, rather than verbal inflection. Both the epistemic and nonepistemic uses of SHOULD (see 3.4.4) are expressed by DEBER rather than the conditional. In

Spanish, speculation about a future event in terms of likelihood, is frequently captured by future or conditional tense marking where English more often uses a modal–adverb of possibility, although the predictive uses of WILL and WOULD are still relatively common.

In addition to lexical modal verbs, Spanish widely uses the subjunctive, a grammatical category for which there is basically no direct equivalent in English grammar. The subjunctive tense system contrasts with the indicative and operates as a generalized marker of modality, conveying an expression of speaker attitude. The complexity of the Spanish tense system and the widespread use of the subjunctive allows for a potentially much wider range of modal distinctions in that language.

Morphologically, the majority of modal adverbs in English derive from adjectives and end in the suffix -LY, although, of course, there are also common simple forms, such as JUST, ONLY and WELL. The -LY adverbs find their equivalents in Spanish, which are also derived from an adjective base, and take the corresponding suffix -MENTE. However, in Spanish, there may be stylistic objections to the use of adverbs ending in -MENTE: 'It is bad style to include too many adverbs in -*mente* in a single paragraph: the final syllables set off ugly rhymes' (Butt and Benjamin 1988: 319). Consequently, forms in -MENTE are regularly replaced by periphrastic constructions, usually adjectival or prepositional phrases, which function adverbially. Hence phrases like ES POSIBLE QUE ('It is possible that') or ES CLARO QUE ('it is clear that') may well be preferred to their adverb equivalents, POSIBLEMENTE or CLARAMENTE. Furthermore, in translation, the latter are often felt to be too 'literal', and the periphrastic constructions more colloquial. Here there is an obvious contrast with English, where the corresponding adjectival or prepositional phrases sound stilted other than in formal contexts.

Spanish has several commonly used adverbs to express possibility, such as ACASO, TAL VEZ, QUIZÁ(S), POSIBLEMENTE which regularly combine with the subjunctive, although in certain contexts they may also occur with the indicative whose use is spreading. The choice of mood is dependent to a large extent on the speaker's perception of the reality or truth contained in the proposition: '[Spanish] native speakers actively exploit the contrast in order to convey different meanings' (Whitley 1986: 129). However, the importance of the subjunctive is not in any doubt and as Butt and

Benjamin (1988: 220) remark: 'there is no conclusive evidence that it is disappearing from the language ... although it is true that spontaneous speech, especially Spanish-American, sometimes uses the indicative where formal language requires the subjunctive.'

5.3.4   An exercise in translation

Some weeks after the completion test, 10 of the original Ss informants, who were trainee translators, were required to translate into Spanish the 10 sentences that had been the focus of the first test. These were now presented in a different order, with minor changes to (e), (f) and (i). Again, the informants were not told the real purpose of the test and the translations were undertaken as a straightforward classroom exercise.

On the basis of the Ss translations, 'model' versions were developed and subsequently verified for accuracy and authenticity by other native speaker experts. With two notable exceptions, involving the idiomatic expressions in sentences (15)(a) and (15)(j), the results of the test showed a high degree of correspondence between the individual Ss and model versions. Alternative renderings and notable deviations are dealt with in the commentary; the percentage of respondents whose translations conformed to the model versions or deviated from them are given in the commentary if considered significant. The purpose of the test was not primarily to assess Ss performance in the translation domain but, rather, to evaluate how two specific linguistic categories – modals and modal adverbs – are translated into Spanish; to assess the grammatical, semantic and stylistic implications the choice of a particular translation has in the context of the given sentence; and to provide some data for the development of class-room or self-access materials. Data obtained from the translation exercise were designed to supplement the results of the completion test and to provide insights into how modal–adverb collocations in the L1 are best formulated in the L2.

The analysis of the Ss translations takes into account the contrasts between the two modal systems and the influence this has on the translation of modal–adverb combinations from the L1 into expressions of equivalent meaning in the L2. 'Equivalence of meaning' implies that the L2 versions should capture as far as possible the concepts and nuances of the originals yet be consistent with the idiomatic expression of modality in Spanish. Where the English adverb is translated by a Spanish adverb (rather than by an adjective phrase, for instance) the labelling of the CGEL classification is used as well; there is, in any case, no comparable framework for the description of Spanish adverbials. For ease of reference, the sentences have been rearranged to coincide with their order of appearance in the completion test and in each case, the L2 'model' version is preceded by the L1 original. The Spanish equivalents of the English modal–adverb expressions are printed in capitals.

(16)   (a)   [I kept thinking when I was doing my revision that I really must look up rickets, but I never did.]
Me quedé pensando cuando estaba haciendo mi revisión que REALMENTE DEBÍA buscar raquitismo, pero nunca lo hice.
(*Emphasizer + Past indicative [Imperfect]*)

(b)   [I shall probably be there by then.]
PROBABLEMENTE ESTARÉ/ES PROBABLE QUE ESTÉ allí para entonces.
(*Content disjunct + Future indicative/Adjective phrase + Present subjunctive*)

(c)   [They might well be pushed off their territories.]
ES PROBABLE QUE los EXPULSEN de sus territorios.
(*Adjective phrase + Present subjunctive*)

(d)   [Perhaps your friend – the fat one – might give some useful leads if subtly approached.]
TAL VEZ tu amigo, el gordo, PUEDA/PODRÍA dar algunas pistas útiles si se le aborda con cuidado.
(*Content disjunct + Present subjunctive/Conditional*)

(e)   [She is much more at home in the town than in the country and would clearly have no problems . . .]
Ella se siente más cómoda en el pueblo que en el campo y SEGURO QUE no TENDRÍAS problemas/CON TODA SEGURIDAD no TENDRÍAS problemas . . .
(*Adjective phrase/Prepositional phrase + Conditional*)

(f)   [In these circumstances, the Government must clearly rely on a full turnout.]

En estas circunstancias, ESTÁ CLARO QUE el gobierno
DEBE confiar/el gobierno SIN DUDA DEBE confiar en
una asistencia completa.
(*Adjective/Prepositional phrase + Present indicative*)

(g) [He surely ought to have arrived in Paris by now.]
SEGURO QUE a estas horas ya HABRÁ llegado a París
(*Adjective phrase + Future perfect indicative*)

(h) [What they are thinking of and what they will
probably come up with at the end of the day need not
concern what we propose here.]
Lo que están pensando y lo que PROBABLEMENTE
CONCLUIRÁN al final del día no tiene porque inter-
ferir en lo que propongamos aquí.
(*Content disjunct + Future indicative*)

(i) [I am sure that with weight reduction his risk of illness
would be much reduced and he would probably not
have to take medication at all.]
Estoy seguro de que si perdiera peso el riesgo de
enfermedad sería mucho más reducido y PROBA-
BLEMENTE NO TENDRÍA que tomar medicinas/ES
PROBABLE QUE NO TENGA que tomar medicinas.
(*Content disjunct/Adjective phrase + Conditional/Present
subjunctive*)

(j) [Rubbish! You can only be about 50 – you can't
possibly have aged that much!]
¡Tonterías! Tú solamente puedes tener alrededor de
50 años. NO ES POSIBLE QUE TENGAS tantos/QUE SEAS
tan mayor.
(*Adjective phrase + Present subjunctive*)

Direct correspondences in grammatical function, semantics,
realization and position are uncommon. (16)(a) and (d) are notable
exceptions: the distinction between VP-adverb (a) and sentence
adverb (d) is upheld in the L2 versions, and the overall structure
of the sentences corresponds almost exactly with the English
originals. In other cases, there are slight deviations, such as in (b),
(h) and (i) where, in the L2 versions, the adverb precedes rather
than follows the modal verb. Elsewhere, and this is more

significant, Spanish resorts to the use of periphrastic constructions whose scope of modification is unambiguously sentential. In (h), for instance, the emphasizer or VP-adverb (SURELY) in the L1 is rendered by an adjective phrase in the L2 whose scope is now the entire sentence rather than primarily the modal–verb. Direct verbal modification is possible, as in (a) for instance, but is not as widespread as in English, where regular syntactic distinctions are made between sentence and VP-modifiers. Butt and Bejamin (1988: 244) note, for instance, that as a direct verbal modifier, POSIBLEMENTE is not particularly colloquial and other forms, such as ES POSIBLE QUE, QUIZÁ(S) or TAL VEZ, are more common. As a result, the majority of the L2 versions involve a degree of syntactic restructuring of the L1 originals.[15]

In the main, the L2 versions captured the nuances introduced by the adverb in the L1, although (16)(c) and (j), which included the idiomatic collocations MIGHT WELL and CAN'T POSSIBLY, were to some extent problematical. In the case of (16) (c), 40 per cent of informants missed the significance of WELL and in their translations either settled on L1 expressions which convey possibility rather than probability, or omitted reference to the L1 adverb altogether. This was the only case where the L1 adverb component was deleted in the L2 version. In (16)(j), a similar number of informants (40 per cent) treated the adverb POSSIBLY as a disjunct rather than as an intensifier and so neglected to convey in the L2 the semantic effect of reinforcement it uniquely provides. Similar problems arose in relation to 16(a), where 30 per cent of informants elected for the prepositional phrase EN REALIDAD rather than the single-word adverb REALMENTE. All informants marked the adverbial off from the rest of the clause so that it functioned as an interpolated disjunct rather than as an emphasizer. REALMENTE, like its English counterpart REALLY, is widely used for reinforcement and there are not the stylistic objections to its use which might prejudice the selection of other forms ending in -MENTE.

It is characteristic of English that adverbs which in other contexts are more loaded for meaning tend to become delexicalized when used in a modal environment, as in the case of CLEARLY in (e) and (f). The corresponding form in Spanish, CLARAMENTE, is not used regularly in this way: it does not undergo a comparable degree of delexicalization. Adverb phrases like SIN DUDA or POR SUPUESTO or adjective phrases like ES CLARO QUE or

ES OBVIO QUE are considered more idiomatic, and they also avoid the risk of becoming too literal in their rendering of the L1 original. Neither (e) nor (f) presented problems to the translators, although each generated a wider variety of adverbial expressions in the L2 than any other sentence in the test.

The semantic content of the L1 collocations can be rendered faithfully in the L2 but the grammatical realization differs considerably because of far-reaching differences in the tense and mood systems of the two languages. For example, in half of the test sentences, (b), (c), (d), (i), and (j), Spanish employs the subjunctive mood to convey nuances of doubt where English has to rely on a small yet versatile group of defective verbs, in addition to a variety of lexical devices. In fact, the subjunctive is always required after statements of doubt or plausibility, and is regularly used after statements expressing emotions and value judgements (see Butt and Benjamin 1988: 220f). Considerations of style are also important: in English the occurrence of several adverbs ending in -LY, even within the same sentence, is considered acceptable whereas in Spanish the practice is condemned.[16] Lindquist (1989: 93) remarks: 'One normally expects the form to be retained as long as it does not interfere with the semantics or clash with TL [L2] syntax or stylistic demands. Semantics is thus seen to have primacy over realization. . . .'

The translation exercise suggests that there is nothing in the L1 modal–adverb system which is conceptually alien to Spanish speakers, although forms of realization in the two languages may differ considerably. A few of the more common modal adverbs in Spanish and English, POSIBLEMENT/POSSIBLY, REALMENTE/REALLY are lexical cognates and share similar properties in their distribution. However, -LY forms have a much wider currency and acceptance in English than their Spanish counterparts ending in -MENTE. This partly explains the difficulties Ss experienced in selecting -LY forms in the completion test, particularly where direct modification of the modal was concerned.[17] Generally speaking, periphrastic adjectival constructions are considered more colloquial than simple adverbs and of course lack the latter's positional mobility. Spanish is less tolerant of direct verbal modification: the nuances introduced by VP-adverbs can often be brought about by switching between the indicative and subjunctive categories of mood, which is a device native speakers actively exploit, depending on their attitude towards the proposition.

The translation exercise highlights important differences between the semantic and syntactic structures of English and Spanish which, of course, partly accounts for the Ss performance in the completion test. Moreover, the translation exercise also indicates that modal–adverb collocations, particularly at the VP-level, are a characteristic feature of the English modal system.

5.4 IMPLICATIONS FOR LANGUAGE TEACHING

The difficulties modal–adverb collocations pose for non-native speakers of English emphasizes the need for them to be taught. The results of the completion test demonstrate that the overriding principle which distinguishes Ns from Ss performance is the trend towards conformity and the respect of collocational ties in the former group and the opposite tendency in the latter. To encourage a response of conformity among Ss or any other non-native speaker group, learners would need first to be made aware of the range of modal–adverb lexical patterns, and the nature and strength of the collocational ties involved. However, the learners' attention needs to be directed towards not only the formal and semantic features associated with modal–adverb interaction at sentence and VP levels, but also to the use of these collocations to perform the type of functions indicated in 5.1.2. Modal–adverb collocations may not be unique to the English modal system but their functions are language-specific. Nowhere is this more true than in the use of modal–adverb expressions in such linguistic rituals as indirect speech acts (see 3.5). The pragmatic category of making a request is not unique to English, of course, and is doubtless a universal function, but its linguistic realization will differ from language to language.[18] The association between modal–adverb combinations and their range of functions is a matter of convention which are thus best seen as both language- and culture-specific.

Exercises designed to improve performance in the modal–adverb domain might initially focus on acquainting learners with the range of basic patterns involved, and then develop expertise in the selection of collocations which are relevant in their contexts of use. The aim is to develop the learners' awareness of the lexico-grammatical status of modal–adverb expressions and to eventually sensitize them to the sociolinguistic factors which determine their rules of use. The types of exercise involved represent a corresponding progression from controlled to relatively free practice.

5.4.1 Teaching modal–adverb patterns

In the case of learners (referred to henceforth as L) whose native language has to some extent grammaticalized the functions fulfilled by modal adverbs in English, the first step is to develop an awareness of the collocational trends and patterns associated with modal–adverb co-occurrence. In the early stages, priority can be given to developing the ability to recognize and produce modal–adverb structures and, while the exercises themselves are not intended as communicative language tasks, they can be designed to engage learners in cognitive problem-solving activities.

5.4.1.1 *Cloze test and multiple choice*

This exercise is very similar in format and task orientation to the completion test. L are given a set of sentences which contain different modal auxiliaries and in each sentence a space is left blank for the insertion of an appropriate adverb. Depending on the level of L, the test may be open choice (Cloze) and L invited to complete the sentences with whatever form comes to mind, or it may require L to select an appropriate item from a list of adverbs expressing a range of semantic roles (multiple choice). If multiple choice, the adverbs can be listed as a random selection, such as: HAPPILY, THEREFORE, WELL, TOMORROW, SIMPLY, JUST, POSSIBLY, EVENTUALLY, FRANKLY, DEFINITELY, HARDLY, PLEASE, VISUALLY, PERHAPS. The sentence frames could well be adapted from texts with which L are already familiar or they could be produced specifically for the exercise:

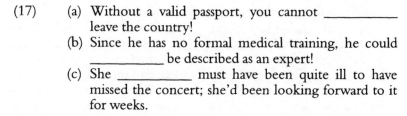

(17)   (a) Without a valid passport, you cannot _____ leave the country!
       (b) Since he has no formal medical training, he could _____ be described as an expert!
       (c) She _____ must have been quite ill to have missed the concert; she'd been looking forward to it for weeks.

(d) _____ he would like to talk to them first before the results are made official.

(e) The size may _____ be the cause of the problem because we've had similar difficulties in the past.

Ideally, the sentences should provide enough immediate context for the learners' selections to be based on a meaningful choice. In (17)(e), for instance, the frame allows for the potential selection of several items (FRANKLY, JUST, PERHAPS, POSSIBLY, SIMPLY, THEREFORE, etc.). The context most plausibly calls for the selection of a modal adverb, although not necessarily WELL; the idiomatic combination must simply be taught and then memorized by L as a fixed lexical phrase or modal 'chunk'. Variations on this 'slot and filler' technique could involve the selection of a modal verb for sentence completion instead of an adverb, in order to test L's awareness of the association in the other direction. For the purpose of reinforcement, modal or adverb items selected by L could then be recycled in a multiple choice exercise where the required collocate is listed with other collocable items whose attraction to the node is weaker and therefore less idiomatic:

(18)   (a) That may _____ be the last time you see her, since she's due to leave for Paris the day after tomorrow. DEFINITELY, PERHAPS, MAYBE, WELL, POSSIBLY.

(b) Can I have some more cake _____? FOR THE PARTY, PLEASE, TOMORROW,

Nattinger and DeCarrico (1992: 116) suggest the use of pattern practice drills as a means of rehearsing a few basic fixed routines, and these could certainly be used as a supplement to the types of exercise outlined above. However, by their very nature, drills are repetitive and, as these authors rightly warn, can become 'mindless' if overused.

5.4.1.2 *Translation*

For the more advanced learner, there are benefits to be gained in adopting an explicitly contrastive approach where L is required to translate from L1 into L2 and vice versa. L are asked to translate a group of sentences, similar to those used in the translation exercise. For example:

(19)   (a) Probably, he'll get the results tomorrow.
         (b) Well, you can't distinguish the images at all.
         (c) We really must get the project completed.
         (d) You couldn't possibly have forgotten the arrange-
             ment, surely.
         (e) Would you kindly send me further information?

The translations are then evaluated in class and a preferred version selected from the various solutions offered. Deviations from the model are then reviewed and the different renderings compared in terms of their respect for the original and the idiom of the L2. For instance, in the case of (16) (a), where some *Ss* translated the English emphasizer REALLY by the adverbial prepositional phrase EN REALIDAD rather than the more appropriate equivalent REAL-MENTE, discussion might focus on sentence versus VP-adverbial and their scope of modification. The process of evaluation would increase awareness of how adverbs interact with their modal verb heads and possibly suggest a variety of solutions to the problems involved with their translation. At a more abstract level, discussion could move away from the assessment of individual examples to the principles and strategies associated with transferring modal concepts from L1 into the L2.

As a diagnostic, translation can be useful in helping to identify particular errors or types of error, such as the failure to recognize the idiomatic sequences MAY WELL or CAN'T POSSIBLY and, certainly, it may be a means of even preventing and remedying errors. The problematic collocations can then become the focus of future translation tasks or completion exercises, such as those outlined above. However, more extensive use of translation exercises is particularly valuable because it can help sensitize advanced learners to matters of style and appropriacy which go well beyond mechanical mastery of the structures and idioms of the L2:

If the advanced learner uses structures which are acceptable, even though in one way or another inappropriate, nobody offers any guidance. He will possibly not even realize that further instruction is desirable. Analysis [on the basis of translation from

L1 to L2] ... may provide the form which such instruction could most usefully take. (Levenston 1971: 121)[19]

5.4.2 Teaching modal–adverb use

While a necessary preliminary, concentration on developing only grammatical competence in the modal–adverb domain is not enough to provide L with the ability to produce combinations in sentences which are appropriate to the context of use. Exercises must also be devised which help L learn which combinations are socially appropriate for which contexts. Tarone and Yule (1989: 18) define this ability in terms of 'sociolinguistic competence' which 'allows the language user to select which utterance form, from any number of possible correct forms, is considered appropriate within a language community on a particular interactive occasion'. The matter of appropriacy has already been raised in discussions on the pragmatic aspects of modal–adverb co-occurrence and particularly their use in polite requests (see 3.5). For instance, while 'Get the wine!' and 'Could you possibly fetch some more wine, please?' are perfectly well-formed, grammatically correct expressions, they are not necessarily interchangeable in the same context. The exercise types outlined previously and those given below are intended to help develop in L the grammatical and pragmatic skills necessary to use the right forms for the right functions in the right contexts.

Lexical phrases and collocations (see 5.2.1 and 5.2.2) are ideal units for exploitation at this stage. Although relatively complex in their syntax, they can be stored and retrieved as prefabricated language chunks, rather like idioms or clichés. In contrast to the latter, however, they are susceptible to analysis by the standard rules of grammar, and can be generated from just one or two basic frames, as we saw in 5.2.2. Their ready-made format requires little processing effort and their association with particular contexts of use makes them relatively easy to learn, understand and produce. In short, they are user-friendly. The simple lexical frame modal + you + (adverb) + VP can be used to generate a range of polite requests which can be optionally marked for increased indirectness according to the degrees of formality required by the context of use. The use of adverbs as politeness markers, for instance, could be warranted in an exchange with a stranger or person in authority:

(20) (a) Can/Could you (please/possibly) let me have the results as soon as possible?
      (b) Will/Would you (kindly/please) refrain from smoking?

Furthermore, modal lexical phrases such as these can be used in conjunction with other types of lexical phrase to signal further degrees of indirectness or politeness. The following could be part of an exchange between a subordinate and his superior:

      (c) I wonder if I might trouble you for a moment. Could you possibly (by any chance) explain to me which of these forms I need to complete first?

There are a variety of permutations available for exploitation, although an indication of the context is necessary to ensure the appropriate use of the appropriate phrase.

Frequently, in language training material, reference to contexts of use are omitted or so contrived as to be virtually meaningless. Tarone and Yule (1989: 90f) recall a textbook, quite popular among teachers in the early eighties, in which L are introduced to four request patterns:

(21) (a) Could I possibly come round into your garden?
      (b) Do you mind if I use your phone?
      (c) You don't mind if I smoke, do you?
      (d) I'd like to open the door. Does anyone mind?

To rehearse their ability to seek permission, L are presented with the following situation and accompanying exercises:

      You have a rented room in Mrs Armstrong's house. Here are some things that you want to do. To be polite, you ask Mrs Armstrong first. You say . . .

(22) (a) Could I possibly have a TV in my room?
      (b) Could I possibly put some pictures on the wall?
      (c) Could I possibly ask some friends to call round on Sunday? Etc.

L are then instructed to ask permission in any of the other ways indicated in (21):

(23)   (a) Do you mind if I ask some friends to call on Sunday?
         (b) You don't mind if I put some pictures on the wall?
         (c) I'd like to have a TV in my room . . .

As drills, these exercises are useful in familiarizing L with basic request patterns in English, but the fixed setting is hardly representative of contexts where the choice between form and function has any meaning. No indication is given of when one type of request strategy is more appropriate than the others. The COULD + POSSIBLY combination is very indirect and its overuse open to potential misinterpretation: L who were to use it repeatedly in one set of circumstances might actually cause offence or be accused of sarcasm! In order for L to exploit the relationship between conventionalized modal–adverb patterns and their associated functions, contextual clues must be provided: 'Knowing these form/function associations, and knowing the contextual constraints on the choice of form, is all part of pragmatic competence' (Nattinger and DeCarrico 1992: 127).

The main problem with producing exercises at this stage lies in establishing appropriate contexts and simulating these in the classroom.

5.4.2.1 *Contextualized exchanges: learning the request function*

The following illustrations are based on examples developed by Nattinger and DeCarrico (1992: 128f). Similar exercises could be developed for practising other types of indirect speech act. Exercises would involve the exploitation of the different lexical patterns associated with the making of a request, most of which are accommodated by the one basic frame: modal + you + (adverb) + VP. Other politeness markers such as MIND or BE WILLING TO ('Would you mind/be willing to . . .') could be substituted for the adverb. Use could be made of the politeness scales cautioned against in 3.5, where pedagogical generalizations should take precedence over demands for accuracy in linguistic description. There is less risk of L being ridiculed or causing offence if they first become familiar with the widely understood and conventionalized patterns which respect the basic socio-cultural conditions of use.

L are provided with a series of contexts, each requiring the use of a different modal pattern, according to the relationship of the participants and the nature of the favour asked:

(24)   *Context 1*
          Two friends, A and B, are in a meeting and A discovers that he has forgotten his pen. Seeing that his friend has two, A asks if he can borrow one and B readily agrees:
          (a) A: Could I borrow your pen?
              B: Sure.

More complex forms can be gradually introduced and different items substituted to demonstrate that the basic request pattern is quite flexible and not an invariable routine:

          (b) A: Could I see your agenda (I've forgotten mine)?
              B: No problem.
          (c) A: Could you pass this note to the Chairman?
              B: Yeh.
          (d) A: Would you mind passing this note to the chairman?
              B: Of course.

Variations in the basic pattern help focus attention on the form of the request as well as on its relevance in the given context. In later stages, functions and contexts can be varied to illustrate that the choice of form is constrained by context.

(25)   *Context 2*
          A is travelling by train to an important conference and wishes to revise his talk but then discovers he has nothing to write with. Seeing that a fellow traveller has a pen in her top pocket, he asks if he can borrow it and she agrees:
          (a) A: Could I possibly borrow your pen?
              B: Of course, here you are.
          (b) A: May I please borrow your pen?
              B: By all means.

It would need to be explained that politeness markers like POSSIBLY or PLEASE (and more complex realizations like BY ANY CHANCE) are appropriate with strangers and that their significance is to make the request more indirect.

At more advanced levels, L could be presented with contexts where the degree of imposition on the addressee would call for even more elaborate (but still idiomatic) request strategies, leading to practice which involves the combination of different types of pattern:

(26)   (a) A: I'm awfully sorry to trouble you, but do you think I could possibly ask you to pull the window up a little?

             B: Yes, of course. It is a little chilly in here.

In this type of exchange, politeness markers are varied, more complex, and 'stacked' together: I'M AWFULLY SORRY TO TROUBLE YOU + DO YOU THINK + POSSIBLY. Simple exchange dialogues could also be expanded into longer conversations to make the exchanges appear more realistic:

    (b) A: Excuse me,

          B: Yes . . .

          A: I'm wondering if you could possibly help me.

          B: What seems to be the problem?

          Etc.

Obviously, a considerable amount of variation can be introduced according to the level of the L and their overall level of fluency.

    A similar methodology can be used for developing the use of modal–adverb combinations in written discourse and rehearsing basic frames, such as WOULD YOU KINDLY . . .?, WOULD YOU PLEASE . . .? Exercises might eventually lead to practice in stacked patterns like I SHOULD BE MOST GRATEFUL + IF YOU WOULD KINDLY . . .. But in all cases an appropriate context would need to be contrived. Nattinger and DeCarrico (1992: 130) summarize the benefits of the approach outlined here: 'The successive stages cycle lexical phrases in such a way that the differing contexts for given functions demonstrate constraints on choices of form, thus providing input needed for acquiring pragmatic competence.'

5.4.2.2 *A matter of judgement*

Modal–adverb combinations also have an evaluating function, as we have seen from our discussion of epistemic modality. They enable a speaker to express his views on the world in terms of probabilities rather than statements of fact. In social interaction, the use of phrases like: 'It might/could well be that . . .' avoids the dogmatism characteristic of a matter-of-fact style which in many contexts can be found offensive. Nattinger and DeCarrico (1992: 88) suggest that such phrases are 'evasive' because they allow participants greater room for manouevre and convey politeness at the same time. The phrase, 'They may well have made a mistake' allows for a tactful retraction, which the blunt assertion, 'They have made a mistake' clearly does not.

The frames which lend themselves to pedagogical exploitation, pronoun + modal + adverb + VP or adverb + pronoun + modal + VP, can readily accommodate the range of speaker assessments discussed in 5.2.3.

(27)   (a) There + could + conceivably + have been a fault in
             the system.
        (b) Probably + they + 'll + be asked to take a resit.
        (c) They must evidently have forgotten.
        (d) You couldn't possibly have been there at the time!

In general, the conviction with which a statement is expressed reflects the status of the available evidence: the clearer the evidence, the more forthright the evaluation.

L are provided with a series of contexts where each invites a different kind of assessment, according to whether the speaker is making a simple speculation; is presenting his assessment as a deduction; or is simply reporting hearsay. In each case, the speaker has to indicate the degree of his commitment to the truth of what he is saying. The contexts outlined below would be suitable only at more advanced levels.

(28)   *Context 1* (Speculation)
        You are a financial consultant specializing in the currency markets. You have to forecast the relative strength of various European currencies in relation to the US dollar over the next twelve months.

        A: What do you think the rate will be for pounds sterling? (the Swiss franc, the German Mark, Spanish peseta, etc.)
        B: Well, there could well be a slight drop in the value of the pound.
            It may possibly fall but not by much.

There shouldn't really be any fluctuation.
Perhaps there might be some slight instability.

(29)   *Context 2* (Deduction)
The results of a local housing survey indicate that there is
enough available rented accommodation to meet market
demand, despite arguments to the contrary from various
pressure groups.

A: Do you agree with the survey's conclusions?
B: Not really, it must be a cover-up. Look at all the
homeless people on the streets.
There could well be some truth in it but the so-called
facts are debatable.
It couldn't possibly have any truth to it.

(30)   *Context 3* (Hearsay)
The local bank manager has disappeared in mysterious
circumstances . . .

A: What do you think could have happened to him?
B: Evidently he must have been having problems at
home and decided to get away from it all.
Apparently, he could have been planning this for
some time, from what I've heard.

An alternative to these contextualized exchanges, which presuppose an already high level of fluency, is to provide L with a series
of different auditory or pictorial stimuli that resist easy identification. L are asked to give their opinion in terms of a pre-taught
hierarchical scale of likelihood.

(31)   (a) It could perhaps be a drill.
(b) It might just possibly be the eye of a needle.
(c) It must be some sort of musical instrument.
(d) It'll be part of a building.

5.4.3 Conclusion

Modal–adverb combinations range from being wholly idiomatic
and invariant to being relatively flexible patterns of regularly

produced language. They therefore represent a cline of idiomaticity, represented at one extreme by such fixed combinations as
MIGHT, MAY or COULD with WELL, and at the other by less fixed but
generally predictable patterns, such as those involving epistemic
MUST and evidential adverbs, like APPARENTLY or EVIDENTLY. In
addition to modal idioms and collocations, we have distinguished
lexical phrases, such as WOULD YOU KINDLY or MAY I JUST; as form/
function composites, these phrases can regularly be associated with
particular pragmatic functions.[20]

The identification and description of modal–adverb expressions
could usefully be incorporated in general works of language
reference, and especially bilingual dictionaries targeted at the non-
native user. The entry for each individual modal would include
details of its collocational possibilities and list its collocational
range; such information would make a valuable contribution to a
more precise description of the modal's meaning and how this is
affected or modified by different types of adverbial collocate. For
instance, it is only in combination with WELL that the modals
MIGHT, MAY and COULD assume a new meaning and express a
higher degree of likelihood than the unmodified forms. Likewise,
certain adverbial combinations with MUST, involving such items as
APPARENTLY or EVIDENTLY, introduce an evidential dimension into
what is otherwise a purely judgemental epistemic system in
English. There is significant potential for making dictionary entries
more explicit by including the kind of syntagmatic information
that the description of modal–adverb co-occurrence yields. The
point is taken up by Nattinger and DeCarrico (1992: 182) who
argue that lexicographical research will increasingly have to take
account of the patterns of words that only analysis of large corpora
can reveal:

> A thorough dictionary . . . would not stop with collocations, but
> would select those that play particular functional roles in the
> language and further label them as lexical phrases. Such a
> dictionary would be a major resource for information about the
> language, for it would list not only the form and reference for
> particular collocations, it would also assign each its function. . . .

The implications for teaching are also significant. Syllabus design
would need to move well beyond purely structural considerations
and the selection and gradation of grammatical items on which so

many foreign language programmes have traditionally been based. Contextual and functional information would also be included and related to the range of discourse functions – exchanging information, voicing attitudes and opinions, using directives – with which modal–adverb expressions are so clearly associated. With pedagogical needs firmly in view, modal–adverb collocations could be defined and effectively presented in teaching materials as 'basic units in strategies of oral and written discourse' (see Nattinger and DeCarrico 1992: 186). They enable the language user to implement strategies commensurate with his need to appear authoritative, uncommitted, vague or polite, and in ways that are always appropriate to and consistent with the particular context of communication. The kind of exercises proposed here are exemplificatory and programmatic, and gradually develop situations that increasingly require genuine communicative practice and rehearsal of the wide repertoire of modal expressions that are available to more experienced speakers.[21]

Of course, it could be objected that the various nuances introduced by modal–adverb expressions and their description are too subtle or refined to warrant inclusion in a teaching programme, because they might appear to make the teaching/learning task much harder than it already is. However, the descriptive categories of idiom, collocation or lexical phrase are naturally derived units of language structure and function, which arise from analysis of accurate data about actual usage. It is hardly surprising that their status does not accord with more traditional views on language education, where approaches dwell on the teaching of pronunciation, basic vocabulary and syntax, and semantics and pragmatics are mostly left to take care of themselves. As de Beaugrande (1996: §77; 532) remarks:

> If the chief unit of language use and language learning is recognised to be the *collocation*, then learning words would be systematically correlated with learning the company they keep, and the latter kind of learning would not be seen as some onerous supplementary job.

5.5 DATA PROFILE OF MODAL–ADVERB CO-OCCURRENCE

The aim of this section is to provide at-a-glance, accessible information on the most significant trends in modal/adverb co-occurrence, primarily with pedagogical needs in view.

Basic statistical information is given in percentages and relates to the spoken and written parts of the Survey of English Usage corpus. The figures cited indicate only broad trends in collocational attraction, they are not definitive statements of association. Statistical minutiae have been omitted for reasons of clarity and readability and the examples, most of which are based on corpus data, have been modified to accord with the outline presentation and purpose of this section.

It is generally the case that co-occurrence is more frequent in the spoken than the written language, although there are important differences, nonetheless, between the spoken and written parts of the Survey: MAY (but not MIGHT), SHOULD, WILL and SHALL are all more common in the written medium, which reflects their wider distribution in relatively formal language registers. Coates (1983: 24), for instance, comments on the relative infrequency of MAY in speech which she attributes in part to 'the formality of its two Root [nonepistemic] meanings (Permission and Possibility), which are found more often in the written material'. WOULD (including 'D), CAN and WILL (including the semantically and historically related contraction 'LL) are the three most common forms in both speech and writing, although their respective frequencies differ according to medium.

Colloquial language favours the more colourful types of expression associated with approximation or reinforcement (see 4.1.3) and, in general, co-occurrence is more frequent in the spoken material. This is particularly noticeable in the case of the more frequent modals CAN, COULD and WOULD, where combinations are roughly twice as frequent than in the written language. SHOULD and WILL are exceptions, where medium seems to have little influence on co-occurrence. We now briefly examine each modal in turn.

5.5.1 Introduction

For ease of presentation, the relevant modals are 'paired'. This also reflects their tendency to share a similar range of adverb collocates. Each entry contains statistical information on the frequency with which different types of modal meaning are expressed by modal–adverb combinations; for example, 86 per cent of combinations involving COULD express nonepistemic modality and 14 per cent epistemic modality. The figures generally correlate with the relative frequencies of modal meanings as these are expressed by the *unmodified* auxiliaries; this is to be expected since the semantic status of the modals determines their collocational ties and tendencies.[22] After the statistical information, the main trends in collocation are outlined under 'Collocational trends', followed by a short list of the *most common* adverb collocates of the modal(s) in question, given under 'Collocational range'. Except for reference to the idiomatic combination of REALLY with MUST (5.4.4), this adverb and the associated forms ACTUALLY and IN FACT, are not otherwise recorded in the lists of collocates, because they freely co-occur with all the modals.

5.5.2 CAN and COULD

	Can	Could
Nonepistemic possibility/ability[†]	91%	82%
Permission	7%	4%
Epistemic possibility (probability)	2%	14%

Collocational trends
(1) Both forms co-occur with a wide range of adverbs when they express nonepistemic possibility, but commonly combine with ALWAYS, EASILY, READILY where these items function as emphasizers.
(2) CAN and COULD of permission combine with JUST, POSSIBLY, PERHAPS to convey additional politeness:

† There is considerable indeterminacy between possibility and ability readings.

    (a) CAN/COULD I JUST speak to you for a moment?
    (b) CAN/COULD I POSSIBLY see that map again?
    (c) PERHAPS you CAN/COULD see your way to lending a hand.
(3) Both forms regularly combine with POSSIBLY (and less frequently, CONCEIVABLY) in nonassertive clauses to express epistemic modality:
    (a) They CAN'T/COULDN'T POSSIBLY be in Paris in time for the meeting.
    (b) CAN/COULD he CONCEIVABLY want to see her again?
    COULD (and exceptionally CAN) combines with WELL to form an idiomatic expression of epistemic probability:
    (c) She COULD WELL be the person for the job.
(4) Both forms combine with POSSIBLY and PLEASE in formulaic expressions of politeness:
    (a) CAN/COULD I POSSIBLY/PLEASE use the phone?
(5) Negated CAN/COULD is frequently emphasized by: HONESTLY, OBVIOUSLY, OF COURSE, and SIMPLY:
    (a) We honestly CAN'T/COULDN'T see a way out of the impasse.
    (b) They OBVIOUSLY CAN'T/COULDN'T understand the implications.
    (c) One OF COURSE CAN'T/COULDN'T anticipate all the questions.
    (d) It seems that they SIMPLY CAN'T/COULDN'T do the job.

Collocational range:
This is wider than for any other modal: ALWAYS (emphasizer), AT LEAST (intensifier), CERTAINLY, CONCEIVABLY, DEFINITELY, EASILY (emphasizer), HARDLY, HONESTLY (emphasizer) JUST, NEVER (negative intensifier), OF COURSE, PERHAPS, POSSIBLY, PROBABLY, SIMPLY and WELL (primarily with COULD).

5.5.3 MAY and MIGHT

	May	*Might*
Epistemic possibility/probability	76%	92%
Nonepistemic: indeterminate	24%	8%

Collocational trends
(1) Both forms regularly combine with WELL in idiomatic expressions of epistemic probability:
   (a) It MAY/MIGHT WELL be that there were faults.
(2) In non-assertive contexts, CAN and COULD replace epistemic MAY and MIGHT: see 5.5.2(3).
(3) When used to seek permission, both forms often combine with JUST in formulaic expressions of politeness:
   (a) MAY/MIGHT I JUST make a few observations?
(4) MIGHT (and to a lesser degree MAY) combine with (JUST) AS WELL in idiomatic expressions typically used to make a circumspect or sardonic recommendation:
   (a) You MIGHT (JUST) AS WELL have asked him to side with the opposition, when you think of the speech he made.
   (b) We MAY AS WELL stay on for another night, given the weather.

Collocational range
Both forms share a similar range of collocates: WELL, JUST, POSSIBLY, PERHAPS, and may also combine with CERTAINLY or OF COURSE in their concessional function: 'CERTAINLY he MAY/MIGHT be there, but I doubt it'.

5.5.4 MUST

	Must
Epistemic necessity	53%
Nonepistemic necessity	47%

Collocational trends
(1) Epistemic and nonepistemic MUST is commonly reinforced by REALLY:
   (a) I suppose it REALLY MUST have been more serious than any of us had anticipated.
   (b) They REALLY MUST get the job finished today or they'll lose the contract.
(2) APPARENTLY, EVIDENTLY, INEVITABLY, OBVIOUSLY all co-occur with MUST and constitute an evidential subsystem of epistemic modality (see 3.4.3).

(3) NECESSARILY occasionally reinforces MUST in subjective epistemic statements:
Any history of art written for the consumption of twentieth-century Europeans must necessarily regard the Giotto–Cézanne period as the most important section of art history. (J 1964: 298)

Collocational range
APPARENTLY, CERTAINLY, CLEARLY, DEFINITELY, EVIDENTLY, INDEED, INEVITABLY, OBVIOUSLY, PLAINLY, OF COURSE, SIMPLY, SURELY. In the environment of MUST, in pre- or post-auxiliary position, these adverbs function as emphasizers, unless marked off by intonation or punctuation.

5.5.5 SHOULD and OUGHT TO

	Should	Ought to
Epistemic (tentative inference)	20%	20%
Nonepistemic (deontic: obligation)	80%	80%

Collocational trends
(1) Slight tendency for SHOULD and OUGHT TO to co-occur with PERHAPS, POSSIBLY (in pre-auxiliary position with OUGHT TO) and PRESUMABLY but otherwise no noteworthy trends:
   (a) PERHAPS they SHOULD/OUGHT TO be kept out of the way.
   (b) You SHOULD POSSIBLY try another type of analgesic.
   (c) They POSSIBLY OUGHT TO be considered.
   (d) PRESUMABLY, there SHOULD/OUGHT TO be no further need for these documents.
(2) In the case of OUGHT TO, there are stylistic objections to the insertion of an adverbial before the TO, which is grammatically and phonologically related to OUGHT:
   (a) */?He is another writer who OUGHT POSSIBLY TO be considered.

Collocational range
CERTAINLY, PERHAPS, POSSIBLY, PRESUMABLY.

5.5.6 WILL and WOULD

	Will	Would
Prediction	70%	61%
Volition	30%	39%

Collocational trends
(1) Both forms have a marked tendency to co-occur with PROBABLY and PRESUMABLY in epistemic contexts:
    (a) He WILL PROBABLY still be there after the meeting.
    (b) PRESUMABLY she WOULD have no hesitation about sacking him now.
(2) Both forms co-occur with courtesy subjuncts such as KINDLY and PLEASE in formulaic expressions of politeness:
    (a) WILL/WOULD you KINDLY/PLEASE answer the question? Both forms may also combine with these adverbs in IF-clauses to convey even greater politeness:
    (b) IF you WILL/WOULD KINDLY/PLEASE sign below . . .

Collocational range
CERTAINLY, DEFINITELY, INDEED, JUST, KINDLY, NEVER (intensifier), OF COURSE, PROBABLY, PRESUMABLY.

5.5.7 SHALL

	Shall
Prediction	47%
Volition	53%

Collocational trends
(1) No notable trends in modern English, but may co-occur with such compound adverbs as HENCEFORTH, HEREUPON, THERE-AFTER typical of legal and other types of formal registers.

Collocational range
Above-mentioned compound adverbs and CERTAINLY, OF COURSE, PROBABLY.

NOTES

1 In Thomas and Short (1996: 232).

2 WELL also combines with CAN but may be ambivalent when the modal co-occurs with main verbs of saying or thinking. See Chapter 3, note 15.

3 Dictionaries differ in the extent to which they recognize the association between common syntactic patterns and a particular sense; there is a growing tendency, especially among bilingual dictionaries, to do so and to include guidance on usage. For example, the Oxford–Hachette bilingual French dictionary (1994) contains quite detailed reference on the use of POSSIBLY (p. 1574) in the environment of CAN and COULD, or the modification of MIGHT and MAY by WELL (p. 1451; p. 1461), and the peculiarities of idiom these associations represent for the translator.

4 In the Chomskyan model of linguistic competence and perform- ance, competence refers to speaker's knowledge of his language and the system of rules which enables him to produce and understand an indefinite number of sentences, and to recognize grammatical errors and ambiguities. In opposition to this idealized conception of language is the notion of linguistic performance, corresponding to the specific utterances actually produced by native speakers and containing all the erratic features of performance, such as hesitations, repetitions, memory lapses and so forth which naturally accompany everyday speech. Although the basic distinc- tion is widely endorsed and accepted by linguists, the dichotomy is often felt to be unnecessarily severe and the demarcation not as clearcut as the standard definitions would suggest. See Nattinger and DeCarrico (1992: 3f) for a full discussion of the contrasts between linguistic and pragmalinguistic competence and perform- ance.

5 The treatment of modal–adverb collocations in this section is based in part on Matthews' discussion of epistemic modality (1991: 33f). He examines a more limited range of modal–adverb combinations in terms of possibility, probability, certainty and necessity. He acknowl- edges the syntactic variation immanent to different types of modal– adverb expression but focuses primarily on the characterization of these and other kinds of modal expression in terms of what he refers to as epistemic 'certainty', involving the 'predictive' uses of the modals, and epistemic 'necessity', involving their inferential uses. The distinction he draws between prediction and inference to some extent echoes our own observations about the confidence–inference axis discussed in 3.3 and under individual entries for the modals in

Chapter 3. See Matthews (1991: ch. 3) for further details of his approach to epistemic modality.

6 The two main branches of elicitation work, 'performance' and 'judgement', consist of different but complementary types of test which are differentiated according to the nature of the task required of informants:

> [The tests] are in a deliberate reciprocal relation, so there is a purposive relation between corpus and elicitation. Not only do we turn to elicitation for information on features that chance to be of fairly rare occurrence: we do so when corpus instances reveal a variation that needs to be explored. (Quirk 1995: 120)

A typology of performance and judgement tests, the relation between them, and their range of applications, are treated in full in Greenbaum and Quirk (1970).

7 In principle, the concept of acceptability applies to what native speakers judge to be possible in their language. In practice, they often differ in their attitudes towards issues of usage because their intuitions are conditioned by variations in their regional and social backgrounds, age, education, personal preferences and so forth. On the basis of research into several important corpora, including the SEU, the CGEL (33f) has found that: 'Assessments by native speakers of relative acceptability largely correlate with their assessments of relative frequency.' The more frequent a particular language phenomenon is, the more likely it is to meet native speaker criteria of acceptability.

8 Greenbaum and Quirk (1970: 2f) draw an essential distinction between elicited usage and attitudes to usage:

> If elicited behaviour is different from the 'actual' behaviour casually observed and (if one is lucky) collected in a corpus, it is at least equally important to distinguish elicited usage from attitudes to usage. And these attitudes can be seen as reflecting three potentially quite distinct but often interacting factors. We may have strong beliefs about the forms we habitually use and we may also have strong views about the forms that ought to be used; these may be in harmony or in rueful conflict, but – needless to say – our beliefs about our own usage in no way necessarily correspond to the facts of our actual usage. Furthermore, we may tolerate usage in others that corresponds neither to the forms we believe we use ourselves nor to the forms that we believe are the most to be commended.

9 Quirk (1995: 147) comments on the advantages of oral elicitation techniques as follows:

> There was in this new [oral] material a much sounder basis [than with written responses] for attributing an 'untidy' response to hesitation, and in addition we now had access to 'silent hesitation' (whether before or during the response), which is not shown at all where subjects make their responses in writing. Most importantly, we could register in the prosodic transcription the changes of tempo (including instances of drawling), changes of tonicity (the location of nuclear tone), types of nuclear tone, and limits of other tone units, which provide essential information on the subject's attitudes to individual sentences and their grammatical interpretation of the sentences as changed on application of the operation task.

Quirk (1995: 156) goes on to conclude that: 'Oral responses yield especially precise clues as to the point of the test sentence at which difficulty seems to be greatest, and fresh parameters become available for determining the subject's reaction and the ways in which his or her response is to be interpreted.'

10 Elicitation techniques involve more complex procedures than our brief treatment might suggest. The aim is to obtain or elicit reliable data in an indirect way by requiring informants to perform tasks which, although seemingly irrelevant to the purpose at hand, produce the kind of data actually sought by the analyst. See Quirk (1995: 129f) for a discussion of current approaches to the elicitation of grammatical data.

11 It could also be argued that the number of informants participating in the test represented only a very small sample of individuals: the native speaker subjects (20) were members of the overseas diplomatic corps, and their non-native (Chilean) counterparts (20) were university undergraduate students. The relative conformity of native speaker responses with the probabilistic tendencies revealed in the data indicated that the sample size was sufficient, even though the exercise was administered only on a small scale. Likewise, the general failure among the non-native subjects to recognize at least the more typical modal–adverb collocations had been largely anticipated. Some of the elicitation experiments referred to by Quirk (1995: 129, 145) also involve comparatively small groups of informants.

12 The five distracter sentences were also taken from the SEU corpus, but they invited a potentially much wider selection of items than the actual test sentences. Responses were correspondingly random.

13 The Romanian informants, undergraduate students of English, were

closer to Ns in their responses to items (b), (e), (f) (g) and (i) than their Chilean counterparts but, again, generally failed to identify the idiomatic associations represented by (c) and (j). For a detailed assessment of the test results, see Hoye (1989).

14 In the context of translation, L1 and L2 are sometimes referred to as the 'source language' (SL) and the 'target language' (TL) respectively.

15 In Romanian, which is also a Romance language, periphrastic constructions are more common than single-word realizations of the adverbial function.

16 With reference to the overuse of Spanish adverbs in -MENTE, Butt and Benjamin (1988: 319) note that 'the barbarous sentence *Evidentemente, todas las lenguas evolucionan constantemente, y sería totalmente absurdo pretender detener arbitrarimente su crecimiento* makes passable English in literal translation – 'clearly, all languages evolve constantly, and it would be totally absurd to attempt to arrest the growth arbitrarily' – but must be recast in Spanish along the lines of *Es evidente que todas las lenguas están en constante evolución, y sería totalmente absurdo pretender detener de manera arbitraria su crecimiento*'. Stylistic objections are not restricted, of course, to adverbs expressing modality, but apply to all -MENTE forms whatever their semantic role. See Butt and Benjamin (1988: 316f).

A similar situation arises in Romanian, although the use of adverbs in -MENTE (the same suffix as Spanish) is restricted to only a few items, such as COMPLETAMENTE, EVIDAMENTE, TOTALMENTE which all function as emphasizers, and tend to be associated with an elevated style. The Romanian equivalent of the above English sentence is similar to the Spanish in its avoidance of -MENTE adverbial forms: '*Evident, toate limbile evoluează constant, și ar fi total absurd să încerci să oprești arbitrar această creștere.*'

17 Levenston (1971), in Nickel (1971: 115-21), suggests that learners tend to overuse or exclude some structures in the L2 according to how similar or different they perceive these to be in comparison with equivalents in their L1:

> One feature of non-native use of a second language, of L2, is the excessive use ('over-indulgence') of clause (or group) structures which closely resemble translation equivalents in the mother tongue, or L1, to the exclusion of other structures ('under representation') which are less like anything in L1. 'Closely resemble' can be more precisely defined as with translation-equivalents which correspond at the level of group (or word) as well as clause; 'less like' means with translation equivalents which correspond at the level of clause (or group) only.

The Ss tendency to avoid using adverbs ending in -LY in the L2 is because there is a general preference for the use of periphrastic structural equivalents in their L1. Although Spanish shares with English a morphological equivalent of almost equal generality (-MENTE), stylistic and other considerations of use place greater restrictions on the frequency and distribution of corresponding adverbial forms ending in -MENTE.

18 The politeness models proposed by Leech (1983), Brown and Levinson (1987) and Fraser (1990) all aspire to universal validity but there is serious theoretical doubt and considerable empirical counter-evidence to contradict their different claims to universality. For example, with regard to the face-saving approach of Brown and Levinson, psychological and anthropological studies indicate that universal conceptualizations of 'face' have no validity because they erroneously presuppose identical assumptions about 'self' across cultures. See Kasper (1994).

19 The use of translation as a didactic procedure is not as widespread as it once was, especially in the case of language learning/teaching methodologies which proscribe or discourage reference to the L1 (cf. the Direct Method; The Audio-Lingual Method). Recently, however, even communicative approaches (where the emphasis is on getting L to *use* the language rather than just rehearse the rules of language *usage*) have started to recognize the advantages of a less doctrinaire, eclectic attitude. It is not being argued here that translation in and out of the L1 should receive a disproportionate amount of attention at the expense of developing language skills as a whole, but it can be used to increase the learner's awareness of what is appropriate and thus help refine the choices of structure or idiom available to him.

20 See Nattinger and DeCarrico (1991: 174f) for further discussion of the relationship between lexical phrases, collocations and idioms.

21 It is beyond the scope of the present study to examine suitable language activities in any depth. As a guiding principle, it is important to develop group work and other situations which encourage the communicative use of language in a very real way. There is now an abundance of commercially available material which focuses on the practical issues of materials writing and especially the development of communicative language activities. The 'Cambridge Language Teaching Library', the Centre for Information on Language Teaching and Research (CILT) 'Pathfinder Series' of handbooks and language teaching guides, the 'Heinemann series of Handbooks for the English Classroom', and the 'Longman Handbooks for Language Teachers' and 'Keys to Language Teaching' are

all valuable sources of guidance, and contain titles which provide a range of practical ideas on materials design and ready-made activities for the language classroom.

22　See Coates (1983: 23f), whose account of the relative frequencies of modal meanings expressed by the unmodified modals is summarized in a histogram. This offers a diagrammatic representation of the relative frequencies of modal meanings as evidenced by the Survey. Although Coates consulted the Survey at an earlier stage in its development, in the late seventies, there are few discrepancies between her findings and our own. The most striking correspondences arise in connexion with epistemic modality, where Coates' figures for .MUST (53 per cent) and MAY (74 per cent) are almost identical to our results. Differences in the interpretation and/ or classification of nonepistemic meanings account for any divergent results in this domain.

Six

Conclusions and implications

6.1 GENERAL SUMMING-UP

At the beginning of this book, it was pointed out that most studies on modality have concentrated on the formal and semantic analysis of the modal auxiliaries to the exclusion of other types of modal expression. The chief reason for this seems to be that, more than any other category of modal expression, the auxiliaries are syntactically distinct and lend themselves most easily to description and analysis. In consequence, the expression of modality by other means has been left largely untouched. Of course, a number of studies do make reference to modal adverbs, as well as to other types of modal expression, such as modal lexical verbs, modal idioms, adjectival, nominal and participial expressions but, with the exception of Bîrä (1979), Perkins (1983) and Matthews (1991), this has been done mostly in passing or where a supposedly synon-ymous paraphrase of the modals has been required for the purposes of elucidation. Contrary to the view that when adverbs occur with the modals they do so pleonastically (see Palmer 1990: 67f), we have argued that modal–adverb combinations function as units of modal expression. This is most clearly demonstrated by idiomatic sequences like MAY WELL and CAN'T POSSIBLY, and various types of lexical phrase (WOULD + YOU + KINDLY; COULD + I + POSSIBLY), where the modal expression operates with a high degree of functional integrity.

The basic modal concepts of mood and modality – the one a formal category, the other a semantic one – can be discussed in terms of the theory of speech acts. Searle's (1983: 166) categories of assertives ('where we tell our hearers [truly or falsely] how things are') and directives ('where we get them to do things') have particular relevance for the description of the two main types of modality known as epistemic and deontic. The first is concerned with the status of the speaker's belief and corresponding degrees of conviction about particular states of affairs, events or actions ('She may well be on her way'; 'She can't possibly have already left, surely?!'), and the second with the speaker's authority in terms of permission granted or obligation imposed ('Can I just say something here?'; 'Will you please answer the question!'). Throughout the book we have drawn a principled distinction between modal–adverb combinations used to express epistemic meanings and those used to express (nonepistemic) deontic meanings, although it is acknowledged that there may be ambivalence between the two and within the broader nonepistemic category itself, where deontic and dynamic readings cannot always be clearly distinguished. Some approaches to the semantics of the modals and associated expressions regard ambivalence as a function of context, external to the semantics of the modals themselves, whereas others view this as a natural consequence of their inherent semantic complexity. The one view is characterized in terms of monosemy, the other in terms of polysemy. This study treads a middle path and, following the practice observed by the CGEL, deals with indeterminacy in terms of gradience: the indeterminate status of the modals is recognized but frequent overlaps in their meaning are also readily acknowledged.

The modal–adverb combinations presented in this study vary in the extent to which they demonstrate idiomaticity; generally, it is only possible to describe co-occurrence in terms of tendencies in association which are more or less predictable, according to the strength of the attraction between the two forms. But our account demonstrates that patterns do emerge and that they represent a continuum ranging from *relatively* 'frozen' units or fixed patterns of modal expression at one extreme to more complex and productive structures at the other.

It has been argued throughout that the category of epistemic modality is more homogeneous and easier to define than those categories related to the nonepistemic domains: the association between the modals and their adverb satellites is correspondingly more transparent and amenable to classification. Modal–adverb synergy is at its most striking where collocations are defined in relation to epistemic scales of likelihood and the corresponding degrees of indirectness or remoteness these represent. Collocational restrictions come into play, disallowing combinations at the extremes of the scale, such as *MAY CERTAINLY or *MUST POSSIBLY on the grounds that they lack modal harmony. The association between modals and adverbs of equivalent epistemic status can be used as a framework for establishing a paradigm of speaker assessments, where each collocation conveys the relative strength or weakness of the speaker's epistemic knowledge. Three broad categories of speaker assessment can be distinguished, in terms of possibility, probability and certainty and a measure of refinement is possible according to the type of adverb selected and where it is placed in relation to the modal verb head. 'They conceivably could have forgotten, I suppose' suggests a more tentative assessment of a given state of affairs, and conveys the speaker's doubt in a more emphatic way, than if the adverb–modal sequence were reversed.

Yet, the dynamic interplay between modal verb head and adverb satellite is not just restricted to epistemic contexts: the conventionalized use of particular combinations to make requests or offers demonstrates their significance in nonepistemic (deontic) contexts as well. The prominence of certain combinations in indirect speech acts, such as COULD and POSSIBLY or WOULD and KINDLY in the making of requests, points to the centrality of such combinations to the deontic system and their conventionalized roles in expressing the associated notions of obligation and permission.

As markers or tokens of speaker presence, modal adverb satellites can be described as 'subjectivity markers': they confirm that the conceptual framework within which the speaker operates, be this epistemic or nonepistemic, is fundamentally subjective. We have therefore taken issue with commentators who (misleadingly in our view) discuss linguistic modality in terms of objectivity. Speaker presence is often marked in an overt way through the use of comment adverbs (content disjuncts) and their strategic placement about the utterance. When the speaker opens with 'Obviously . . .', what follows may well not be obvious at all. As Halliday (1994: 355) remarks: 'Speakers have indefinitely many ways of expressing their opinions – or rather, perhaps, of dissimulating the fact that they *are* expressing their opinions.' The interpretation of modal–adverb use, whether manipulative or otherwise, brings us firmly into the realm of pragmatics.

We have been careful to underline the significance of context in assessing the role and function of modal–adverb expressions, particularly with regard to the pragmatic interpretation of such features as indirectness or remoteness mentioned above. The relationship between modal–adverb use and environment of use is highly complex and an area we have touched on only briefly in our discussion of modality and power, and modality and politeness. Abstract scales used as frameworks to establish degrees of politeness or formality have to be treated with extreme caution because, ultimately, context provides vital clues as to how any utterance should be interpreted.

In covering new ground and exploring familiar territory, there have been a number of issues raised in this study which require an airing before we draw to a close. These are primarily concerned with the theoretical assumptions on which the study has been based and the implications of our findings for modality-centred research in particular and linguistics in general.

6.2 THEORETICAL AND METHODOLOGICAL IMPLICATIONS

In order to establish a coherent framework within which to analyse and describe modal–adverb co-occurrence, this study has relied heavily on traditional and, in the main, widely accepted definitions of what constitutes the class of verbs referred to in the literature as 'modal auxiliaries'. Although some scholars continue to argue against the recognition of either auxiliaries or the modals as a separate verbal category, distinct from main verbs, there is much greater controversy surrounding their semantics and how the various meanings they convey can be most satisfactorily accounted for.

The evidence provided by co-occurrence is that a valid distinction can and needs to be made between the epistemic and nonepistemic meanings of the modals, and corresponding modal–adverb expressions. The identification of epistemic modality as a distinct category is further enhanced by the collocational patterns that emerge when both epistemic modals and adverbs combine. In particular, the association between MUST (and to a lesser extent WILL and WOULD) and evidential adverbs like APPARENTLY or EVIDENTLY suggests that English has not one but two types of epistemic system, the one judgemental, the other evidential. Whereas the first also involves the unmodified modals, the evidential system is synthetic and requires the co-occurrence of an appropriate adverb form. In strictly formal terms, of course, English has only judgements as the evidential component is not grammatically encoded. But, in functional terms, English clearly makes it possible for the speaker to qualify the degree of his commitment by making reference to the quality or type of evidence at his disposal (be it visual or non-visual). Recognition of an evidential subsystem of epistemic modality in English, even if expressed synthetically, facilitates cross-linguistic comparison. Palmer (1986: 54f) notes a range of languages where particles exist to mark epistemicity and where distinctions made on the quality and type of the available evidence are also encoded; by establishing a functional typological category, it then becomes possible to compare modal systems which formally may be very different. In a similar way, the inference–confidence distinction made in relation to MUST and its potential association with collocates like CERTAINLY, DEFINITELY or OF COURSE contrasts with the situation in other languages where, again, a particle may be used to signal that the speaker's judgement is more a matter of confidence, more a matter of deduction (see Palmer 1986: 64f). In both instances, the adverb collocate brings about a change in the modal status of the auxiliary and heralds a refinement in the way epistemic contrasts are expressed.

Modal–adverb collocations in deontic environments also play an important role and especially in expressions used for making offers or requests. Yet there is much less to be said with regard to the nuances adverb collocates introduce once these instances of conventionalized use are accounted for. It is true that adverbs such as PERHAPS or POSSIBLY combine with past tense forms of the modals in both epistemic and deontic contexts and that their role is broadly similar: to mitigate impositive force as opposed to rendering a judgement more tentative or less dogmatic. But the fact remains that the nuances adverbs introduce in nonepistemic contexts are less extensive and, typologically, less significant.

We have discussed at some length the enormous difficulties surrounding the description of adverbial behaviour. We have largely avoided the vexed issue of adverbial classification by adopting wholesale the system developed by the CGEL. In principle, there is nothing very controversial about drawing the distinction between adverbs which have a marked tendency to focus the verb phrase (what we have referred to variously as VP-adverbs or subjuncts) and adverbs which extend their focus over an entire clause (so-called S-adverbs, or disjuncts). In practice, however, a whole complex of factors comes into play and precise delimitations of adverbial scope can all but be impossible to uphold. When two or more modal elements are present in the same clause, the synergy produced often permeates the whole construction and it is simply impossible to identify the precise locus of modification. For this reason, modal adverbs have often been relegated to the S-class by default. This is a mistake. There are prototypical instances of VP-modification, which mostly correspond to the more idiomatic modal–adverb combinations: COULD/MIGHT/MAY + WELL and COULDN'T + POSSIBLY. There are also other cases where the scope of modification has an intermediate value and is neither co-extensive with the clause or solely confined to the verb phrase. This is where the analysis of attested spoken data comes into its own because intonation and stress patterns correlate directly with the part(s) of the utterance the speaker has chosen to focus. By contrast, the clues offered by punctuation (when it is present) are decidedly primitive.

The semantic processes associated with approximation – thematization, interpolation, tagging – which involve sentential modification and the role of disjuncts are more distinct than those associated with reinforcement – emphasis, intensification and focus – which involve some form of VP-modification and the role of subjuncts. The explanation is not hard to find. By its very nature, reinforcement demands that the reinforcing item contribute not so much individual meaning as a discernible heightening effect on the item so modified. In modal environments, the finer distinctions between emphasizer, intensifier and focusing subjunct become somewhat blurred and hard to maintain: they all share a similar function and they are all maximally redundant in terms of their lexical content. There is a case for classifying the items concerned as reinforcement particles.

For the purposes of this study, the range of items included in the notional category of modal adverb has been kept deliberately broad. This has been done for reasons of coverage and to facilitate comparison between modal–adverb collocations where there are marked differences in the strength of their mutual attraction. The implication of this methodological decision is that a principled distinction can be made between a central and more peripheral class of modal adverb, where the terms central and peripheral relate to semantic rather than syntactic status. The central category might consist of those items which themselves express modal meanings of likelihood (POSSIBLY, PROBABLY, CERTAINLY) and which tend to operate sententially, and those items which carry no particular meanings themselves but reinforce and focalize the verb head to which they are attached (JUST, WELL, POSSIBLY [intensifier]). The latter group are of particular interest because, of all the items discussed in this study, they are the most likely candidates to be assigned the status of particle, chiefly on the grounds of their lexical redundancy and reinforcing role in the closed modal environment. By contrast, the peripheral class would include those comment adverbials (such as style disjuncts and content disjuncts not directly concerned with the expression of modal values) which impinge in no obvious way on modal meanings and are therefore not subject to the usual collocational restrictions. These items are the least interesting from the point of view of co–occurrence. However, the tendency for otherwise quite lexically loaded items to become delexicalized in modal environments must not be ignored: to wit the behaviour of adverbs like CLEARLY in combination with MUST.

In sum, while this study has targeted an area of modality that has attracted little attention elsewhere, the description and analysis of co–occurrence places the modals in a new perspective, and is a further defining characteristic of this verbal category. It could be argued that, if language description is to take into account units of language use, then the modals are only incompletely described unless due attention is paid to their typical collocates and the way both elements behave once they are combined. No language description is complete if it dwells on matters of form alone; the wider range of functions with which modal expressions can be meaningfully associated also warrants attention. For instance, the manipulative use of modal–adverb expressions could well be the focus of a broader study which explores the relationship between modality and power at a general level.

One of the main drawbacks of much previous work on modality, and language description in general, has been its heavy reliance on invented example and introspection. In the past this was often unavoidable, at least where the gathering of spoken data was concerned. But today, the arguments in favour of approaches which are corpus-based are overwhelming as the techniques of corpus compilation become increasingly sophisticated and the corpora themselves continue to grow. It is important, too, to have in mind the crucial role that elicitation experiments have to play in corpus-based descriptions. They are a necessary adjunct and an indispensable means of investigating rare features of occurrence or apparent quirks of usage.

Although the informant tests in this study played a relatively minor role – and certainly lacked the sophistication of those used in the preparation of the CGEL – they have proved to be a fairly reliable and independent means of confirming particular features of modal–adverb co-occurrence. There is considerable scope for extending their role in the investigation of co-occurrence, particularly in those cases where the combination of the two elements is relatively infrequent or where no attested examples are found in the data.

The scope of this book has been highly focused and there is clearly much work to be done in this most fertile of language areas. Modal–adverb expressions play an important part in the expression of modal concepts in English, possibly finding their equivalence in the (subjunctive) mood components of other languages. While modality will remain an elusive area of human language and thought and continue to defy ready definition and analysis, it can be best served, perhaps, by extending research well beyond treatment of just the modals themselves. The aim of this study has been to demonstrate the benefits of such an approach. Scrutinizing the dynamic interplay between two independent carriers of modal meaning at all levels of language description – grammatical, semantic and pragmatic – provides us with fresh insights into the workings of the English modal system as a whole. Ultimately, what is needed is a comprehensive grammar of modal expressions which not only seeks to examine the formal and semantic aspects of the system but which also attempts to explain how modal elements combine and interact at a pragmatic level. This is what constitutes modality in language.

Corpus bibliography

The books listed below supply supplementary data. Illustrative material drawn from these sources is indicated in the text by the appropriate letter code, followed by the relevant page number(s), e.g. (AA/304). The place of publication in all cases is London.

AA   ARMSTRONG, C. (1992) *Agents of Darkness*. Coronet
BS   BROCKBANK, P. (ed.) (1985) *Players of Shakespeare I*. Cambridge University Press
BB   BURDEN, P. (1991) *Bury Him Kindly*. Headline
CG   CRISPEN, E. (1977) *The Glimpses of the Moon*. Gollancz
CP   CRITCHLEY, J. (1992) *Hung Parliament*. Headline
MD   MICOU, P. (1992) *The Death of David Debrizzi*. Bantam
DM   DICKSON, C. (1951) *And So To Murder*. Penguin
EK   ENDLER, F. (1989) *Herbert von Karajan: My Autobiography*. Sidgwick & Jackson
FC   FRANCIS, D. (1992) *Comeback*. Pan
HB   HARE, C. (1946) *With a Bare Bodkin*. Faber
HT   HIGGINS, J. (1994) *Thunder Point*. Signet
PH   PETERS, E. (1992) *Never Pick Up Hitch-Hikers*. Headline
SB   SAYERS, D. (1977) *Whose Body*. Four Square

Ec   *The Economist*
THES   *Times Higher Education Supplement*

Bibliography

AIJMER, K., and ALTENBERG, B. (eds) (1991) *English Corpus Linguistics: Studies in Honour of Jan Svartvik.* London: Longman

ALCONCHEL, J.L.G. (1991) *Tiempo, Modalidad y Adverbio.* Salamanca: Universidad de Salamanca

ALLERTON, D.J. and CRUTTENDEN, A. (1974) English sentence adverbials: their syntax and their intonation in English. *Lingua* 27, 1–29

———— (1976) The intonation of medial and final sentence adverbs in British English. *Archivum Linguisticum* 7, 27–59

———— (1978) Syntactic, illocutionary, thematic and attitudinal factors in the intonation of adverbials. *Journal of Pragmatics* 2, 155–88

ANDERSON, J. (1971) Some proposals concerning the modal verb in English. In A.J. AITKEN, A. MCINTOSH, and H. PÁLSSON (eds) *Edinburgh Studies in English and Scots.* London: Longman, 69–120

ANTINUCCI, F. and PARISI, D. (1971) On English modal verbs. In *Papers from the Seventh Regional Meeting of the Chicago Linguistics Society.* Chicago: Department of Linguistics, University of Chicago, 28–39

ASHER, R.E. *et al.* (eds) (1994) *The Encyclopedia of Language and Linguistics,* 10 vols. Oxford: Pergamon Press

AUSTIN, J.L. (1961) Ifs and cans. In *Philosophical Papers,* 205–32

———— (1962) *How to Do Things with Words.* London: Oxford University Press

AYER, A.J. (1973) *The Central Questions of Philosophy.* London: Weidenfeld & Nicolson

AYERS, M.R. (1980) Austin on Could and Could have. In *Philosophical Quarterly* 16, 15–21

BACHE, C. and DAVIDSEN-NIELSEN, N. (forthcoming) *An Advanced Learner's Grammar (Working title).* Berlin and New York: Mouton de Gruyter.

BARDLEY, R. and SWARTZ, N. (1979) *Possible Worlds: An Introduction to Logic and its Philosophy.* Oxford: Basil Blackwell

DE BEAUGRANDE, R. (1996) The pragmatics of doing language science: The warrant for large-corpus linguistics. *Journal of Pragmatics* **25**, 503–35

BELLERT, I. (1977) On semantic and distributional properties of sentential adverbs. *Linguistic Inquiry* **8**, 337–51

BERGMAN, G. (1960) The philosophical significance of modal logic. *Mind* **69**, 466–85

BÎRĂ, E. (1979) *Aspects of Modality in English.* Bucharest: University of Bucharest Press

BLACKBURN, S. (1986) *Spreading the Word in the Philosophy of Language.* Oxford: Clarendon Press

BLAKE, N.F. (1988) *Traditional English Grammar and Beyond.* London: Macmillan

BLAKEMORE, D. (1992) *Understanding Utterances: an Introduction to Pragmatics.* Oxford: Blackwell

BLUM-KULKA, S. (1987) Indirectness and politeness in requests: same or different? *Journal of Pragmatics* **11**, 131–46

BOLINGER, D. (1972a) *Degree Words.* The Hague and Paris: Mouton

————— (1972b) Linear modification. *Publication of the Modern Language Association of America* **67**, 1117–44

————— (1975) *Aspects of Language,* 2nd edn. New York: Harcourt Brace Jovanovich

————— (1977) *Meaning and Form.* London: Longman

BOUMA, L. (1975) On contrasting the semantics of the modal auxiliaries of German and English. *Lingua* **37**, 313–39

BOYD, J. and THORNE, L. (1969) The semantics of modal verbs. *Journal of Linguistics* **5**, 57–74

BROWN, K. (1991) Double modals in Hawick Scots. In P. TRUDGILL and J.K. CHAMBERS (eds) (1991)

BROWN, P. and LEVINSON, S. (1987) *Politeness: Some Universals in Language Usage.* Cambridge: Cambridge University Press

BURCHFIELD, R. (1985) *The English Language.* Oxford: Oxford University Press

————— (1992) *Points of View: Aspects of Present-Day English.* Oxford: Oxford University Press

BUTT, J. and BENJAMIN, C. (1988) *A New Reference Grammar of Modern Spanish.* London: Edward Arnold

BUYSSCHAERT, J. (1982) *Criteria for the Classification of English Adverbials.* Brussels: Koninklijke Academie

CALBERT, J.P. (1975) Towards the semantics of modality. In *Aspekte der Modalität.* Tübingen: Verlag Gunter Narr

CLARK, H.H. and CLARK, E.V. (1977) *Psychology and Language.* New York: Harcourt Brace Jovanovich

CLOSE, R.A. (1975) *A Reference Grammar for Students of English.* London: Edward Arnold

———— (1977) *English as Foreign Language.* London: Longman

COATES, J. (1980a) On the non-equivalence of MAY and CAN. *Lingua* 50, 209–20

———— (1980b) Review of Palmer 1979. *Lingua* 51, 337–46

———— (1983) *The Semantics of the Modal Auxiliaries.* London and Canberra: Croom Helm

COATES, J. and LEECH, G. (1980) The meanings of the modals in modern British and American English. *York Papers in Linguistics* 8, 23–34

COMRIE, B. (1989) *Language Universals and Linguistic Typology,* 2nd edn. Oxford and Cambridge, Mass.: Blackwell

CORUM, C. (1975) A pragmatic analysis of parenthetic adjuncts. In R.E. GROSSMANN et al. (eds) *Papers from the Eleventh Regional Meeting of the Chicago Linguistic Society.* Chicago: Department of Linguistics, University of Chicago, 131–41

CRYSTAL, D. (1966) Specification and English tenses. *Journal of Linguistics* 2, 1–34

———— (1967) English word classes. *Lingua* 17, 24–56

———— (1969) *Prosodic Systems and Intonation in English.* Cambridge: Cambridge University Press

———— (1980) Neglected grammatical factors in conversational English. In S. GREENBAUM, G. LEECH, and J. SVARTVIK (eds) (1980), 153–66

———— (1991) *A Dictionary of Linguistics and Phonetics,* 3rd edn. Oxford: Blackwell

CRUTTENDEN, A. (1986) *Intonation.* Cambridge: Cambridge University Press

———— (1994) *Gimson's Pronunciation of English,* 5th edn. London: Edward Arnold

DAVIDSEN-NIELSEN, N. (1990) *Tense and Mood in English: A Comparison with Danish.* Berlin: Mouton de Gruyter

DEVITT, M. and STERELNY, K. (1987) *Language and Reality: An Introduction to the Philosophy of Language.* Oxford: Basil Blackwell

DIVER, N. (1964) The modal system of the English verb. *Word* 20, 322–52

DONNER, H.W. (1951) *Två kapitel engelsk grammatik II: adverbets plats i engelskan.* Helsingförs: Söderstroms

EHRMAN, M.E. (1966) *The Meanings of the Modals in Present-Day English.* The Hague: Mouton

FAIRCLOUGH, N. (1989) *Language and Power.* London: Longman

———— (1991) *Language in the News: Discourse and Ideology in the Press.* London and New York: Routledge

————— (1995) *Media Discourse*. London: Edward Arnold

FIRTH, J.R. (1957) *Papers in Linguistics 1934-51*. Oxford: Oxford University Press

————— (1967) The Anatomy of Certainty. *Philosophical Review* 76, 3–27

FRASER, B. (1990) Perspectives on politeness. *Journal of Pragmatics* 14, 219–36

GIMSON, A.C. (1980) *An Introduction to the Pronunciation of English*. London: Edward Arnold

GIVÓN, T. (1982) Evidentiality and epistemic space. *Studies in Language* 6, 23–49

GOFFMAN, E. (1967) *Interaction Ritual: Essays on Face to Face Behaviour*. New York: Anchor Books

GÓMEZ, L.G. (1988) *Perífrasis Verbales*. Madrid: Arco/Libros, S.A.

GREENBAUM, S. (1969) *Studies in English Adverbial Usage*. London: Longman

————— (1970) *Verb–Intensifier Collocations in English*. The Hague and Paris: Mouton

————— (1988) *Good English and the Grammarian*. London: Longman

GREENBAUM, S. and QUIRK, R. (1970) *Elicitation Experiments in English Linguistic Studies in Use and Attitude*. London: Longman

————— (1990) *A Student's Grammar of the English Language*. London: Longman

GREENBAUM, S., LEECH, G. and SVARTVIK, J. (eds) (1980) *Studies in English Linguistics for Randolph Quirk*. London: Longman

HAEGMAN, L. (1984) Pragmatic conditionals in English. *Folia Linguistica* 18, 485–502

HAKUTANI, J. (1972) English modal auxiliaries: a reconsideration. *Linguistics* 90, 11–19

HALLIDAY, M.A.K. (1970) Functional diversity in language as seen from a consideration of modality and mood in English. *Foundations of Language* 6, 322–61

————— (1985) *An Introduction to Functional Grammar*. London: Edward Arnold

————— (1994) *An Introduction to Functional Grammar*, 2nd edn. London: Edward Arnold

HARRIS, Z. (1957) Co-occurrence and transformation in linguistic Structure. *Language* 33, 283–340

HARTMANN, D. (1986) Context analysis or analysis of sentence meaning? On modal particles in German. *Journal of Pragmatics* 10, 543–57

————— (1994) Particles. In R.E. ASHER *et al.* (eds) (1994), 2953–8.

HARTVIGSON, H. (1969) *On the Intonation and Position of the So-Called Sentence Modifiers in Present-Day English*. Odense: Odense University Press

HEIDELBERGER, H. (1963) Knowledge, certainty and probability. *Inquiry* 6, 242–50

HERMERÉN, L. (1978) *On Modality in English: A Study of the Semantics of the Modals*. Lund: CWK Gleerup

HINTIKKA, J. (1973) *Logic, Language-Games and Information: Kantian Themes in the Philosophy of Logic*. Oxford: Clarendon Press

HOCKETT, C.F. (1958) *A Course in Modern Linguistics*. New York: Macmillan

HOFFMANN, T.R. (1966) Past tense replacement and the modal system. In J.D. McCawley (ed.) (1976) *Syntax and Semantics 7, Notes from the Linguistic Underground*. New York: Academic Press

———— (1979) On modality in English and other languages. *Papers in Linguistics* 12, 1–31

HORN, L. (1972) *On the Semantic Properties of Logical Operators in English*. Unpublished PhD Thesis: University of California at Los Angeles

HOUSE, J. and KASPAR, G. (1981) Politeness markers in English and German. In F. COULMASS (ed.) *Conversational Routine*. The Hague: Mouton

HOYE, L.F. (1984) *On Modal Auxiliary–Adverb Co-occurrence in English*. Unpublished MA Thesis: University of Reading

———— (1988) Aspects of epistemic modal–adverb co-occurrence in English. *Studia* 2, 3–13. Cluj-Napoca: University of Cluj-Napoca

———— (1989) *A Grammar of Modal Auxiliary–Adverb Co-occurrence in English*. Unpublished PhD Thesis: University of Bucharest

HOYE, L.F. and ZDRENGHEA, M. (1995) Modals and adverbs in English with reference to Romanian. *Rask* 2, 25–50. Odense: University of Odense Press

HUDDLESTON, R.D. (1971) *The Sentence in Written English: A Syntactic Study Based on an Analysis of Scientific Texts*. Cambridge: Cambridge University Press

———— (1976) *An Introduction to English Transformational Syntax*. London: Longman

———— (1984) *Introduction to the Grammar of English*. Cambridge: Cambridge University Press

———— (1994) Sentence types and clause subordination. In R.E. ASHER et al. (eds) (1994), Vol. 7, 3845–57

JACKENDOFF, R. (1972) *Semantic Interpretation in Generative Grammar*. Cambridge, Mass.: The MIT Press

JACOBSON, S. (1964) *Adverbial Positions in English*. Stockholm: Studentbok

———— (1975) *Factors Influencing the Placement of English Adverbials in Relation to Auxiliaries*. Stockholm: Almqvist & Wiksell International

———— (1978) *On the Use, Meaning, and Syntax of English Preverbal Adverbs*. Stockholm: Almqvist & Wiksell International

————— (1981) *Preverbal Adverbs and Auxiliaries: A Study of Word Order Change*. Stockholm: Almqvist & Wiksell International

JENKINS, L. (1972) *Modality in English Syntax*. Bloomington, Indiana: Indiana University Linguistics Club

JESPERSEN, O. (1909–49) *A Modern English Grammar on Historical Principles I-VIII*. Heidelberg: Karl Winter; Copenhagen: Einar Munksgaard

————— (1924) *The Philosophy of Grammar*. London: George Allen & Unwin

JOHANNESSON, N.L. (1976) *The English Modal Auxiliaries: A Stratificational Account*. Stockholm: Almqvist & Wiksell International

JOOS, M. (1964) *The English Verb: Form and Meanings*. Madison and Milwaukee: The University of Wisconsin Press

KARTTUNNEN, L. (1972) Possible and must. In J.F. KIMBALL (ed.) *Syntax and Semantics*. New York: Seminar Press

KASPER, G. (1994) Politeness. In R.E. ASHER *et al.* (eds) (1994) Vol. 6, 3206–11.

————— (1990) Linguistic politeness: current research issues. *Journal of Pragmatics* 14, 193–218

KATZ, J.J. (1966) *The Philosophy of Language*. New York: Harper & Row

KEMPSON, R.M. (1977) *Semantic Theory*. Cambridge: Cambridge University Press

KENNY, A. (1975) *Will, Freedom and Power*. Oxford: Basil Blackwell

KEYSER, S.J. (1968) Review of Sven Jacobson: adverbial positions in English. *Language* 44, 357–74

KLINGE, A. (1993) The English modal auxiliaries: from lexical semantics to utterance interpretation. *Journal of Linguistics* 29, 315–57

————— (1995) On the linguistic interpretation of contractual modalities. *Journal of Pragmatics* 23, 649–75

KNOWLES, G. (1987) *Patterns of Spoken English: An Introduction to English Phonetics*. London: Longman

KOKTOVÁ, E. (1986) *Sentence Adverbials*. Amsterdam: John Benjamins

KRESS, G. and HODGE, R. (1979) *Language as Ideology*. London: Routledge & Kegan Paul

LAKOFF, R. (1972) The Pragmatics of Modality. In *Papers from the Eighth Regional Meeting of the Chicago Linguistic Society*. Chicago: University of Chicago Press

LEBRUN, Y. (1965) *Can and May in Present-Day English*. Brussels: Presses Universitaires de Bruxelles

LEE, D. (1987) The semantics of just. *Journal of Pragmatics* 11, 377–98

LEECH, G.N. (1971) *Meaning and the English Verb*. London: Longman

————— (1983) *Principles of Pragmatics*. London: Longman

LEECH, G.N. and COATES, J. (1980) Semantic indeterminacy and the modals. In S. GREENBAUM, G. LEECH and J. SVARTVIK (eds) (1980)

LEVENSTON, E.A. (1971) Over-indulgence and under-representation –
aspects of mother-tongue interference. In G. NICKEL (ed.) (1971)

LEVINSON, S.C. (1983) *Pragmatics*. Cambridge: Cambridge University
Press

LINDQUIST, H. (1989) *English Adverbials in Translation: A Corpus Study of
Swedish Renderings*. Lund: Lund University Press

LYONS, J. (1968) *Introduction to Theoretical Linguistics*. Cambridge: Cambridge University Press

————— (1977) *Semantics* (I and II). Cambridge: Cambridge University
Press

MARINO, M. (1973) A feature analysis of the modal system of English.
Lingua 32, 309–23

MATTHEWS, P.H. (1981) *Syntax*. Cambridge: Cambridge University Press

MATTHEWS, R. (1991) *Words and Worlds: On the Linguistic Analysis of
Modality*. Frankfurt: Peter Lang

MCCAWLEY, J.D. (1975) The category status of the English modals.
Foundations of Language 12, 597–601

————— (1981) *Everything that Linguists have Always Wanted to Know
about Logic but were Ashamed to Ask*. Chicago: The University of
Chicago Press

MCDONALD, C. (1981) *Variations in the Use of Modal Verbs with Special
Reference to Tyneside English*. Unpublished PhD Thesis: University of
Newcastle upon Tyne

MEY, J. (1985) *Whose Language? A Study in Linguistic Pragmatics*. Amsterdam
and Philadelphia: John Benjamins

————— (1993) *Pragmatics: An Introduction*. Oxford: Blackwell

————— (1994) Pragmatics. In R.E. ASHER *et al*. (eds) (1994), Vol. 6,
3260–78

MILLER, G.A. and JOHNSON-LAIRD, P.N. (1976) *Language and Perception*.
Cambridge: Cambridge University Press

MINDT, D. (1996) English corpus linguistics and the foreign language
teaching syllabus. In J. THOMAS, AND M. SHORT (eds) (1996) 232–47

NAGLE, S. (1989) *Inferential Change and Syntactic Modality in English*.
Frankfurt: Peter Lang

NATTINGER, J.R. and DECARRICO, J.S. (1992) *Lexical Phrases and Language
Teaching*. Oxford: Oxford University Press

NEY, J.W. (1979) Capability, possibility and permission in the English
modals CAN and COULD. *General Linguistics* 2, 115–30

NICKEL, G. (ed.) (1971) *Papers in Contrastive Linguistics*. Cambridge:
Cambridge University Press

PALMER, F.R. (ed.) (1968) *Selected Papers of J.R. Firth 1952–59*. London:
Longman

————— (1974) *The English Verb*, 1st edn. London: Longman

———— (1979) *Modality and the English Modals*, 1st edn. London: Longman

———— (1986) *Mood and Modality*. Cambridge: Cambridge University Press

———— (1987) *The English Verb*, 2nd edn. London: Longman

———— (1990) *Modality and the English Modals*, 2nd edn. London: Longman

PERKINS, M.R. (1981) The development of modal expressions in the spontaneous speech of 6–12 year old children. In *Work in Progress* 14, 54–61. Department of Linguistics, University of Edinburgh

———— (1982) The core meaning of the English modals. *Journal of Linguistics* 18, 43–81

———— (1983) *Modal Expressions in English*. London: Frances Pinter

PLANK, F. (1984) The modals story retold. *Studies in Language* 8, 305–64

POUTSMA, H. (1926–9) *A Grammar of Late Modern English*. Groningen: Noordhoff

PULLUM, G. and WILSON, D. (1977) Autonomous syntax and the analysis of auxiliaries. *Language* 53, 741–88

QUIRK, R. (1965) Descriptive statement and serial relationship. *Language* 41, 205–17

———— (1986) *Essays on the English Language, Medieval and Modern*. London: Longman

———— (1995) *Grammatical and Lexical Variance in English*. London: Longman

QUIRK, R. and SVARTVIK, J. (1966) *Investigating Linguistic Acceptability*. The Hague: Mouton

———— (1979) A corpus of modern English. In H. BERGENHOLTZ and B. SCHAEDER (eds.) *Empirische Textwissenschaft*. Königstein: Scriptor

QUIRK, R., GREENBAUM, S., LEECH, G. and SVARTVIK, J. (1972) *A Grammar of Contemporary English*. London: Longman

———— (1985) *A Comprehensive Grammar of the English Language*. London: Longman

RADFORD, A. (1981) *Transformational Syntax: A Student's Guide to Chomsky's Extended Standard Theory*. Cambridge: Cambridge University Press

———— (1988) *Transformational Grammar*. Cambridge: Cambridge University Press

RAMON, E. (1977) *On the Representation of Modality*. Bloomington, Indiana: Indiana University Linguistics Club

RESCHER, N. (1968) *Topics in Philosophical Logic*. Dordrecht: Reidel

RIVERO, M.L. (1972) Remarks on operators and modalities. *Foundations of Language* 9, 209–41

ROBERTS, P. (1954) *Understanding Grammar*. New York: Harper & Row

ROSS, J.R. (1973) Slifting. In M. GROSS et al. (eds) *The Formal Analysis of Natural Language*. The Hague: Mouton

SCHREIBER, P.A. (1971) Some constraints on the formation of English sentence adverbs. *Linguistic Inquiry* 2, 83–101

———— (1972) Style disjuncts and the performative analysis. *Linguistic Inquiry* 3, 321–47

SCOLLON, R. and SCOLLON, S.W. (1983) Face in interethnic communication. In I.C. RICHARDS and R.W. SCHMIDT (eds) *Language and Communication*. London: Longman

———— (1995) *Intercultural Communication*. Oxford: Blackwell

SEARLE, J.R. (1969) *Speech Acts: An Essay in the Philosophy of Language*. Cambridge: Cambridge University Press

———— (1979) *Expression and Meaning: Studies in the Theory of Speech Acts*. Cambridge: Cambridge University Press

———— (1983) *Intentionality*. Cambridge: Cambridge University Press

———— (1989) How performatives work. *Linguistics and Philosophy* 12, 535–58

———— (1995) *The Construction of Social Reality*. New York: Free Press

SINCLAIR, J. (1991) *Corpus Concordance Collocation*. Oxford: Oxford University Press

SMITH, N. (1989) *The Twitter Machine: Reflections on Language*. Oxford: Basil Blackwell

SOLANO-ARAYA, J.M. (1982) *Modality in Spanish: An Account of Mood*. PhD Thesis. University of Kansas. (1988) Ann Arbor: University Microfilms International.

SPERBER, D. and WILSON, D. (1986) *Relevance: Communication and Cognition*. Cambridge, Mass.: Harvard University Press

STEELE, S. (1975) Is it possible? *Stanford University Working Papers on Language Universals* 18, 35–58

STRANG, B. (1968) The Tyneside Linguistic Survey (paper read at International Congress on Dialectology, Marburg, 1965). *Zeitschrift für Mundartforschung*, 788–94

STUBBS, M. (1983) *Discourse Analysis: The Sociolinguistic Analysis of Natural Language*. Oxford: Basil Blackwell

———— (1996) *Text and Corpus Analysis*. Oxford: Basil Blackwell

SWAN, T. (1981) Modal adverbs. In S. JOHANSSON and B. TYSDAHL (eds) *Papers from the First Nordic Conference for English Studies*. Oslo: University of Oslo, 424–37

———— (1987) *Sentence Adverbials in English: A Synchronic and Diachronic Investigation*. Tromsø: University of Tromsø

SWEET, H. (1892-8) *A New English Grammar*, Vols I and II. Oxford: Oxford University Press

TARONE, E. and YULE, G. (1989) *Focus on the Language Learner: Approaches to Identifying and Meeting the Needs of Second Language Learners.* Oxford: Oxford University Press

THOMAS, J. and SHORT, M. (eds) (1996) *Using Corpora for Language Research.* London and New York: Longman

TREGIDO, P.S. (1982) MUST and MAY: demand and permission. *Lingua* 56, 75–92

TROSBORG, A. (1995) *Interlanguage Pragmatics: Requests, Complaints and Apologies.* Berlin and New York: Mouton de Gruyter

TRUDGILL, P. and CHAMBERS, J.K. (eds) (1991) *Dialects of English: Studies in Grammatical Variation.* London: Longman

TWADDELL, W.F. (1963) *The English Verb Auxiliaries.* Providence, Connecticut: Brown University Press

VAN ELS, T., BONGAERTS, T., EXTRA, G., VAN OS, C. and JANSSEN-VAN DIETEN, A.M. (1984) *Applied Linguistics and the Learning and Teaching of Foreign Languages* (trans. R.R. VAN OIRSOUW). London: Edward Arnold

VIRTANEN, T. (1992) *Discourse Functions of Adverbial Placement in English.* Åbo: Åbo University Press

VON WRIGHT, G.H. (1951a) *An Essay in Modal Logic.* Amsterdam: North Holland

——— (1951b) Deontic logic. *Mind* 60, 1–15

WELLS, G. (1979) Learning and using the auxiliary verbs in English. In V. LEE (ed.) *Language Development.* London: Croom Helm

WIERZBICKA, A. (1986) Precision in vagueness. The semantics of English approximatives. *Journal of Pragmatics* 10, 597–613

WHITAKER, S.F. (1966) The mighty must: some suggestions concerning the modal auxiliary. *English Language Teaching* XXI, I, 12–15

——— (1987) Might may be right? *English Today* 11, 35–6

WHITE, A.R. (1975) *Modal Thinking.* Oxford: Basil Blackwell

WHITLEY, M.S. (1986) *Spanish/English Contrasts: A Course in Spanish Linguistics.* Washington, DC: Georgetown University Press

WIDDOWSON, H. (1990) *Aspects of Language Teaching.* Oxford: Oxford University Press

WITTGENSTEIN, P. (1958) *Philosophical Investigation.* Oxford: Basil Blackwell

Indices

There are three indices, Index of Authors, Index of Modal Expressions, and Subject Index, which cover Chapters 1 to 6. In all entries, references are to pages. References to chapter end notes are indicated by page and note number, for example, 'adverbial frequency 277n6'.

Three kinds of entry are included: the names of authors cited in the text (Index of Authors); simplex and complex items which have been treated and classified in lists, or which have been the focus of analysis and discussion (Index of Modal Expressions); and general concepts (Subject Index).

Index of Authors

Index of Modal Expressions

Items listed as modal expressions include modal auxiliaries, modal adverbs, modal–adverb combinations, adjectival, participial and nominal modal expressions, and modal lexical verbs. Spanish modal expressions are given in italics.

In the case of modal–adverb combinations, the symbol (~) is used to indicate the place of the headword: for instance, under CAN, (~ EASILY) should be read as CAN EASILY; (POSSIBLY ~) as POSSIBLY CAN. In some entries, dots (...) are used to signal omission of part of a construction: for example, under CAN, OF COURSE (...) ~ refers to a clause/sentence beginning with the adverbial OF COURSE and followed by unspecified text and then the co-occurrence of the modal CAN; conversely, ~ (...) POSSIBLY refers to a clause/sentence beginning with the modal CAN followed by unspecified text and then the co-occurrence of the adverbial OF COURSE. Therefore two types of modal–adverb expression are indexed: adjacent and disjunctive modal–adverb/adverb–modal combinations.

Subject Index

Cross-reference to multi-word entries treats the first item as the headword. Thus reference to the entry 'focus, focalization, focalize' is given as 'focus'. Reference to a sub-entry is signalled by the headword followed by the appropriate sub-heading in parentheses. Thus, the sub-entry 'and language use' under 'modality' is given as: 'modality (and language use)'. Where the headword is a constituent of a multi-word sub-entry, the symbol ~ is used to indicate its place in the reference: for example, under 'discourse', (~ functions) should be read as 'discourse functions'.

Individual modal expressions, such as modal auxiliaries, modal adverbs, and modal–adverb combinations, are listed alphabetically in a separate index, Index of Modal Expressions, for ease of reference.

Key references are given in bold.